SOFTWARE
PROJECT
MANAGEMENT

SOFTWARE PROJECT MANAGEMENT

A GUIDE FOR SERVICE PROVIDERS

S. RAMANATHAN

PARTRIDGE

ISBN: Hardcover   978-1-4828-7013-8
             Softcover   978-1-4828-7012-1
             eBook   978-1-4828-7011-4

Print information available on the last page.

To order additional copies of this book, contact
Partridge India
000 800 10062 62
orders.india@partridgepublishing.com

www.partridgepublishing.com/india

Contents

Preface xi

1   Understanding a Project 1

1.1 Lesson objectives 1

1.2 Understanding Software Project Management 1

1.3 What causes a software project to succeed? 9

1.4 Program management 15

1.5 Project management standards 16

1.6 Project management defined 17

2   Stages of Project Management 21

2.1 Lesson objectives 21

2.2 Stages of project management 21

2.3 Project management knowledge areas 29

3   Project Initiation 35

3.1 Lesson objectives 35

3.2 Scope management 35

3.3 Business case 52

3.4 Presentation to management 54

4 Project Planning 69

   4.1 Lesson Objectives...69

   4.2 Project Planning – Coverage 69

   4.3 Specifying user requirements...70

   4.4 Estimating duration 71

5 Time Management: Software Measurement...................93

   5.1 Learning objectives..93

   5.2 Why measurement?... 94

   5.3 Metrics...95

6 Software Estimation 121

   6.1 Learning objectives 121

   6.2 What is estimation? 121

   6.3 Challenges in Estimation 122

   6.4 Can software be estimated at all? 124

   6.5 Approaches to software estimation 125

   6.6 Metrics for software estimation.......................................128

   6.7 Automation of estimation 129

7 Project Scheduling and Tracking.....................................135

   7.1 Learning objectives...135

   7.2 Project scheduling 135

   7.3 Assigning staff to activities 147

   7.4 Tracking the schedule...148

8   Quality Management..154

8.1 Learning objectives 154

8.2 What is quality?..154

8.3 Quality management 155

8.4 Quality control 169

9   Risk Management..181

9.1 Learning objectives..181

9.2 Risk defined..181

9.3 Risk management life-cycle – Phases..182

10   Project Cost Management 202

10.1 Lesson objectives 202

10.2 Importance of project cost management..202

10.3 Project cost management processes..203

10.4 Project Plan..212

11   Project Execution..219

11.1 Learning objectives..219

11.2 Launching the project..219

11.3 Stakeholders of a project..220

12   Project Staffing..224

12.1 Lesson objectives..224

12.2 Project staffing..224

12.3 Project organization structure 229

12.4 Project Management Office (PMO) 231

13   Procurement Management 237

13.1 Lesson objectives 237

13.2 Growing importance of Outsourcing 237

13.3 Request for Proposal (RFP) 238

13.4 Vendor evaluation 239

13.5 Contract preparation 240

13.6 Vendor Management 241

14   Profile of a Project Manager 247

14.1 Lesson objectives 247

14.2 Skills required of a project manager 247

15   Monitoring and Controlling a Project 296

15.1 Learning objectives 296

15.2 Activities during this phase 296

15.3 Project status reporting 297

15.4 Cost control 299

16   Change Control and Configuration Management 305

16.1 Learning objectives 305

16.2 What is configuration management? 305

16.3 What is software configuration? 306

16.4 Challenges in software configuration management 306

16.5 Baseline 307

16.6 Functions of configuration management 307

16.7 Software Configuration Management (SCM) tasks 308

17 Release Management 318

    17.1 Learning objectives 318

    17.2 What is release management? 318

    17.3 Why is release management challenging? 319

    17.4 Release identifier 320

    17.5 Release package 320

18 Expectation Management 323

    18.1 Lesson objectives 323

    18.2 What is expectation management? 323

    18.3 When is expectation management important? 326

    18.4 A technique for expectation management 327

    18.5 Prerequisites for managing expectations 329

    18.6 Technology – a tool in managing expectation 330

19 Closing a project 335

    19.1 Lesson objectives 335

    19.2 Steps in project closure 335

Annexure I: Techniques of Cost-Benefit Analysis 343

Bibliography 345

Index 349

Preface

It was a mail from Singapore totally out of the blue; I did not recognize the sender till he introduced himself to be an old colleague. He referred to a set of slides on information security, which I had shared with my students and asked me whether these were mine. The title slide had my name. I was glad to know that several of the people preparing for the CISA examination were using those slides.

In one of the executive training programs, I was asked if I could record my entire sessions on a CD and circulate. I am sure several of my colleagues in academics would have had such experiences. Students clamour for the text books that explain the concepts in free-flowing easy-to-understand style. Many text books choose an intimidatory style in an effort to demonstrate their academic rigour and in the process fail to establish a connect with the readers – be it students or the working executives. This book intends to address this gap.

Stephen Covey says that all things are created twice – first mentally and then physically. This book was taking shape during the past fifteen years of teaching of this course. Or should I say in Maya Angelou's words that I was bearing the agony of this untold story in me? The long class room testing has contributed to refining and perfecting the contents.

Rome was not built in day nor by a single hand. While the cover shows me as the sole author, there are several others, who directly and indirectly contributed to realizing my long-cherished dream of writing this book. First my thanks are due to my students, who by their incisive questions influenced the contents and the style of this book. This volume is a small addition to the vast literature available in this domain and I have liberally used many of the thoughts expressed by these authors. I am thankful to those authors and publishers, who generously permitted me to use some portions of their published work and some of them even wrote back encouraging me in my endeavour.

The illustrations were created by Ms. Nivedita Ramanathan and these went through several iterations to improve their communication and she patiently worked with me in evolving these. She was also helpful in laying out the text with proper numbering. In the painful effort of proof-reading to create a readable and error-free output, Mrs. Usha Vaidyanathan and Dr. Nirupama Ramanathan lent their helping hand. Mr. R.K. Ajay too chipped in to resolve any technical glitch in the word processing. All those deserve my gratitude.

My thanks are due to Partridge Publishing India, who came forward to publish this book.

I request the faculty members who teach this course, the students and the practitioners to give their comments and feedback. After all, the project management is a lot experiential and we are continuously learning!

S. Ramanathan
ram1951@hotmail.com

1

UNDERSTANDING A PROJECT

If you wish to converse with me, define your terms. - Voltaire

1.1 Lesson objectives

In this lesson we will learn the following:

- What is a project?
- How is a software project unique?
- Factors for the success of a software project
- What is program management?
- What are the recognized standards in the project management?

1.2 Understanding Software Project Management

If we have to understand Software Project Management, we need to understand each of the terms in it. Apparently all the three terms contained in it sound familiar, but do we understand each of them?

Could we define what *software is?* May sound an audacious proposition to an audience, predominantly of the software professionals. Software is the most misunderstood and hence the misused term by the software professionals. We tend to use the terms program and software synonymously and that is not correct. However we are not going define software now and will return to this fairly late in this book.

We will discuss in detail what a project is and also what the project management is in this chapter. In the manufacturing organizations, you will find two roles – Project Manager and Production Manager. How are these roles differentiated? Have you ever wondered why two such roles do not exist in a software organization and there is only a Project manager? Also try to explore these questions:

- Why do we call all the software production activities as projects?

- In software also, we use the term 'production'. For instance we have a production environment or a production directory. We call the software development as a project whereas when it is installed in the user organizations, it is called the production environment. Does it give you any indication of the difference between a project and production?

- Now that you have an idea – vaguely though – of what a project is and how it is different from production, could you classify the following activities into these two categories?:

  - The publisher of a newspaper brings out millions of copies every day, without fail, at 4 am with as much of the current news as feasible.
  - You have taken the responsibility of conducting your sister's wedding.
  - An event management company, which regularly organizes weddings, has been entrusted with the conduct of the wedding.
  - Every day you drive to your office through chaotic traffic for about an hour.
  - A team of surgeons performs a complicated surgery.

A discussion of these questions should lead you to define the characteristics of a project.

1.2.1 So what is a project?

A project has the following characteristics:

Non-routine tasks: While in production, we repeat the same tasks again and again, a project will consist of non-routine tasks. That is why the plant erection and the pilot production are under the purview of the project management; once the production process stabilizes, it is handed over to the production manager. With the processes standardized, the tasks become repetitive. For the same reason, the software development is termed a project. If the software development process is defined, how could the tasks be non-routine? A software development activity, despite all the definitions of the processes, might encounter several uncertainties and that makes the tasks non-routine. A technical problem could stall the development of a program and may require several rounds of consultations and discussions to solve it. So is a conversion of a business process into code. On the other hand, a developed and tested program handed over to a user is expected to run repeatedly without fail. That is why it is called the production environment.

Defined objectives and deliverables: The success of a project is determined by the extent of the fulfilment of the pre-defined objectives. Associated with the objectives are a set of deliverables. These deliverables are also pre-specified and in most instances in a written form and maybe in the form of a legal contract.

Pre-determined time duration: Uncertainties in a project may well be handled if time is no constraint. The challenge arises because of the deadline fixed for the deliverables. Managing time is an important task of a project manager and a critical factor in deciding his / her success.

Involvement of several specializations: Several specialists come together in completing a project. That is why a complicated surgery could be called a project. A project manager should show the capability to coordinate between different specializations. It is no mean task to elicit compliance from the experts in different fields to achieve the project goal.

Several phases: A project goes through several phases. Phases are differentiated by the processes and the tasks. With repeated runs, a production process is made smooth and thus the day-to-day control of such processes is left to the lower level employees. But in the case of a project, the changes in the processes and the tasks across its different stages make its management challenging and requires continuous supervision by a qualified project manager.

Constrained resources: If for the fulfilment of the project objectives, your management is willing to provide an unlimited budget with no questions asked on the amount of the resources utilized and with an option to specify your own delivery date(s), you are a lucky project manager. But alas! Life is tough; your management and the client will have a definite say on the budget, the resource allocation and the deadlines. The requirement of the ability to deliver the results with the constrained resources makes this a management discipline and hence the name project management.

Size and complexity: By their very nature, projects tend to be large and complex. How are size and complexity different? Aren't the large duration projects inherently complex? Complexity is defined by the interdependency of the components. Such an interdependency makes the planning and the allocation of resources challenging.

With the knowledge of the characteristics of a project, you may revisit the activities mentioned in 1.2 above and try to classify them as to which of them may be called projects.

So we may define a project as *"a set of connected activities with a pre-specified goal and with a set of pre-specified deliverables, which need to be fulfilled with reference to the specifications within the specified time duration and the budget, optimally using the allocated resources."*

A project manager thus has to manage the following factors:

- Scope: Specifications
- Quality

- Time
- Cost
- Resources

The relationship among these factors is represented by a scope triangle Fig 1.1.(Wysocki, 2010).[1]

Fig. 1.1 Scope Triangle

1.2.2 Software Project Management – how is it unique?

If projects are well-defined, cutting across different fields from construction to machine building to rocket launch and if the project management has evolved as a formal discipline, what could be so special about the software projects that make their management unique? It is not our contention that software projects are totally different from the other projects, but there are some aspects exclusive to software..

What are the factors that make the software projects unique?

Product intangibility: In a software project, the final product is intangible. Does intangibility create serious challenges in its management? Compare the intermittent progress measurement in a civil construction project and a software project. Except when

---

[1]   Other ways of representing this triangle has been proposed by several other authors. This seems to be the most appropriate representation with the deliverables inside the triangle and the inputs / constraints as the sides of the triangle.

the foundations are being laid, the progress in a construction project is visible and thus easily measurable. The invisibility of the software product has given rise to what is popularly known as the '90% syndrome'[2,3] in the software industry. This syndrome is the consequence of the immeasurability of the software progress. From the project management perspective, this is serious because the project manager has no way to cross-check the progress reported by a team member. Could a civil construction project manager be misled by his / her subordinates in this manner?

Limited experience: Software development is an infant science. Our experience in this domain spans a few decades[4], while the other disciplines have amassed a great body of knowledge over hundreds or even thousands of years[5]. Based on the theories of science, engineering disciplines evolve with experience. That experience was available to software only for a very limited period – compared to civil engineering, it may be called miniscule. Software development was recognized as an engineering discipline only as late as 1968[6]. It was at that time it was recognized that software development was no art and it needed to be based on some standard tested processes[7]. We are in the process of transitioning software into an engineering discipline – with many pessimistic about such a total transformation – and till such time,

---

[2] Whenever a progress review takes place, the software project team members have a tendency to report "90% done". This is referred to as the 90% syndrome. "Coding .... is "90 percent finished" for half of the total coding time. Debugging is "99 percent complete" most of the time" - Frederick Brooks (Brooks, 1975)

[3] The trouble with programmers is that you can never tell what a programmer is doing until it's too late.—Seymour Cray

[4] The basis of software – algorithm – was designed by Ada Lovelace in the nineteenth century, but no software was created on this basis at that time. The first theory about software was proposed by Alan Turing in 1935. However software as we know today – programs stored in digital computers - was first created in 1946 (Source: Wikipedia).

[5] For example pyramids were constructed around 2600 BC and these demonstrate the evolution of civil engineering discipline from such an early period.

[6] Margaret Hamilton of MIT Instrumentation Laboratory is credited with coining the term 'Software Engineering'.

[7] This is still not a settled debate in the software field. You will find several research papers to blogs arguing on either side or taking a via media approach to the question.

the uncertainties in managing the software development process will remain.

No standard process: This is allied with the issue we raised above. Defined processes and strict compliance to the defined processes ensure the product quality. Every other engineering discipline has evolved over a period and standardized its basic processes and these processes have also been made simple enough to minimize error-proneness. The unit operations in chemical engineering have been standardized and have suffered limited changes in the last several decades. The leaf level processes like brick-laying in civil construction have been simplified and standardized so well that any unskilled labourer may learn them in a short time. These standardizations and simplifications have helped the engineers in these disciplines to undertake massive projects and complete them with ease and confidence. Such a standardization is in a very early stage in the software industry. The knowledge as to what extent the process parameters will affect the product quality has been gained by a chemical engineer over several experimentations and iterations. Such a knowledge base is unavailable to the software professionals at least as of now.

Rapid technology changes: In no other discipline, tools and technologies change at such a rapid pace and as a consequence, render the professionals redundant fast. The knowledge gained with one technology becomes useless – at least partially – when a new technology gains the popular acceptance. It might be argued that the project management is independent of technology. While this may be true in theory, there is an increasing trend in the industry to assign the project managers on the basis of technology (apart from domain) and so it has become a necessity for a project manager to be proficient in a technology. The project management is more impacted by the methodology changes. How far is the experience gained in the waterfall model projects useful in agile projects? Can the project manager take charge of an agile project without any new learning? More importantly without unlearning what (s)he has already learnt and practised? The basis of an earlier model is challenged by the subsequent evolution. The gospel truths supporting the relational approach are questioned in object-oriented design.

New and innovative projects: The type of applications to which software is put to use is changing drastically. Computers were initially confined to the scientific applications. Business became the major user soon and accounting the main application. The monopoly of number crunching soon gave room to word processing. Inventors of computers and computing would have rarely imagined that letter writing would be a major application on computers. Financial accounting and inventory control gave rise to the integrated applications. Internet changed the face of business and more e-commerce applications followed. Gaming and entertainment soon constituted our major portfolio. Now mobile apps challenge the desktop applications in every field.[8] All these dramatic changes have taken place in less than seven decades! Could we cite even a fraction of this level of changes in any other discipline?

People dependency: While there is a continuous effort in the industry to streamline and standardize the processes, software development is still far from becoming totally independent of the people developing it. Nor is it feasible to make the lowest level of the processes as simple as in the construction industry. Programming is the lowest level of the processes and even at this stage, the intellectual content of the job is of a high order. Thus one single programmer's coding failure could lead to disastrous results in the product. While testing should be rigorous to identify such errors, it is a known fact that exhaustive testing is never feasible to ensure that no bug exists in the final delivered product. If one such error that has escaped testing were to prove disastrous, then it will be a reflection on the project manager. One of the early US spacecrafts, Mariner 1 failed disastrously because of a missing hyphen in the code![9] Manufacturing has perfected the assembly line production

---

[8]   From 2010 onwards the smart phones have started outselling the personal computers. This may give an indication of the type of the software projects that would be handled in future.

[9]   New York Times reported the news with the headline 'For Want of Hyphen, Venus Rocket is Lost'.

with the standardized processes and the stage wise inspections. The software industry is still far from such a regimented development approach. For want of a nail, a battle may be lost; but is it reasonable to expect the captain to check each and every nail? Ironically, the industry, with a mission to automate the processes to save labour in its customer organizations, itself is highly labour dependent!

Accommodating change: In all the other projects such as civil construction, the requests for change from the users are accepted till the design is frozen. After this stage, the project managers will decline to accept any change. In the software development life cycle too, we have a stage called freezing of the design. But that is not a stage at which the change requests are stopped, but they are formalized. By their very nature, the software projects will attract changes and such change requests will keep flowing till the product reaches the delivery stage. And that is not the end of the change requests; even after the software is implemented, the requests for change keep flowing in. This challenge is unique to the software projects. If changes were to be accepted throughout the lifecycle of the development and quite frequently in the running of the software, the design should have the flexibility to accommodate changes and at the same time the design should be robust to execute with resilience after so many changes. Flexibility and robustness are normally the characteristics that are antithetical to each other. The challenge of a software designer is to make them coexist in the product.

1.3 What causes a software project to succeed?

If the software projects are so challenging to execute, it may be worthwhile to understand, based on the industry experience, the factors that contribute to the success of a software project:

User involvement: The users play an important role in explaining the business processes, providing feedback on the submissions such as the SRS (System Requirement Specification) and the Design document and also in conducting the user acceptance tests. Many projects have suffered because of the user indifference. Particularly, the mission-critical applications such as ERP demand a high user involvement and that is why joint application development, in which the user representatives become a part of the implementation team, is recommended for such projects.

Top management commitment: Wherever the top management fails to own the projects and abdicates the responsibility totally to the IT management, it is a guaranteed prescription for failure. Responsibility of the top management does not end with the provision of the budget. Applications such as ERP and core banking might require business process changes – sometimes quite drastic - as a pre-requisite for the software implementation and such changes will normally be resisted by the middle management. This is where the top management needs to throw its weight around and exercise control. As a parody to what Georges Clemenceau[10] said of war, we may say "the software projects are too serious business concerns to be left to the IT managers"! Such large projects will be closely overseen by a steering committee, which will have among its members the functional heads and be headed by the CEO himself / herself or by a senior management representative who has the confidence of the CEO.

Project management expertise: The role of the project manager cannot be overemphasized in this whole exercise. (S)he is the kingpin. Could one person make or mar a project – wonders Kishen (See the case study at the later part of this chapter). Many multinational organizations use their off-shore development centres (ODC) in the countries like India, the Philippines or China for the purpose of coding only and the higher end services including the project management are rendered from the US or Europe. Brykczynski (2006) cites India, Hungary, Russia, the Philippines and the Middle East – many of them emerging as important software development centres - as being weak in the project management skills and practices - all the more the reason why the service provider nations need to concentrate on this area.

---

[10]   Georges Clemenceau (1841-1929), the French statesman and journalist is credited with the quote "War is too serious a thing to be left to the generals"

Formal methodology: Software development is no more a trial and error exercise to be left to the individual excellence. With software evolving into an engineering discipline, several formal methodologies have been developed and a process focus is emphasized. More importantly, the organizations involved in the software development should ensure compliance to the formal methodologies. Many IT professionals, including those at the senior levels view these methodologies as an impediment to fast development. Quick and dirty and trial and error methods do not ensure sustainability of a product. Commitment to a formal methodology is an important requirement for the success of a software project.

Usage of tools: We discussed the people factor in software development, which introduces uncertainties in the development process and hence in the quality of the final product. Automation is one way to reduce the dependence on people, For example testing tools can ensure more exhaustive testing than the manual testing. Templates and checklists can ensure better compliance. There are tools available for the project management itself (e.g.) MS Project.

Case Study

The Three Muscateers at the Crossroads – Is Project Management the Key?

The problem:

When Kishen Nayak was called into the Chief Executive's cabin, little did he realize that the CEO Krish was going to hand him over an issue, which was of critical importance to the organization. Being a business school whiz kid newly joined in the Strategic Management Group, he should have expected that less important issues would not come to him.

"What do you understand by Project Management?" asked the CEO. Kishen did not know how to handle such a general question. The CEO was not expecting an answer from him. "We know nothing about it – that is what everybody thinks – our clients, our principal – everybody" Krish, the CEO continued in a tone echoing frustration.

Kishen was all ears. He was still waiting for the problem to unfold. Krish and Arvind, Director, Marketing were just back from the DemonOS (Distributed Environment Management and Online Operational System) user conclave. Something must have gone wrong there, Kishen surmised. He was not wrong.

The organization:

It is three months since Kishen joined the newly formed Strategic Management Group of ReSearch – an ERP implementation firm, promoted by three IIT, Delhi graduates – Krish, Leo and Arvind. Because the trio worked for sometime in Muscat before starting the company, the three were jocularly referred to as the Three Muscateers.

ReSearch was focussed on implementation of the ERP software DemonOS, a product from D365 and has been in this niche area for the past ten years. While the technical and the functional competence of the ReSearch consultants were not in doubt, project management was identified as a major weakness of the company. Every time they were called for a review by the principal, D365, this deficiency was a point of a prolonged discussion, at times bitter.

Problem detailed:

"The meeting with Ramsay is the one I would love to forget, but I cannot afford to" Krish continued. Ramsay was the Head of Sales, the Americas in D365. "He did not mince words" "Krish, we have had enough with you guys. The latest horror story is your implementation or should I say attempt to implement in Brazil? Could you guys not learn something called project management? All your projects are getting delayed eating into our margins and perhaps your margins as well. Why are you guys not doing something about it? Deviations are not reported in time. Worse, when things go out of control your people blame the product and the principal. Where is the accountability?" While Krish and Arvind did not expect the meeting to go smoothly, this was more than what they could take. Obviously things were going out of control. "If this continues, you may forget all the orders from us" Ramsay seemed to mean what he said. Project management had become an issue of life and death for ReSearch.

"We have to do something about it" Krish said in a serious tone. Arvind nodded.

Kishen could not believe that one project manager could make or mar a project. But he did not want to counter the senior management, when they were seized of a grave situation. "So we have to understand Project Management" Krish smiled wryly. "At least Solomon was milder" Solomon Gray was Ramsay's deputy. During the boisterous meeting with Ramsay, Solomon tried to ease the situation by suggesting "When we say your people are poor in Project Management, what we mean is that they have to improve in the communication management and the escalation management". Was that all or more expected of our staff - Krish wanted an answer. Failure to arrive at the right answer could be catastrophic for ReSearch.

Options available:

"As a person with a good business school background and a fresh perspective of our organization, tell me what we should do. How do we improve our Project Management skills?"

Kishen did not have an immediate answer. If the problem has been persisting in an organization for ten years, it could not have easy and obvious answers. Kishen wanted to test out some ideas with the CEO, whom he admired a lot, before coming with a set of concrete proposals.

"Why don't we recruit from the organizations which have expertise in construction or from ISRO[11], known for their project management capabilities?"

"But software project management is different" Krish interjected. 'Is that true?' Kishen wondered. He did not opt for the second year elective Software Project Management, because he had studied Project Management as a part of Operations Research in the first year. He did not expect anything new in Software Project Management. Was he wrong?

"We have two people with PMI certification. We can showcase their capabilities to D365 to gain more orders" said Krish. That was something positive, thought Kishen, but his hopes were dashed when Krish said "But I am not sure that all their projects would be successful". Now Kishen was confused. So the certified project managers also cannot save a project.

"We should look for people from other software organizations" Kishen suggested meekly. "But they should not be people who have handled SDLC projects. We want people with product implementation capabilities." 'Is that right to suggest that different environments require different project management capabilities?' Kishen wondered.

"Taking all these into account, can you prepare a white paper on the software project management appropriate for us? That is your project" Krish ended the meeting.

'That is what I do not understand' Kishen had more questions than answers as he left the CEO's room.

---

[11]   India's space research organization

1.4 **Program management**

A group of related projects is referred to as a program. This relating of different projects could be based on technology, domain or customer. It makes sense to group the projects under one domain to develop a knowledge base and expertise in that area. This has given rise to what we call the "verticals" [12] in the software industry.

Another way is to assign a program manager to a client. This is alternatively called the account management. When multiple projects are executed for a client, a program manager is assigned to the client. This program manager is expected to manage the projects cutting across application areas, technologies and business domains. For example, a software company may be developing different applications for a client – document management system for their administration function, workflow management across the organization, ERP implementation and treasury for their financial services business. While each of these projects may have a project manager, all of them will report to a program manager. A program manager is expected to understand the business of the client, keep a tab on the newer technologies and applications available in the market, suggest to the client of their need to adopt some of these technologies and applications and ensure the successful completion of the projects. In scouting for such new projects, the program manager keeps in mind his / her organization's interests as well.

1.4.1 **Project management vs. Program management**

It is natural for every project manager to aspire to become a program manager as a part of his / her career progression. So how do the perspectives of a project manager and a program manager differ?

As the above discussion shows, program management aims at the realization of the strategic objectives of the client organization as well as the software

---

[12]   In the software industry, the technology specializations are referred to as horizontals and business domains as verticals. So if you develop software for retail using Java. Java is your horizontal and Retail is your vertical.

development organization. The business objective determines the choice of the applications and in making these choices, a program manager is expected to show managerial skills apart from a broad understanding of technology. A project manager, on the other hand executes the project with an aim to control the cost, the time and the resources in a project to deliver the scope with the desired quality (Recapitulate scope triangle Fig. 1.1). The following table will show the difference clearly.

Project Management	Program Management
Focus on the content	Focus on the context
Management at the tactical level	Focus on the realization of the strategic objectives
Limited cross-functionality	Extensive cross-functionality
Technical and managerial skills	Extensive managerial skills with peripheral understanding of technology

Table 1.1

1.5 Project management standards

As a professional, it is important for you to learn about the standards in the profession. Some of the professional standards for project management are

- PMBOK (Project Management Body of Knowledge): This standard is developed and maintained by PMI (Project Management Institute). This institute conducts a certification examination called PMP (Project Management Professional), which is widely popular, particularly in the USA. Many large companies and multinationals insist on this certification for a project management position. PMI has another certification called PgMP (Program Management Professional) targeted at the program management practitioners.

- PRINCE 2 (An acronym for Projects IN Controlled Environments Ver. 2) was developed as a UK government standard for information systems and thus is popular in the UK.

- IEEE standard: IEEE has adopted PMI's PMBOK – Fourth edition (2008) and this is referred to as IEEE 1490 – 2011.

- IPMA (International Project Management Association) certifications: IPMA offers certifications at four levels, one of which is the Certified Project Manager (Level C).

1.6 **Project management defined**

We will close the chapter with a formal definition of project management

Project Management is the application of knowledge, skills, tools and techniques to project activities to meet the project requirements – PMBOK definition

In the coming chapters we will discuss

- the conceptual knowledge required by the project managers,
- the skills – technical and managerial – to be developed by the project managers,
- the technology tools that are available for the project managers and
- the techniques that the project managers should be familiar with.

Practice Questions

1. State whether true or false:

    a. A project usually has unconstrained resources.
    b. Project is a set of non-routine activities.
    c. Finance is a resource for a project.
    d. A project is normally large in size.
    e. Product intangibility makes the software project management challenging.
    f. Technology changes are rapid in the software industry.
    g. Once the requirements are frozen, no change should be permitted in the software project.
    h. A PMP qualification is a must for a project manager.
    i. Managing the software projects is impossible because software is intangible.
    j. Quality of the deliverable in a software project is independent of the quality of the people in the team.
    k. PMP is the certification offered by IPMA.

2. Fill in the blanks with the most appropriate terms:

    a. The most popular certification program for project management is offered by ----.
    b. ---- is the project management technique popular in UK.

3. Choose the most appropriate answer:

    a. Which of the following may be called a resource for a project?
        i.   Cost
        ii. People
        iii. Programs
        iv. Quality

b. To successfully manage the deliveries, on which of the following does the project manager have a maximum control to manipulate?

   i. Duration of the project
   ii. Project funding
   iii. Person hours input
   iv. Scope of the project

c. MS Project could be classified as a

   i. concept
   ii. skill
   iii. technology
   iv. tool

d. Which of the following could bring tangibility to a software product?

   i. Documentation
   ii. Schedule
   iii. Defining scope
   iv. Usage of tools

e. Which of the following is a needed skill for a project manager?

   i. Effective communication
   ii. PERT / CPM
   iii. Programming
   iv. PMP

4. Discuss the following questions

a. Project management comes with experience. Why should it be learnt formally?

b. If Fig. 1.1 is redrawn with scope, cost and schedule as sides and
    Resource at the centre
    Quality at the centre
how would you interpret these triangles?

c. Order the resources in their order of criticality for a project.

5. Comment on the following statements

    a. Managing an agile project is very similar to managing a waterfall project.
    b. How well the software meets the requirements of the customer is the responsibility of quality assurance.
    c. Innovation, cost-effectiveness and quick delivery are the reasons why teams choose agile methodology.

6. Why is a formal methodology important for the successful development of software?

2

STAGES OF PROJECT MANAGEMENT

First we need to understand what needs to be done. Then we decide how to do it. Then we do it. Any other sequence is asking for grief. — Paul Oldfield

2.1 Lesson objectives

In this lesson we will learn

- the different stages a project goes through and
- the tasks performed in each of these stages.

2.2 Stages of project management

PMBOK identifies five stages of project management:

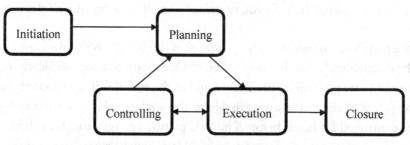

Fig 2.1 Stages of Project Management

These stages indicate a chronological sequence of the processes in a project; among these, execution and controlling take place concurrently.

2.2.1 Project initiation

A task well begun is half done – very true of all the projects. This is the phase in which the user requirements are gathered and the success of the project depends on how well the project team has understood the user requirements and delivered a product to address all those requirements.

2.2.1.1 Eliciting user requirements

In the software world, we no more use the term *gathering* the requirements, but our business analysts are urged to *elicit* the requirements. The choice of the term is deliberate to emphasize that a business analyst has to draw out / extract the requirements from the users, who may not voluntarily provide them. The situation is analogous to a doctor performing a diagnosis. A doctor is not content with what the patient states; (s)he knows that what the patient lists are all the symptoms and for recommending a lasting remedy (s)he needs to identify the cause(s). Towards this the doctor keeps probing, mentally sets his / her hypotheses and with each question and test keeps validating / invalidating these hypotheses. Eliciting the requirements is an analogous exercise. A business analyst normally tries to find out the tasks performed by each user and his / her pain areas. Does it not sound paradoxical that the analyst needs to probe to identify the tasks that the user is performing on a day-to-day basis? It is not because the user does not know the tasks that he fails to provide the right inputs. Ironically it is because of his close familiarity that he misses out the steps in describing the tasks. For example how many of us will be able to detail each step, if we are asked "how do you breathe?" and all of us breathe all the time!

Take a peep into a business analysis discussion (box) – this is just the beginning of the discussion. What do you find here? Details are coming out slowly with more and more probing by the analyst and at the end of this questioning, only a few pieces of the jigsaw are available to the analyst. The exercise may have to be continued for hours before a holistic picture emerges and even then one cannot be sure that this is comprehensive. There may be omissions because the user makes assumptions about the knowledge of the analyst and also jumps steps without getting into the details so vital for a software system design. And whenever the user mentions 'case-to-case basis', a further probe is required to understand the underlying logic. Humans are capable of discretion; computers need algorithms.

This is a critical step in the software life cycle. Poor requirement gathering has been found to be one of the top reasons for the unsatisfactory deliverables.

Scenario: Business analyst (BA) trying to gather requirements from a purchase manager (user).

BA: I am here to understand your function.

User; (silence)

BA: Could you say what you do?

User: Well, we purchase.

BA (with a smile): That is what I want to know: how do you purchase?

User: Nothing unique; like how all the other companies purchase.

BA: Could you please tell me the tasks involved in purchasing?

User: Same – indent, order and then .... Order amendment etc. I am sure you know all these.

BA: I want more details; who raises the indents?

User: Who else? Only the users.

BA: Users from?

User: Any department can raise the indent; but mainly production; even administration can raise...

BA: For all the purchases, the indent is a must?

User: Well, not for the MRP items.

BA: That means for the direct items.

User: Not all the direct materials are covered in the MRP.

BA: Which are not covered?

User: Some materials; there is a separate list available. But the list is not exhaustive. Sometimes engineering advise the specification change to the items in the MRP at the time of the purchase.

BA: Are the packaging materials included in the MRP?

User: No, only for the large items.

BA: Large means?

User: Over a period of time by our experience we know the classification. There is no criterion specified by the company.

BA: Import items?

User: They are bought in bulk.

The discussion continues....

2.2.1.2 Documenting user needs

Documentation ensures clarity in the requirements and also the agreement between the development team and the client on the requirements. It acts as a communication tool across the team through the development life cycle and also acts as a basis for testing whether the deliverables are in accordance with the user requirements.

The analyst documents the requirements using the standard tools and techniques. UML[13] is one of the most popular techniques, though other notations too are in use. Software organizations specify the standards for

---

[13]   Unified Modelling Language is a system specification technique associated with object oriented analysis and design.

documentation and in some cases, the client organizations have their own specifications.

2.2.1.3 Negotiating requirements

All the requirements of the client may not be accepted. In their enthusiasm to make the system all-encompassing, the users will tend to include a large number of requirements. The ambitious requirements list may render the deadlines infeasible and put a strain on the budgetary allocation. There could also be diverse views among the users on how a business process should be designed and sometimes these requirements could be conflicting with each other. Thus the requirements need to be resolved for appropriateness and consistency, pruned and prioritized.

Once all the requirements are collected and analyzed, the analyst makes the classification of vital, essential and desirable (VED) - from the business point of view and not from the technical or the development perspective – and discusses with the client to retain the vital aspects, combine some requirements, drop the redundant requirements and be flexible on the desirable features. This process has to be iterated till the list of requirements is pruned to a level achievable in the pre-specified timeline and budget. Because of this reason, the project manager has a stake in this exercise, though the analyst may lead the negotiations.

2.2.1.4 Preparing scope document

A document delineating what is proposed to be achieved in the project with a cost-benefit analysis is prepared. This is submitted to the management for approval.

2.2.1.5 Approval by the management

The scope document is scrutinized by the management based on the factors such as the criticality of the client to the business, the domain expertise available, the strategic importance of the domain to the business, availability of the necessary resources, feasibility of meeting the deadlines specified by the customer and the profitability assessment and then approved / declined.

2.2.2 Planning

Planning is an important phase in the project management. Success of the execution depends a lot on the soundness of the plan. This is an elaborate exercise.

2.2.2.1 Estimation

Two important parameters that need to be estimated fairly accurately are time and cost – the two critical factors identified in the scope triangle. Towards this, the project has to be broken down into detailed tasks and the effort input for each task estimated to arrive at the total effort estimate of the project.

With identification of the tasks, the human resources required for each of these tasks may be identified and their cost too estimated. Apart from the human resources, which form the major proportion of the project cost, other costs such as hardware, travel, training and overheads too need to be included in the cost estimate.

The tasks should then be sequenced taking into account the interdependencies which will help estimate the total duration of the project. This sequence of the tasks called the *schedule* needs to go through several iterations to optimize the duration of the project.

2.2.2.2 Risk management plan

All these estimates are subject to some assumptions. The estimates prepared as above may be achievable, if everything goes right. That is one assumption which never works. Any activity in real life – a project much more so – is subject to several uncertainties and to expect that none of these uncertainties, also known as risks, will materialize is unrealistic. So all the above estimates have to take into account the risks involved and accordingly be reworked. The risk management plan involves identifying the most likely risks in a project and working out the mitigation plans for the same.

2.2.2.3 Project Plan

The extensive planning exercise done on several aspects of the project are documented in a project plan. Quality plan, which details the proposed steps to achieve the desired quality level, is also a part of the project plan. This plan acts as a bible for the execution of the project and is the standard reference material for the entire team. The project plan, however, undergoes changes through the life of the project and it is the latest version of the plan that is the reference material for the team.

2.2.3 Execution, Monitoring and Controlling

In terms of duration, the execution phase is the longest.

2.2.3.1 Progress monitoring and reporting

In this phase, the progress of the project is monitored continuously and reported periodically to the management and the client. Fixing the reporting responsibilities, standardizing the forms and their formats and defining the appropriate media for different reports are all the tasks in this phase. The stakeholders being spread in different locations is also a consideration in defining the media for reporting.

2.2.3.2 Monitoring risk

The risks identified at the planning stage may not remain static. As the project progresses, some risks may become ineffective and some may be accentuated. There is also a possibility that new risks may arise. So the risks need to be monitored continuously and the mitigation plans may also need to be reworked.

2.2.3.3 Managing scope changes

We identified this as a unique challenge in the software project management. At no point of time during the project duration can the project manager put a hold on changes. Unless these changes are managed properly, it might create instability in the project and its deliverables. A proper procedure needs to be put in place for the change requests and the actions on them.

2.2.3.4 Managing people

To ensure the successful delivery of the scope with quality, a project manager has to manage three aspects: Technology, People and Process (Fig 2.2). Of these, our understanding of the technology is the highest and people are the least understood component of the software projects. Maximum uncertainties are created through the people factor and the problem with the people issues is that they keep simmering beneath the surface and suddenly explode. That is why a project manager should discover and solve the problems.

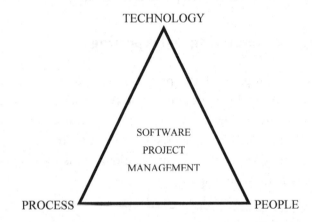

Fig. 2.2 Factors in software project management

2.2.4 Closure

This is the last phase of the project.

2.2.4.1 Installing deliverables

The deliverables, as agreed in the contract, need to be delivered in the appropriate forms to the satisfaction of the client organization.

2.2.4.2 Data migration

The data in the old environment need to be converted to the new format to make it amenable to the processing by the new software.

2.2.4.3 Sign off

The client sign-off that the project has been completed to their satisfaction is an important task in this phase.

2.2.4.4 Post implementation audit

At the initiation stage, the project success criteria were identified and agreed upon with the client. Now is the time to test whether those criteria have been fulfilled, which will indicate the successful completion of the project.

2.3 Project management knowledge areas

What are the different things that a project manager should know to be effective?

Turning to the classical wisdom

> *I keep six honest serving-men*
> *(They taught me all I knew);*
> *Their names are What and Why and When*
> *And How and Where and Who.*
> — Rudyard Kipling[14]

Let us look at the questions that need to be addressed by a project manager to manage projects effectively:

- *What* has to be done: This is what we call the **scope** of a project.

---

[14]   From 'Just So Stories' (1902)

- *Why* should it be done?: The project manager needs to understand the **business justification** of the project. During the course of the project, the scope undergoes several changes. In making these changes and in all the other decisions affecting the project scope, the project manager should ensure that the purpose for which the project was originally proposed to be undertaken is not altered. If a substantial deviation from the original justification is unavoidable, then it has to be done only after a detailed discussion with the client – particularly the project sponsor (For a definition of this role see 11.3) - highlighting the changes and obtaining his / her concurrence.

- *When* is it required? The **schedule** will decide the duration of the project and the delivery timeline for the different deliverables.

- *How* will it be done? The **process methodology** to be adopted and the **quality** criterion of the project are addressed in the quality plan.

- *Where* will it be done? The proportion of the on-site and the off-site activities needs to be understood which will have an impact on the costing.

- *Who* would do the job? – the **human resources** and the **skills** assigned to the project.

- *How* should the people be organized? – **Organization structure** and **team management.**

- If the needed technical skills are not available within the organization, what should we do? In such cases, outsourcing of the skills or the project becomes necessary and that makes **procurement** and the **vendor management** the necessary knowledge areas for a project manager.

- For whom is the project created? Addressed by the **stakeholder management.**

- How much will it cost? **Budgeting** and the **cost control** will address this question.

- What are the uncertainties? This will be addressed in the **risk management** plan.

- How will the different stakeholders come to know about the progress of the project? – **Communication management.**

(Adapted from Managing the Project Team: The Human Aspects of Project Management, Volume 3, by Vijay K. Verma (Project Management Institute, 1997)

Project management is thus an integration of all these knowledge areas. PMBOK identifies ten knowledge areas:

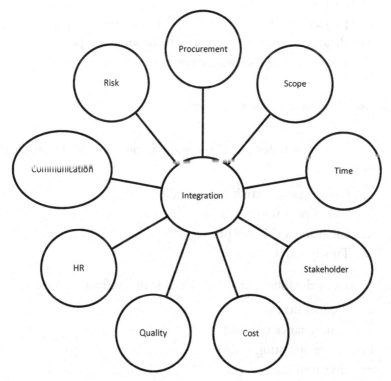

Fig 2.3. Project Management Knowledge Areas

Practice Questions

1. State whether true or false:

   a. All the requirements of the client have to be accepted by the analyst.
   b. Once a project plan is finalized, it cannot be changed.
   c. During the course of a project, the risks may change.

2. Fill in the blanks with the appropriate terms:

   a. The document that contains all the requirements of the users is called ----.
   b. The process of effectively responding to change requests is called ----.
   c. Budget is a ---- control tool.
   d. In a project, uncertainties are referred to as ----.
   e. The detailed sequence of activities is shown in the project ------.
   f. The role collecting the requirements from the users is -----.

3. Choose the most appropriate answer:

   a. Which of the following is the most important for the success of a project?
      i.   Doing several activities in parallel
      ii. Sound planning
      iii. Choosing a risk-free project
      iv. Timely start

   b. Which of the following is a deliverable in a software project?
      i.   Product license
      ii. Maintenance contract
      iii. Server operating system
      iv. User training

c. Which of the following is the last activity chronologically in a software project?

   i. Eliciting the user requirements
   ii. Estimating the resource requirements
   iii. Installing the deliverables
   iv. Submitting the progress reports to the management

d. Which phase of the project life cycle has the greatest degree of uncertainty?

   i. Initiation
   ii. Planning
   iii. Execution
   iv. Closure

e. Which is an important input for sequencing activities?

   i. Duration of the project
   ii. The multitasking capability of the project organization
   iii. Dependencies among the activities
   iv. Availability of the resources

f. Which could be a source of problems for a project?

   i. Duration of the project
   ii. Reduction in the risk intensity
   iii. Sequence of the activities
   iv. Staff

g. Why is the post-implementation audit necessary?

   i. To check the financial irregularities
   ii. To check if the project has achieved the originally specified objectives
   iii. To compensate for the activities omitted during the project
   iv. To get the customer sign-off

h. Which of the following is not a Project Management Knowledge Area?

   i. Procurement
   ii. Quality
   iii. Schedule
   iv. Scope

4. Match the following with the phases of a project

    a. Managerial control is high
    b. Customer sign-off
    c. Needs identification
    d. The success of this phase impacts the other phases.
    e. High degree of uncertainty

5. Discuss the following questions:

    a. Distinguish between a plan and a schedule.
    b. Why is it that while the execution takes the maximum time in a project, planning will consume more time in the project management training?
    c. Technology, process and people are the three factors a project manager has to manage. Suggest some methods of managing these.
    d. Documents that undergo changes during the progress of a project are called the configuration items. Which of the following are the configuration items?
        i.   Project plan
        ii. Schedule
        iii. Risk plan

    e. Identify the parameters that need to be estimated at the beginning of a project.
    f. How are the PMBOK process areas different from the SDLC activities? Why do we need the PMBOK over and above the SDLC?
    g. Why do monitoring and controlling run concurrently with the execution phase and not with the other phases?
    h. The project staff work as teams. What are the important attributes that are required to be an effective team?

6. Identify the high level requirements for a mobile commerce application.

3

PROJECT INITIATION

I believe that this nation should commit itself to achieving the goal,
before this decade is out, of landing a man on the moon
and returning him safely to the earth.
- President Kennedy, Address to Congress, May 25, 1961

3.1 Lesson objectives

In this lesson we will learn the following:

- How is the scope of a project defined?
- What are the contents of a scope document?
- What is a business case and how is it created?

3.2 Scope management

The most important activity in this phase is defining the scope of the project. Scope is what we propose to do towards the achievement of the objective in the execution of a project. Unlike in a civil construction and similar projects, wherein the scope may be defined in concrete terms, the abstract software needs to be defined in terms of its functionalities and also the non-functional requirements such as performance, security etc. Scope defines the extent of work and the precision with which the scope is defined determines the success of a software project. Any ambiguity in defining the scope could become a matter of dispute.[15]

3.2.1 Problems in defining scope

- **Generality:** The user tends to make general statements and that makes the requirements ambiguous. Statements such as 'we need regular MIS' cannot be converted into the software specifications without further elaboration.

- **Ambiguity:** Related to generality is the ambiguity of requirements. A statement such as 'the software should be user-friendly' could have different meanings to different people.

- **Incoherence:** In an oral interview, the user cannot be expected to give the requirements in a coherent logical fashion. The user will give the requirements as it comes to his / her mind and the analyst may have to make sense out of it. (See Box: Material issue report – Gathering requirements)

- **Conflicting requirements:** Different users give the requirements which conflict with each other. While the Head of Sales might think that it is his / her prerogative to sanction a special discount, the CFO might suggest that this approval falls in his / her domain.

- **Poor understanding of capabilities and limitations of computers:** Many users have a hazy understanding of what computers can and cannot do. In every organization you will find sceptics who feel that computers are useless and error-prone. Successive exposures to the programming errors only reinforce their belief. And on the other hand

---

[15] Ambiguity in the scope has been the reason for many failed software projects and tortuous court cases. Some examples are
Polaris Software Labs Vs. Bank Arthagraha, Indonesia (2003)
De Beers UK Limited Vs. Atos Origin IT Services Limited (2010) (discussed in detail in the case study at the end of this chapter)

are the users, who have a romantic notion of computers. Their ideas of computers and what they can do are all imported from the sci-fi movies. A customer wanted pre-printed numbers in the cheque leaves to be read automatically from the printer. Many users are wary of codes and want the application to recognize the customers from their names.

- **Communication gap**: Analysts should recognize that users will not be able to understand their technical jargons just as analysts might find the terminologies specific to the business domain difficult to understand. Look at the following transcript from a requirement gathering interview:

> User: We charge a declining interest rate depending on the period and the amount and this rate is tied to the bank's basic rate. The interest is compounded annually except for some special schemes. While the pre-specified interest rate is applicable till the maturity date, for the balance period a marginal rate is only applicable.
>
> Analyst: Client level cross validations are recommended for the interest rate and the amount - period combination. Key customer variables will be validated at the back end.

- Imagine the level of understanding reached between the User and the Analyst at the end of this conversation!

- **Omitting the 'obvious' information**: Because of his / her close familiarity with the processes, the user assumes many of them to be obvious and known to everybody and thus does not specify in sufficient detail some of those processes during the discussions with the analyst. That a computer requires all the details without any omission and thus an analyst needs to record all of them without exception is not understood by the user. If the analyst fails to fill these gaps with his / her domain knowledge or by incisive probing, the final deliverable will fall short of the customer expectations.

- **Non-testability**: Requirements such as 'interface with pleasing colours' and 'easily navigatable menus' fall in this category. Translating these into test cases and proving the fulfilment of these requirements are difficult.

Material issue report – Gathering Requirements

User: We need a daily material issue report.

Analyst: What will it contain? From where will the data be collected?

User: A list of the materials issued from the stores. The issue notes will be the source.

Analyst: ok. Can I get a format?

(User gives a format of the report)

User: In ascending order of value; no, descending order.

Analyst: The model format you have given does not contain value.

User: ok. You could provide item code wise. You may have to segregate the raw materials and the indirect items.

Analyst; How do we identify the items as direct or indirect?

User: It is a part of the item code – first digit; no, the second digit represents it. When the issue is for different plants, it has to be shown separately.

Analyst: So the order is item code wise, plant wise.

User: No plant wise, item code wise. Oh I forgot to mention: the return notes have to be offset against the issues.

Analyst: ok.

User: If the return relates to the previous days' issue, it has to be tagged.

The conversation continues…

3.2.2 Consequences of poor scope definition:

Expectation mismatch: At the end of an arduous development activity spanning months, when the final delivery is made, if the user says 'this is not what we wanted', that would be the most traumatic experience for any project manager, leaving his / her position vis-a-vis his / her management and the client management vulnerable

Scope creep: Formal changes to software are implemented through an established procedure called change control and go through a technical evaluation and a formal approval. Bypassing this procedure (an undesirable practice a project manager should resist), the users tend to enforce changes in the software under the pretext that they are minor or are included in the originally specified scope. The ambiguous wording of the scope often facilitates such creeps. Unless controlled, creeps could grow at the rate of 3.5% per month in a commercial software development (Jones, 1995). Imagine in an eighteen month project, almost half the requirements would have changed that too without any formal procedure.

3.2.3 Process of scope definition

3.2.3.1 Identify the problem / opportunity

A software application is created to address a business problem.

Example: A retail chain finds its operations unprofitable and the inventory is identified as a major cost area. A sound inventory management system with tight replenishment measures could be a solution.

In such a case, the user interviews form an important part of the problem identification in addition to the secondary research on the industry and optionally the expert interviews.

Alternately, a software organization could identify a business opportunity and develop a product.

Example: Compliance with the Basel norms[16] is an important requirement for the commercial banks and a software organization might see a business opportunity in developing an application to ensure this regulatory compliance.

In this case, the secondary research and the domain expert opinions are the important inputs.

3.2.3.2 Identify user needs

Not all that the user states are his / her requirements and some of his / her needs remain unexpressed. An experienced business analyst identifies the expectations of the client and using the expectation as a critical parameter, distils the expressed wants to what the user needs, which are then translated into the features of the software.

The relationship between expectations, wants and needs is shown in Fig. 3.1. Take the famous adage by Henry Ford: "If I had asked people what they wanted, they would have said faster horses."[17].

In this case, the customer expectation is to have fast movement.

Towards this, the customer specifies that (s)he needs a robust, powerful, healthy horse which can run @ 20 mph without any interruption for 4 hrs.

Customer need, however, is to have a reliable contraption – can we call it an engine? - which can run at 20+ mph fitted into an arrangement providing a convenient seating for two persons (Later generations referred to this as a car!).

---

[16] Basel norms are a set of supervisory standards formulated by a group of central banks.
[17] It is said that Ford never uttered these words. However, this is one of the most popular quotes. Since the quote helps us distinguish among expectations, wants and needs, we will use this disregarding the authenticity of the quote.

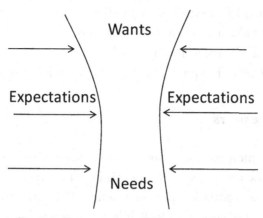

Fig 3.1. Expectations, Wants and Needs

For a software application, let us differentiate these three:

User expectation: Using typewriters to create a text requires a special training. Could we have an easier method of creating a text?

User wants: ability to input a text, modify and delete a part or the whole of it at will without any trace, restore the text if needed and print it in a presentable format.

User needs:

Ability to

- create a text with automatic word-wrapping without the usage of carriage return.
- modify any portion of the created text without trace; however with trace if the option is preferred.
- delete a text – again with a trace option.
- save the deleted text in a separate location for retrieval (Could we make such a storage optional with an option other than delete – may be 'cut'?).
- reformat the text automatically, whenever a modification / deletion occurs.
- set margins, header and footer.

- provide the left, centre and right alignments.
- have the bold, italics, underlines options.
- print in the WYSIWYG[18] mode.
- Store the text, if required, for future reference / change.

3.2.3.3 Involve users

This needs generation exercise is done with an active user involvement. Every requirement of the user is put through this exercise, negotiated and the need agreed upon. The negotiation process should not be seen by the user as an effort to cut down the project work. While we mentioned earlier that the users may not know their requirements or they may not know how to express them, the negotiating process should not be conducted as if the project manager and the business analyst are educating the user. Such an exercise will leave the user in a defeated mode and that is a prescription for the disastrous start of a project. On the contrary, the project manager should show empathy and try to understand why the user is saying what (s)he is saying and should make his / her suggestions not as a counter but as an alternate way of achieving what the user desires.

3.2.3.4 Communicate to the client

Managing the expectations is said to be the major task of a project manager. As the project progresses, the user expectations tend to change – normally expand; with a better appreciation of the software and its capabilities, the user starts reimagining his / her requirements. The project manager has to be cautious that the revised expectations do not result in the scope creep or in the expectation mismatch.

Once the scope is defined, the project manager should communicate to the users what they may expect from the software. The needs statement above for a word processor clearly delineates the capability of the software when delivered.

---

[18]   What You See Is What You Get: the acronym is used to describe the capability of any software to present the pre-view of the document exactly as it would look like in the print-out.

At the same time, the project manager should not hesitate to include a truly enhanced functionality in the product, even if this has not been specified in the beginning. Throughout the project, the project manager should keep the communication channels with the users open so that at any point of time any user can check with the project manager whether his / her new idea may be included in the software or not.

During the course of the project, selected users, identified by the client organization, may be kept updated of the progress of the project and their feedback obtained. This is over and above the formal progress report submitted to the client.

3.2.3.5 Documentation

Contents of a scope document:

1. **Problem / Opportunity identified**

2. **Project objectives**: In the above-mentioned retail chain, the inventory management is the problem; the cost reduction or the profit increase is the objective.

3. **Functional requirements**: What the software is required to do is included here.

4. **Exclusions**: Scope document is referred to as a *bounded* description of the functionalities, which means that the document describes not only the functionalities to be addressed, but also the ones that will not be included in the project. This makes the automation boundary well-defined and reduces ambiguity and the future disputes between the users and the developers.

5. **Interface requirements**: In the production environment, the developed software may have to work in conjunction with another application. There may even be data transfer requirements between these applications. For example, the team that develops ATM application needs to understand the core banking software, already

installed, broadly – particularly the structures of the data files accessed need to be understood; the exercise may become challenging, if the technology platforms are different.

The interface could also be a hardware device: an attendance monitoring system with a barcode reader might be interfaced with a payroll application.

6. **Data to be processed**: The intent is not to describe all the input requirements in detail here, but to broadly indicate the source and the volume of the data that will be processed towards fulfilling the stated objective. Exceptions such as the source of some or all of the data being external and the difficulty in obtaining them need to be highlighted here. Volume and rate of the data flow are the necessary inputs for the hardware sizing; also in conjunction with the performance requirement, this will decide the extent of optimization required in the software.

7. **Technology environment**: An indication of the likely choice of the technology is mentioned here. This could be determined by the application requirements and could also be influenced by the technology currently in use in the client organization. With technology evolution, the technology specifications go beyond the hardware and the software. Issues like whether the application will be hosted within the premises or in the cloud environment, whether the cloud will be private or public and the technology environments in the different layers of the cloud all need to be mentioned here.

8. **Impact on the organization**: Any impact this application is likely to have on the organization structure and the staffing need to be mentioned here.

The extent of the impact an application will have on the organization will determine its criticality. Imagine a highly visible application like the passenger reservation system in the railways. Any loophole in the application will invite the immediate attention of the public and the press. Any failure will have an adverse consequence on the service of the railways as well as on the reputation of the development organization. Not only that, a computerized reservation system changes the work styles at the operating level and one can imagine the challenges, if the work style changes are to be implemented in an organization like the Indian Railways, employing more than a million people across 7000 plus stations. The project management in such cases goes much beyond managing the software development.

9. **Control requirements:** Major validation requirements are included here – these are particularly important in the financial and the security applications. Requirements imposed by the statutory and the regulatory agencies also need to be mentioned here. KYC[19] norms for new depositors for a bank, credit card authentication requirement in online commerce are good examples worthy of inclusion here.

10. **Performance requirements:** The customer-facing parts of an application may have stringent response requirements. In B2C e-commerce applications, this can even be a deciding factor in maintaining a competitive edge; thus it becomes a non- negotiable requirement. There have been some large project implementations in which the software development organizations were required to sign performance bank guarantees[20] against the promised performance. Penalties are stiff for not meeting this requirement.

It may also be noted here that the control requirements tend to impede the performance and thus stringent control requirements may render meeting the performance specifications more challenging.

---

[19]   KYC means Know Your Customer – This is a procedure mandated by the central banks on the commercial banks to collect all the relevant details about the customer while opening an account.

[20]   A performance bank guarantee is a surety bond, issued by a bank or any lending institution, to guarantee the satisfactory completion of a project by a contractor. On the non-fulfillment of the contract requirements, the buyer of the services may invoke the guarantee, in which case the guarantor institution is liable to pay the pre-specified penalty amount.

11. **Reliability requirements**: This might look like a surprising inclusion in a scope document. Do we need to specify reliability as a requirement? Is it not required for all the software applications? True, but the degree of the reliability required is not the same for all the applications. A web design application may go through quick and dirty, trial and error method and even if the final deliverable has a bug, it would not have such a serious consequence as in the case of a rocket-launching application.

The question then arises as to how the reliability requirement impacts the scope of a project. Would it in anyway affect the effort, the duration or the cost of development? An application with a high reliability requirement will need to go through several rounds of rigorous testing and thus will need a significantly increased effort. NASA specifies that the testing effort should be thrice over the coding (Waligora and Coon).

12. **Assumptions**: The analyst makes some assumptions in defining the scope. These assumptions should have been vetted with the customer. All these assumptions need to be stated explicitly. For example, 'at any point of time more than a thousand users will not be logged into the system' is an important assumption to state, particularly when the performance target has been specified. Again 'a dedicated server will be provided for this application by the customer' is an assumption that needs to be stated explicitly.

13. **Risks**: While all the possible risks will be identified and its impact will be analyzed in detail under the risk management, here we will mention the risks specific to this project. Some industries or some applications, by their very nature, are vulnerable to some specific risks. For example telecom billing is a highly volatile application, which undergoes many quick changes to meet the challenge of market competition. Being a real- time application, the changes need to be implemented within a stipulated short period and thus become risky.

14. **Constraints**: Constraints are the limitations imposed by the management of the client organization or the development organization. Technology could also impose some constraints. For example, an

application that may have to be interfaced with a legacy application may have to be developed using the legacy technology, though it may not be optimal. Insufficient budgetary allocation is the most often encountered constraint in the software projects.

15. **Success criteria**: On which basis will the success of this application be decided? Project success should not be viewed from the perspective of technology, but should be expressed in the business terms. "This will be the first application that will be rolled out in the latest version of Java in a multi-tier architecture" is not a good success criterion. "On the implementation of this software, the inventory turnover ratio will move from 6 to 9" is an appropriate one.

16. **Cost-benefit analysis**: Any project in a business has to be justified in terms of the costs associated with the project and the benefits accruing out of the installation of the software, monetized through appropriate techniques after applying valid assumptions. Only when the cumulative benefits outweigh the total cost, the project is undertaken. Annexure I provides different techniques of cost-benefit analysis. Even in the case of the not-for-profit organizations, a cost-benefit analysis is recommended, though it may be less rigorous,

A model scope document is shown below:

Scope document – an example
Creation of a social networking website

Opportunity identified: Social networks such as Face book, Twitter etc. provide access to everybody and allow sharing of trivia across different people without any restriction. Such a wide, undefined audience is not conducive for intensive discussions on specific subjects. The present project aims to create a site which will allow different interest groups to create sub network groups and interact. Such a need is felt by the serious users of social networks and it is expected that such a site will have a good patronage.

Objective: Provision of a platform for the groups with common interests is expected to facilitate migration of these people from the existing networks. The value-add in this site would be contents that would be of interest to these groups on a chargeable basis. For the advertisers, such a targeted segment is a great opportunity and the revenue model will include the advertisements and the transaction-based charges as well.

Functionalities:

User registration with capture of their background and interest details

Profile maintenance by the users

Creation of forums and subgroups within forums

User authentication

Administrative controls over the creation and the maintenance of the users and the forums

User's ability to define friends in the group – alternately 'unfriend' some people in the group

Real-time chats within the group

Asynchronous messaging within the group

Ability to share different types of messages – text, audio, video contents – among the members of the group

Ability to host surveys / polls

Ability to post links to the related forums

Ability to host advertisements

Administrative control to suspend a forum after a specified period of inactivity or due to any other cause

Exclusions: Integration with mobile, SMS, the webcam feeds and the live meetings are excluded in the current phase of the development. However, since these are proposed in the future versions, the design should have the flexibility to include these features.

Interfaces: The software should have the ability to replicate the data into the existing popular social media sites and should also be able to pull the data from them. As indicated in the previous paragraph, the software design should take into account the future requirements of interfacing with mobile, SMS, the webcam feeds and the live meetings.

Data to be processed:

User profile data collection should have a segregation as mandatory data and optional. Mandatory data should not include any data, considered intrusive into the user privacy.

Privacy of the data collected from the users should be ensured. Any data that is proposed to be used for the commercial purposes should have a prior user permission.

Filters for spam and monitors for the objectionable content need to be a part of the design.

Depending on the user groups, RSS[21] feeds from the sites of interest to these groups may be provided.

The database is expected to expand exponentially and the servers with adequate back-up will be needed. An archival policy also needs to be put in place.

Technology environment: It is recommended that we use the open source technologies for the creation of the site. The choice is not only based on the cost consideration, but also because of the proven capability of these technologies for such high volume, high velocity social networking sites. Server banks located across the globe with replication in the cloud are the preferred option.

Impact on the organization: This project is likely to bring high visibility to our organization and hence the management is totally committed to this as a high priority project.

Control requirements: The distinguishing feature of this site from the other popular social network sites is the need for the entry authentication for the users. Based on the profile submitted by the user (this may require the corroborative

---

[21] Rich Site Summary

testimonials as well), his / her membership for a group is approved by the administrator. The extent of verification and the documentation requirements need to be identified. Anonymous ids are not permitted.

Performance requirements: The response time should not exceed eight seconds. With the increasing volume of the posts, this may become challenging and the architecture should take this requirement into account.

Reliability requirements: The site should ensure that no data corruption takes place. Hanging of the site is annoying to the users and should be minimized. The site should ensure high availability.

Assumptions: The site will initially be designed with an assumption that no group will have more than hundred thousand members and no group will have more than ten thousand concurrent users logged in. However, this assumption needs to be revisited once the site goes live.

Risks:

The social media space has quite a few heavyweights and a new entrant in this segment may have a long gestation period before gaining acceptability / popularity. During this period the project might continue to demand higher and higher investment without any return.

Emergence of a similar product also might blunt our USP and thus our competitive edge.

Sustainability of the groups depends on the extent of the intelligent use by the subscribers; as a result initially several forums may die an early death. The success of the site will depend less on our efforts and more on our users and hence not in our control.

Our organization has not worked in a similar project and this inexperience may prove to be a risk.

It should be ensured that no copyrighted material is fed into the site without the needed permission.

Constraints:

The available staff trained in the open source technologies is inadequate for this project.

The initial allocation of $10 million is adequate to create the product. Aggressive promotion may be required from the second year onwards and this requires heavy additional funding.

Success criteria:

The membership and the usage of the site are the most important criteria to judge the success of the site. We have set a target of hundred thousand members in the first year and twofold increase in the second and third years.

The advertisement revenue is another measure to judge the popularity of the site.

Cost-benefit analysis:

(In thousands of dollars)

	Year 1	Year 2	Year 3	Year 4	Year 5
Revenue					
Membership	0	0	1000	2000	4000
Advertisement	0	0	1000	50000	100000
Transactions	0	0	40	400	1000
Total revenue	**0**	**0**	**2040**	**52400**	**105000**
Cost					
Development	7500	2500	0	4000	2000
Promotion	0	7500	20000	20000	20000
Maintenance	0	2500	5000	10000	10000
Copyright	0	1000	2000	5000	5000
Total cost	**7500**	**13500**	**27000**	**39000**	**37000**
Profit	**(7500)**	**(13500)**	**(24960)**	**13400**	**68000**

Assumptions:

The membership is assumed at $10 per member per annum.

The membership is free for the first two years.

The transaction commission is assumed at 4% of the transaction value.

With the popularity of the site increasing, the cost of promotion is expected to come down.

The maintenance cost includes introduction of additional features in the product.

At a discounted rate of 10%, NPV is calculated:

$$NPV = -7500 - (13500/1.1) - \{24960/ (1.1)^2\} + \{13400/ (1.1)^3\} + \{68000/ (1.1)^4\} = 16111$$

3.3 Business case

As an alternate to the scope document, a business case is sometimes recommended as a project initiation document. While the scope document focuses more on the technical aspects, the business case emphasizes on the business justification. To that extent, a business case covers the technical and the functional aspects of the project only at a macro level and stresses on the cost / benefit analysis more. The business case is also useful, when multiple solutions are available and a choice has to be made on some criteria.

A business case has the following format:

- **Executive summary**: This is a one page summary of the report covering the salient points such as the recommendations and the costs involved. Often the senior managements may not have sufficient time to read the entire report; they will go through only the executive summary. So it is important that the executive summary captures the essence of the report.

- **Problem / Opportunity identified**: The business problem that is proposed to be solved is stated here.

- **Different options available to solve the problem**

- **Criteria identified for the evaluation of the solutions**: Typical examples are the cost, ease of implementation, acceptability by the staff etc. All criteria may not have equal importance. So a weightage is assigned to each of the criteria identified.

- **Evaluation of the solutions**: The criteria identified are applied to the options and the best option is chosen.

- **Cost of the solution**: For the solution chosen, the associated costs are identified.

- **Benefits of the solution**: The benefits are quantified in monetary terms. The problem is that all benefits are not quantifiable easily. A benefit such as a better inventory management can be quantified by calculating the interest cost saved on the reduced inventory. But how do we quantify a benefit like the increase in the customer convenience? We may have to identify some proxy variables for this such as the increase in the number of the customers or the reduction in the customer interaction time in offering the service and thus may have to compute the monetary value of the benefit.

- **Disbenefits**: This term may sound strange. How are these different from costs? To cite an example, implementation of the software may result in the reduction of the employees, which might have an impact on the employee morale. This cannot be termed as a cost. The amount to be spent for restoring the morale could be the monetary equivalent of this disbenefit.

- **Cost-benefit analysis**: We have already discussed this in detail and the methods are also shown in Annexure I.

- **Risks**

- **Assumptions**

- **Constraints**: These three are the same as in scope document.

3.4 **Presentation to management**

The scope document and / or the business case is presented to the software organization management and to the client management for their review and approval.

3.4.1 Important considerations from the management point of view

The managements would like to evaluate whether the problem / opportunity identified are of importance to them to make an investment. They would like to assure themselves that the document is internally consistent and logical in the sense that the solution identified addresses the problem adequately. The risk analysis is an area the managements would like to focus on: if the project has too many risks, the management might reassess the need of the project and might even decide to drop it.

Case Study

De Beers Vs. Atos Origin

The parties

The De Beers (DB) Group of Companies is a leader in the diamond exploration, mining, retail, and trading and the industrial diamond manufacturing sectors.

Atos is a French multinational IT services corporation headquartered in Bezons, France that provides the managed services, hi-tech transactional services, the consulting & technology services and systems integration.

Background

In May 2006, De Beers Diamond Trading decided to move a major part of its operations from South Africa to Botswana. This transfer required a software system to support the diamond supply chain management and DB decided to take the opportunity to upgrade its existing software systems, which were obsolete and were not properly integrated across the departments.

History of IT systems in De Beers

Since DB's business concerns diamonds, for reasons of security, it had always been anxious to ensure that its internal processes were kept confidential; with the result each department treated its business processes as a secret. For the same reasons, the company was reluctant to use the third party consultants or the service providers and instead used the in-house resources for the development of the IT systems. These systems tended to be configured specifically for each department and thus ended up in the islands of automation with a limited interaction and high redundancy. These were obviously inefficient.

There was a strong case for updating and integrating the IT systems throughout the company. Previously, in 2000, DB had engaged Accenture to redevelop its integrated stock management systems, but the project did not go well and after three years it was terminated without achieving most of its objectives. Accenture complained that the project had gone badly because their team had not received sufficient cooperation from the relevant personnel within DB. Thanks to this unsuccessful project, DB came to recognize how unusual the nature of its business was and how difficult it was for the outside consultants to understand it.

Proposed IT system: Aggregation in diamond supply chain – business process

Aggregation is the process by which the operators combine and blend the batches of sorted uncut diamonds. The identification, classification and valuation of the diamonds take place before they get into the aggregation process. This sorting and blending process requires a set of highly trained experts because there are over 16,000 different categories of the uncut diamonds based on the stone's size, shape, quality and colour. This gives an indication of the complexity of the operation.

Processes in aggregation supply chain:

1. Export for Aggregation: this covers the steps, which need to be taken for the diamonds to be transported (exported) from the local sorting office (LSO) to their destination, for aggregation (which was to be in Botswana).

2. "Import for Aggregation: covers the steps taken when the diamonds are received for aggregation.

3. Rolling Management: here the diamonds from the different mines, which have been imported, are aggregated or "rolled" together.

4. Splitting: After the stones have been aggregated, they are split up into the groupings in which they will be presented for sale.

5. Export for Sight: Once the diamonds have been split up (into boxes), they are then exported for the purposes of sight by the customers.

6. Import for Sight: consists of the steps to be taken at the LSO (now a local sales office) when the boxes of diamonds are received.

7. Prepare and Hold Sight: the steps to be taken in order to prepare for sight by the customers from around the world.

The IT system was proposed to be designed to keep a precise check on the diamonds as they moved through the process so as to ensure that no stone is lost and to provide the facilities for valuing the stones (or groups of stones) as well as to provide a proper audit trail of the movements of the stones.

Splitting was originally excluded from the contract and was later included through a change request.

Vendor selection

In April 2007, DB put the software contract out to tender against which Atos won the bid.

Initiation and Analysis

Recognizing the unusual complexity of its operations, De Beers allowed Atos a six week pre-contract period (the "Initiation and Analysis Phase" or "IAP") for the requirements gathering and to assess the project before committing to a fixed price. The output of the IAP was to be a detailed requirements definition and a high level design, leaving the detailed design to be fleshed out under the main contract. The system was to be developed on an iterative basis through an ongoing cycle of delivery, the customer feedback and improvement.

IAP was completed in October 2007 and the fixed price contract for £ 2.9 m was signed in November 2007, with the delivery deadline fixed as June 2008.

At the end of the IAP, Adelman, the lead business analyst alerted the project manager Wong that the requirements collected were at a high level and may not truly reflect DB's processes. Wong asked Adelman to make suitable assumptions and proceed. Thus Atos took a calculated risk.

On its side, DB too had a feeling that Atos had not fully understood its business processes. The problem was exacerbated by the fact that the Atos business analysts never saw the relevant processes in operation on the ground: Still DB did not do anything to alleviate this and allowed Atos to be on its own in the development of the software.

Project progress or lack of progress

The identification of the slippage in the gathering of the functional requirements first appeared in an Atos internal project status report dated 7th November 2007. The summary in this report recorded that five requirement areas had some form of delay, but this was said to have no impact on the next iteration schedule. Only the delay in one process requirement (PR), Container Management, was said to have a potential impact on the Phase 1 schedule and was therefore under investigation. It seemed that in the case of that PR and some of the others that had fallen behind, the delay was probably caused by a lack of information from the DB users.

The Steering Group Meeting held on 23rd November 2007 showed the project to be in the red status - *significantly behind the schedule on seven core requirement areas*. Two of these referred to the lack or late provision of the information from the DB business users, and one referred to the non-availability of the DB staff. The other three reasons were the matters that were primarily within Atos's control, such as the activities taking longer than expected owing to the complexity or the identification of the new requirements that were "*in scope*", but which required further elaboration.

The Steering Group meeting on 12th December 2007 noted in addition

- "amendments to requirements still being advised by the business e.g. Export for Aggregation still not nailed down.

  Further action needed to make a productivity leap required including
  - the freezing of all the functional requirements by the end of Jan 2008.
  - the streamlining of the development with a renewed focus on building as much of the detailed specification alongside the analysis.
  - further tuning of the delivery approach, which may include bringing some Atos India resource on-shore. (Visas / Space etc will need to be considered).

- revision of the plan in line with the activities above and a further review to identify any additional action.
- Non-functional requirements still in the RED status, but expected to be finalized by the day end.
- Splitting Process has been assessed and it is clear that this will be a significant project in its own right. Impact Assessment expected at the end of this week for review."

Resource availability was a problem in the Atos side also in some cases. On Jan 2nd, Atos inducted six more business analysts, which brought the total number of BAs to 10.

One important reason for the delay in the project was the non-availability of the subject matter experts (SMEs) for providing the functional inputs. Also the users were coming to the requirement gathering workshops with conflicting requirements and this dragged the development process on. And during this period the scope also started increasing.

5th February 2008 Atos internal report:

Build phase is not progressing to the plan. [Atos India] have delivered a number of modules which are now in system test, but core pipeline process areas have not started due to a need to review the technical architecture issues as a result of the elaborated requirements.

Mid- Feb status:

o DB's Finance requirements still remained undefined. Atos had indicated a hefty price increase for the finance requirements.
o Splitting was added as an additional module. Price was agreed at £415,000. However, the formal change request had not been signed and the impact assessment was still in progress.
o Requirements for Large stones still require the information from DB.

Fast track requirements gathering workshops had thrown up many more process requirements than Atos had envisaged. The original 65 PRs had increased to 128 PRs (106 excluding Splitting). Not only the number of PRs, but also the number of steps in each PR increased substantially. Apart from the additional work for this development, there was likely to be an impact on the design of the technical architecture.

Request for deadline extension

By March 2008, it was clear to Atos that the project cannot be delivered by the committed date. Atos requested DB to extend the date to mid October 2008 on the grounds that the elaborated requirements had revealed significantly more complex and intricate business processes than it had originally envisaged. Atos asserted that these changes led to redesign, recoding and retesting, thus needing a substantial additional effort.

But the change of date was not acceptable to DB. DB asked Atos to separate the priority modules – called the Gold Bundle - from the others. On 4th April, Atos presented a plan, in which the delivery of the Gold Bundle was committed in mid-August and the rest in October 2008. And the plan did not contain the contingencies for the activities in the non-priority modules.

Remedial measures in project management

In early April 2008, Atos commissioned an "in-flight review", whose purpose was *"to determine if the project management approaches being used are adequate to deliver the "Gold Bundle" on time and to the budget, and to recommend changes where necessary.*

The in-flight review suggested

- the replacement of the current project manager.
- the assignment of an experienced software architect.
- a detailed review of the existing plan to understand the estimates behind the various activities . . .
- a review of the development approach and the quality of code being produced.

Longer term action is to look at how to address the contract management and the proficiency of DB Program Management.

The findings stated that there was "hands off" interaction with the offshore development (Atos India). It recorded that Atos India was reporting RED consistently.

Precipitation of conflict

Atos raised its fourth invoice for £320,000 on 3rd March 2008, which was due for payment in April. DB refused to pay, citing the inadequate quantum and the poor quality of the work as the reasons. The Atos management was by then concerned with the cost overrun of the project. And added to that was the significant enhancement of the scope.

On May 21st, Atos sent a mail to DB asking for a renegotiation of the contract, agreeing to complete the project on time and material basis on its own internal terms without any claim of profit and suggested an additional price of £ 4 m, failing which it threatened to terminate the work. Since DB was not willing to negotiate, Atos terminated the work by June 2008.

DB raised the matter in England and Wales High Court with a claim of £8.3 m from Atos. The Court had to establish whether the withholding of the payment by De Beers, or the termination of work by Atos, constituted a repudiation of the contract.

The judgment

Based on an assessment by a veteran technical employee of Atos, the judge observed:

1. The application turned out to be much larger than the originally envisaged, in terms of the function points.
2. The application was much more complex than was originally thought: a huge end-to-end multi-country workflow, with many of the sub processes not originally identified.

3. The detailed requirements finalized in January 2008 were much larger than envisaged in the high level design.
4. The agile approach was not suitable for this application. The decision was subsequently taken to move to the waterfall model, but the team organization was not compatible with the methodology chosen.
5. The team was divided into the functional silos and was not appropriate for developing an integrated system.
6. The team was busy defining how to define the system, but was not clear about what was to be designed – in short the system analysis was missing. For a project of this size, this was an important activity.

And then went on to observe that

7. contracts should specify the customer obligations as well (reverse SLAs), which were absent in this case. Even otherwise a customer could not hide the material information from the service provider under the guise of secrecy or inability to communicate the complex processes to an outsider. The customer had an obligation to ensure that the service provider had understood all the requirements clearly.
8. while the non-availability of the functional experts for providing the inputs was attributable to the De Beers management, Atos also was to blame for its failure to give the advance notices for such meetings.

The court categorized change requests into two
    a. Changes in breadth: changes in the functionality – scope creep
    b. Changes in depth: changes in the scale or the complexity of work

The Judge ruled that only the changes in breadth were the true changes and deserved an extra payment. The Court criticized the behaviour of both the parties. Nonetheless, it was established that whilst De Beers was clearly in the breach of the contract by withholding the payment, this did not constitute a repudiatory breach. De Beers was even prepared to make an extra-contractual payment to Atos to ensure that the project did not fail. The enhancement of the scope could also not be viewed as a breach of the contract, but has to be viewed as an extension of the work for which Atos could claim an additional cost, but not damages.

In contrast, the Court held that Atos' behaviour had amounted to a clear repudiatory breach. Atos did have a contractual right to suspend the work until the payment of the invoice by De Beers, but the demands made by Atos did not reflect its contractual entitlements. By suspending the work until De Beers would enter into a new commercial agreement, Atos was showing an intention to only complete the work on different terms and not upon the terms originally agreed in the contract. Since Atos suspended the work, DB was forced to upgrade and maintain the legacy system. The Judge agreed that these costs were recoverable from Atos. DB was also entitled to recover the cost of the replacement systems.

The judge decreed Atos to pay a damage of £ 1.4 m after netting the amounts due to them under the contract plus DB's legal fees.

Post script

Till 2010, when the judgment was delivered DB had not moved its aggregation operations to Botswana and a clear target date was also not in sight.

A clear lose-lose case!

(Case prepared by the author on the basis of the judgment delivered by Justice Edwards- Stuart in England and Wales High Court http://www.bailii.org/ew/cases/EWHC/TCC/2010/3276.html).

Practice Questions

1. State whether true or false:

    a. A software project is triggered only by the user requirements.
    b. Wants are a subset of needs.
    c. Wants and not needs are what a project manager needs to fulfil.
    d. 'The project will be delivered in three months' is a good example of a success criterion.

2. Fill in the blanks with the appropriate terms:

    a. ----- is the only part in a report the senior management may read sometimes and hence it should capture the essence of a report.
    b. What is not covered by the project is addressed under the title ---- in the scope document.
    c. The time by which a project reaches the break even stage is called ----.
    d. Some organizations prepare a ------ instead of a scope document as a project initiation document.

3. Choose the most appropriate answer:

    a. Technology obsolescence is a(n)
        i.   assumption
        ii. constraint
        iii. objective
        iv. risk

    b. What could be a good technique for an investment analysis?
        i.   PERT
        ii. PMP
        iii. RoI
        iv. Risk analysis

c. That a maximum of only 1000 users will log in concurrently at any time is a(n)

    i.   assumption
    ii. objective
    iii. risk
    iv. success criterion

d. Constraints may be

    i.   financial
    ii. organizational
    iii. technological
    iv. all the above

e. Which of these could be a good example of a disbenefit?

    i.   The project requires an investment of 100 million.
    ii. The application will result in an inventory reduction by 30%.
    iii. At no time the number of concurrent users will exceed 1000.
    iv. Some employees may feel redundant due to the introduction of the new package.

f. Business value is reflected in

    i.   assumptions
    ii. benefits
    iii. costs
    iv. risks

g. Which of the following is not a consideration in the management approving a project?

    i.   Business justification
    ii. Market demand
    iii. Project feasibility
    iv. Technology advances

h. The important part of a business case is ------

    i.   constraints

    ii. cost-benefit analysis

    iii. project overview

    iv. scope document

i. Which could have an effect to stop a project?

    i.   Assumptions

    ii. Objectives

    iii. Risks

    iv. Scope

j. Software is being created for a non-profit voluntary organization. Which of the following could be the most likely success criterion for the project?

    i.   Improved capability of community service

    ii. Service cost increase

    iii. Increased profitability

    iv. Implementation of new technology

k. Staff attrition is an example of a(n) ----

    i.   assumption

    ii. constraint

    iii. objective

    iv. risk

l. Which of the following is not a financial analysis?

    i.   Break-even analysis

    ii. Cost-benefit analysis

    iii. Discounted cash flow

    iv. Risk analysis

m. Identify the most appropriate problem statement.

    i.   Response time for the application should not exceed 4 seconds.

    ii. To develop the application in the latest version of Java.

    iii. Delivery of the project within 18 months.

    iv. Customer turn-around time in billing counter exceeds half an hour.

n. Which of the following defines a project goal?

i.   How the problem is intended to be addressed
ii. A problem needing resolution
iii. Project success criteria
iv. What is in and what is not in the project

o. Which of the following may be considered a constraint in a project?

i.   The project needs to be completed within $ 5 million.
ii. The client organization's culture may not be compatible with that of the development organization.
iii. Possibility of a major change in the client management during the project.
iv. Technology new to the company.

p. Which of the following is covered in a scope document?

i.   Parameters that will be monitored in the project
ii. Problem / opportunity
iii. Requirements document
iv. Service requirements

q. It is most important that the project goals should align with the

i.   budgetary allocation
ii. business case
iii. business objectives
iv. cost-benefit analysis

r. What has to be done in a project is defined by its

i.   assumptions
ii. objectives
iii. schedule
iv. scope

4. Organizations require a different orientation to develop a product than to execute a software project – elaborate on this statement.

5. Are there situations when an organization decides to go for a project even when the NPV is negative? Why?

6. What could be the scope, objective, constraints of a(n)

   a. electricity billing system
   b. alumni system of a college
   c. treasury system for a bank
   d. automobile service centre system

7. Create a scope document for a(n)

   a. mobile banking application
   b. college admission system
   c. hotel reservation system
   d. online food ordering and delivery system

8. Prepare a business case for

   a. automation of the operations in a FMCG retail store
   b. a CRM system for a manufacturing company

4

PROJECT PLANNING

Plans are nothing; planning is everything. – Dwight D. Eisenhower

4.1 Lesson Objectives

This lesson introduces the Project Planning phase and lists the activities conducted in that phase.

We will also learn about a technique called the Work Breakdown structure in detail.

4.2 Project Planning – Coverage

The planning phase will cover

- the estimation of the duration of the project.
- the preparation of a schedule for the project.
- the estimation of the resource requirement.
- the estimation of the cost.
- the preparation of a quality plan.
- the preparation of a risk management plan.

At the end of this phase, a project plan will be prepared, which will act as a bible in the execution of the project.

4.3 Specifying user requirements

A clear set of the user requirements is an input to the planning phase. By this time, the business analyst has collected all the requirements of the users, consolidated similar requirements, reconciled the conflicting requirements, negotiated the requirements and zeroed in on the final set of requirements. Negotiating the user requirements is important because the users normally specify an ambitious set of requirements to get everything done through the software. With the constrained resources and with a deadline specified, a project manager will not be able to fulfil all the requirements.

One of the techniques suggested is MOSCOW, which stands for

Must have: these are the vital features of the product without which it will not work or it will not be complete.

Should have: the essential features. Without these features the product will work, but these will add value to the final product. The statutory requirements such as the reports to the government and the regulatory agencies will also fall into this category.

Could have: the useful feature, but does not significantly add value to the product.

Won't have: unimportant; could wait for the next release.

This categorization should be done based on the inputs provided by the users. In other words, these categories are based on the business requirements and not from the software development or the technology perspective.

These negotiated set of requirements are consolidated in a document called the Software Requirements Specification (SRS).

4.4 Estimating duration

4.4.1 Work Breakdown Structure (WBS)

Work Breakdown Structure is a technique that is used for estimating the duration and the resource requirement of a project. The underlying idea is that a project as a whole is difficult to estimate and the margin of error will be high and this can be overcome by breaking down the project into tasks, the duration of each of which is small and hence its estimation is prone to a lesser margin of error.

WBS is a hierarchical description of all the work that must be done to satisfy the requirements of the customer. There are two ways of constructing the work breakdown structure:

- Top down
- Bottom up

While the top down is the most widely adopted method, the bottom-up is preferred in specific cases.

4.4.1.1 Top down approach

Steps in the top down approach

1. Objectives are the starting point of a WBS.
2. Identify the deliverables towards achieving these objectives.
3. Break down the deliverables into the activities that need to be performed to create these deliverables.
   For this breakdown, a rule called the 100% rule is recommended:
   The 100% rule states that the sum of the work at the "child" levels must equal 100% of the work represented by the "parent"; neither less nor more, which means that if a(n) deliverable / activity A is broken down into A_1, A_2 and A_3, these three together should wholly represent the requirement of A – there should neither be overlaps among A_1, A_2 and A_3 nor should there be omissions. To put it differently A_1, A_2 and A_3 are *necessary* and *sufficient* to achieve A.

This decomposition should be continued to the successive levels till we reach a level where
- each component is logically distinct.
- the time estimates of these components can be arrived at with reasonable accuracy.
- each lowest level of entry is of duration of 1 – 10 days.
- the components at the lowest level are such that their mode of implementation does not lack clarity, which means that each of these components have an identified start, an identified end and a deliverable.

This successive decomposition is known as the Progressive Elaboration. In this decomposition exercise, we need to be careful about the frequently encountered omissions:
- Often the reviews and the documentation get omitted.
- The testing and the trainings get overlooked.
- Also whenever the documents such as the SRS or the design document are submitted to the users, there is a delay – often substantial – in their giving approval.
- The software installation does not take place instantaneously. If the installation needs to be done in several locations, then the time requirement is even higher.

Each of these activities requires considerable time and any omission might affect the duration estimate substantially.

4. Once all the activities are identified, trace bottom up to see all the deliverables have been accounted for.
5. Estimate the duration of the activities at the lowest level and sum them up to arrive at the project duration.

4.4.1.2 Bottom up approach

In the projects, in which the final deliverable is not fully clear, the bottom up method is used. Would we undertake any project in which the deliverable is not clear? In the research projects, for example, the team may only have a broad idea of what the final product is going to look like. In the gaming projects also, the product evolves as the development goes along. In such cases, the top down is infeasible. So we start identifying some features of the product through the techniques such as brainstorming and build the product by successively adding more and more features.

Take the case of a driverless car. The development team may not have the full specification defined *ab initio*. Such projects do not get started with a clearly defined SRS. Alternately, the team might brainstorm and come up with some features such as identifying the route from the Google Maps, receiving the traffic information from the control room and the ability to slow down on recognizing an object within ten feet and may start developing the application. At that point of time, the team may not know how the traffic signal will be sensed by the car, but still the development starts and goes on[22].

The gaming projects also follow such an evolutionary approach[23].

4.4.1.3 Constructing a WBS

A typical WBS looks like this:

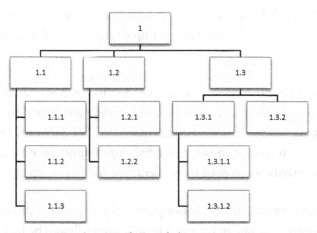

Fig. 4.1. Work Breakdown Structure

---

[22] A development model known as the spiral model is used for such R & D projects instead of the traditional waterfall model.

[23] This approach is known as the agile model.

The structure is made of levels. Level 1 is the list of deliverables. Each of the boxes in the diagram is referred to as a WBS entry. The deliverables are specified by nouns with or without adjectives such as Design specifications.

Each of these deliverables is then broken down into the activities needed to obtain these deliverables. In this breaking down, initially the macro level activities are identified, which are progressively split into the component activities. Activities are specified by a verb followed by a (adjective) noun – Update specifications.

The golden rule of 7±2 is applicable in this break down exercise. The rule states that human mind can absorb only seven discrete facts at any time, at the most nine. Thus we should ensure that no entry is broken into its components fewer than five or more than nine in number. Towards achieving this, their combination or splitting should be performed. Ideally the structure should be balanced in breadth and depth – meaning there should neither be a large number of the first level entries with a few levels nor a few first level entries decomposed into several levels.

Numbering: The WBS entries should be numbered in such a way that it is easy to identify the parent of each child. Activity 1.1 will have its children numbered as 1.1.1, 1.1.2 and 1.1.3. From the number of digits in the identification number, the level is also known. For example 1.1.3 is a level 3 activity (see the Fig 4.1).

Risk events: These are the events associated with some uncertainties. These events need to be highlighted - may be with a different colour. The duration of these events may increase, if the risk becomes a reality. Not only should there be an enhanced tolerance in the estimated duration of these events, but the contingency activities also need to be identified for each of them.

Milestones: Milestones are the major points of progress in a project and thus are the appropriate points for review. The milestones should be included in the WBS, though they will be the activities of zero duration. These are normally referred in the past tense – 'Acceptance Test Completed'.

4.4.1.4 Validation of WBS

Once completed, the WBS is validated bottom up.

4.4.1.5 Testing WBS

How do we know that we have constructed a WBS properly? If at any point of time during the project execution, the completion status can be illustrated through the WBS without any ambiguity, then we have identified the right components at the right level of granularity.

4.4.1.6 Benefits of WBS

In Chapter 1, we identified the intangibility of the software as a big challenge in measuring the project progress. The WBS aims to break a project into a set of identifiable components and thus the completion of the project is more measurable now. In the review presentations, the project manager may present the WBS with a colour code for the completed entries and this could act as a good visual tool in appraising the management of the extent of completion of the project.

The components identified may also be used for the work assignments, because each of these components is fairly independent of the others in its execution.

4.4.1.7 Work Breakdown Dictionary

The project manager should create a work breakdown dictionary, in which each entry has a separate page. A typical dictionary page looks like this:

Project Name		
WBS Name	WBS id	Parent id
WBS Owner	Start Date	End date
WBS Detail		
Description of Deliverable		
Acceptance Criteria		
Assumptions		
Resources Assigned		
WBS Dependencies		
Time		
Approved by	Date	

Fig 4.2. Work Breakdown Dictionary

WBS name: Each entry should have a name such as 'code development for profit & loss statement'.

WBS owner: the person who is responsible for the completion and the delivery of the particular WBS entry. For a program, it should be a programmer or a set of programmers. At the beginning of the project, when the manager creates the dictionary, the specific names may not be available. These entries will be made as the project progresses.

Start and end dates: again these dates will be finalized only when the schedule is ready.

WBS detail: The WBS name may not be sufficiently explanatory. So the details about the WBS – what is proposed to be done – is entered here.

Deliverable: Each component should have a clearly identifiable deliverable. The tested code will be the deliverable for a program.

Acceptance criteria: Please note that in the previous paragraph we were careful to mention not just 'code' but 'tested code'. Completion of the testing and the certification by a tester as bug-free is the acceptance criterion for a program. Similarly the completion of the reviews could be for the software design or for a document.

Assumption: Any assumption associated with this entry needs to be specified here. Explicit documentation of the assumption is necessary because the assumption may be revisited for its validity as the project progresses.

Resources assigned: Along with the human resource, any other resource such as the hardware specifically required for the WBS entry may be mentioned here. This information may not be available for all the entries at the time of the preparation of the work breakdown dictionary, but will be added as the project progresses.

Dependencies: Even though we have specified that each component is independent of another, it may not always be possible. Also a WBS entry may be dependent on some external activity. For example, the installation of the software may be possible only when the new machine is installed. Stating this assumption will help the project manager in the appropriate follow-ups.

Time: Duration of this task

Practice Questions

1. State whether true or false:

    a. The work breakdown is always top down.
    b. The top down approach is more widely used than the bottom up in constructing WBS.
    c. Each entry in a WBS should preferably be capable of independent execution.
    d. In a WBS, the duration of an activity at every level is ≤ 10 days.
    e. Work breakdown dictionary is created for each WBS entry.
    f. The top down WBS is validated bottom up.
    g. The assumptions need to be recorded because they need revalidation during the course of the project.
    h. A milestone is a risk event.

2. Fill in the blanks with the appropriate terms:

    a. A WBS shows a parent activity A contains children A1, A2 and A3. Then A1+A2+A3 is exactly equal to A. This is called ------.
    b. ----- approves WBS dictionary entries.

3. Choose the most appropriate answer:

    a. Which could be the most scientific way of estimating the duration of a project?
        i.   Break the project into tasks and estimate the duration of each task.
        ii. Ask your colleagues who have done a similar project.
        iii. The project duration will be fixed by the customer expectation.
        iv. Get the estimate from the team members.

b. In a software project, the user training is a(n)

   i.   activity

   ii. deliverable

   iii. objective

   iv. resource

c. Work breakdown structure is an example of

   i.   deliverables

   ii. inputs

   iii. milestones

   iv. tools

d. Which is the parent activity of the activity 1.2.3?

   i.   1

   ii. 1.2

   iii. 1.2.2

   iv. 1.2.3.4

e. Duration of the lowest level of activity should be < 10 days because

   i.   no activity will have a duration of 10 days or more.

   ii. when the duration is more than 10 days, it is not called an activity in WBS.

   iii. the estimates are more accurate when the duration is less than 10 days.

   iv. the number of levels will remain at an unacceptable level if the duration is more than 10.

f. Which is the technique that is followed in the bottom up approach but not in the top down?

   i.   100% rule

   ii. Brainstorming

   iii. Progressive elaboration

   iv. Work breakdown dictionary

g. The successive decomposition of the parent activities into their children is known as the

    i.   100% rule

    ii. bottom up

    iii. progressive elaboration

    iv. top down

h. Design specification is a(n)

    i.   activity

    ii. deliverable

    iii. milestone

    iv. risk event

i. Which of the following activities is least likely to be included in a WBS?

    i.   Documentation

    ii. Estimation of the duration

    iii. Training

    iv. Reviews

j. When a task is broken down to the lower level tasks, for the completion of the task, the lower level tasks are

    i.   necessary, but not sufficient.

    ii. sufficient, but not necessary.

    iii. either necessary or sufficient.

    iv. necessary and sufficient.

k. What is the duration of a milestone, as represented in a WBS?

    i.   0

    ii. 1 – 10 days

    iii. 7±2

    iv. Depends on the duration of the project

l. When is a program said to have met the acceptance criterion?

    i.   When the program is passed on from the developer to the tester.

    ii. When the tester completes the testing and prepares the bug report.

    iii. When the programmer has completed the debugging.

    iv. When the tester certifies that there is no bug in the program.

m. Which is not shown in a WBS?

    i. Deliverables

    ii. Milestones

    iii. Task hierarchy

    iv. Task sequence

n. It is recommended to have 7±2 activities in each level because

    i. no activity can be broken down beyond this number of activities.

    ii. the human mind can absorb only 7±2 discrete points at any point of time.

    iii. that makes it easy for converting into a schedule.

    iv. that is the standard imposed by PMI.

o. Which should be the necessary requirement for a milestone?

    i. Documentation of activities completed

    ii. Review checklist

    iii. No specific requirement

    iv. WBS

p. In a typical WBS, which of the following is most likely to be in level 1?

    i. Activities

    ii. Deliverables

    iii. Milestones

    iv. Reviews

q. Contingency activities are required for

    i. deliverables

    ii. entries

    iii. milestones

    iv. risk events

r. In the top down approach, which is the right sequence?

    i. Activities, deliverables. objectives

    ii. Deliverables, objectives, activities

    iii. Objectives, activities, deliverables

    iv. Objectives, deliverables, activities

s. What are milestones?

    i. List of deliverables

    ii. Any WBS entry

    iii. Major points of progress

    iv. A risk event

t. 'Acceptance Test Completed' is a(n)

    i. deliverable

    ii. milestone

    iii. noun

    iv. risk event

4. The development methodology will have an impact on the activities in the WBS – Discuss

5. Create a work breakdown structure for a

    a. movie ticketing system

    b. FMCG retail store

    State your assumptions and constraints clearly.

Case Study

Share Registry – Shareholder Services

Scope

The Registrar system will maintain the shareholder information of the Issuer Company, for whom the Registrar acts as the administrator.

The Registrar system will provide the following:

- Shareholder services
- Depository services
- Company services
- Corporate events.

Here we will discuss only the shareholder services in detail.

Shareholder services

The following are the shareholder services available with the Registrar:

- Share transfer
- Certificate management
- Revalidation of cheques
- Power of Attorney request
- Change of the shareholder details

All the requests for the above services will be monitored through the Back Office. After receiving the request, a basic verification shall be made, following which an Inward Number will be generated.

In the event of the services involving the submission of the certificates, the shareholder and the certificate details will be checked. For the services without the certificates, only the shareholder details will be checked. At any point of time, the service request can be tracked using the inward status.

Each of these services with the associated business processes are discussed below:

Share transfer

Share transfer is the process of transfer of the physical certificate and the ownership from one shareholder to another. The Registrar system will support the following types of transfers:

- Stock Exchange (SE) transfer: The approval of the SE will be a mandatory input to effect these transfers. The SE will allocate a transfer number for the approved requests. The Back Office user will capture this transfer number for reference.
- Normal transfer
- Inheritance: The shareholders can transfer their certificates to their heirs. The submitted certificate will be issued to all the heirs, in the proportion set out in an appropriate legal instruction.
- Subscription transfer: After a new issue allocation and printing, the shareholders belonging to the same group can request for a subscription transfer. All the certificates issued for the Shareholder Identification Numbers (SIN) in the specified group will be transferred to the SIN requested by the shareholders.

Business Processes

- The Back Office user (BOU) will capture the transfer details in the Registrar system.
- The status of the certificate will be verified by the system.
- On the failure of any of the validations, the request will be rejected and the certificates will be returned to the shareholder with the reasons for rejection.
- On successful manual verification, the new certificate details will be generated and the old certificate will be cancelled in the system.
- The new certificates will be printed with the transferee and the transfer date. The status of the inward entry will be updated to 'Servicing Complete'.

- The Back Office user must verify the details of the despatching certificates in the outward register. The system will update the inward entry status to 'Delivered'.
- A report of the transfers, with the transfer number, the transfer type, the transferor's identification number and the transferee's identification number can be generated.

Certificate management

The Registrar will provide the following certificate management facilities to the shareholder:

- Printing and maintaining the certificates
- Merging and splitting of the certificates
- Replacement of the lost and the stolen certificates
- Replacement of the damaged certificates

The Certificate Management process will support all the procedures involved with the issuing of the physical certificates.

Print and maintain certificate details

- The Registrar system will print the certificates for the new issues, transfers and replacement for the lost, stolen and damaged certificates. Whenever a despatch / issue of a physical certificate occurs, the details will be stored in the Registrar system. The various service requests received by the Registrar system regarding the certificates will be verified against the certificate details stored.

Business Processes

- All the inward register entries with the status 'To Print' will be taken up for printing.
- After completion of the printing, the status for the entry in the inward register will be updated to 'Servicing Complete' and the outward register details will be captured.

- On despatching the certificate, the Registrar will verify the outward entry details and the inward entry will be updated to 'Delivered'.
- The printed certificate will be manually checked and in case of faulty printing, the same certificate can be printed again only with the supervisory approval. A log will be maintained in the system for all the printings.
- The Back Office user must confirm the details of the delivery of the certificates in the outward register. The system will update the inward entry status to 'Delivered'.

Merging of certificates

The Registrar will issue a certificate of consolidated denomination for two or more certificates of same or different denominations. This will be done on a request from the shareholder. On successful validation, the old certificates will be cancelled and a new certificate will be issued with the same status as the old certificate.

Business Processes

- The Back Office user will capture the details of the merging in the system.
- The Registrar system will check for the existence of the certificate number and the certificate status.
- The old certificates will be physically marked as cancelled and the new certificate details will be captured with the consolidated denomination. The old certificate status will be updated to 'Cancelled' with the reason as 'Cancelled due to Merging'.
- A new certificate will be generated with a new number.
- The status for the entry in the inward register will be updated to 'To Print'.
- The certificates will be printed and the inward register status will be updated to 'Servicing Complete'.
- The Back Office user must verify the details of the new certificate issued in the outward register.
- The inward entry status will be updated to 'Delivered' on despatch of the certificates.

Splitting of certificates

The Registrar will issue the certificates of different denominations from one single certificate. This will be done on a request from the shareholder. On successful validation, the old single certificate will be cancelled and several certificates of requested denominations would be issued with the same status as the single certificate.

Business Processes

- The Back Office user will capture the details of the split in the system.
- The Registrar system will check for the existence of the certificate number and the certificate status.
- The old certificates will be physically marked as cancelled and the new certificates will be captured with the requested denominations. The old certificate status will be updated to 'Cancelled' with reason as 'Cancelled due to Splitting'.
- New certificates will be generated with new numbers.
- The status for the entry in the inward register will be updated to 'To Print'.
- The certificates will be printed and the inward register status will be updated to 'Servicing Complete'.
- The Back Office user must verify the details of the new certificate issued in the outward register.
- The inward entry status will be updated to 'Delivered' on the despatch of the certificates.

Replacement of lost and stolen certificates

The Registrar system will have an entry for the requests for the replacement of the certificates. The Registrar will send the certificate details to the Ministry (designated agency) at the end of the day. On manual verification of the lost and the stolen certificate details, published by the Ministry (designated agency), the Registrar will issue a new certificate for the lost / stolen certificates. In such cases, a new certificate will be created with a new number. In the event of there being a block on the old certificate, the blocking will remain on the new certificate as well.

Business Processes

- The Back Office user will capture all the request details in the system.
- On manual verification of the lost and the stolen details published by the Ministry (designated agency), the system will create the details for the new certificate and the old certificate status will be updated to 'Lost'.
- The inward register status will be updated to 'To Print'.
- On successful printing of the certificate, the status in the inward register will be set to 'Servicing Complete'.
- The Back Office user must verify the details of the new certificates issued in the outward register.
- The inward entry status will be updated to 'Delivered' on despatch of the certificates.

Replacement of damaged certificates

The Registrar will generate new certificates as a replacement of damaged certificates. The replacement will be on a request from the shareholder. If the validation is successful, all the details of the original certificate will be maintained for the new certificate.

Business Processes

- The certificate details and the status will be validated by the system.
- On successful validation, the new certificate details will be generated and a new entry will be created in the certificate details.
- The status of the old certificate will be updated to 'Cancelled' with the reason for cancellation as 'Cancellation due to replacement'.
- The inward entry for the replacement request will be updated to 'To Print'.
- On completion of the printing of the certificate, the status for the entry in the inward register will be updated to 'Servicing Complete'.
- The Back Office user must verify the details of the new certificate issued in the outward register.
- The inward entry status will be updated to 'Delivered' on the despatch of the certificates.

Revalidation of cheques

Shareholders can request the Registrar for the revalidation of cheques. On successful validation, the Registrar will stamp the cheque with a future date.

In the event of the shareholders' delay in presenting the cheques made out to them (e.g. for dividends) to their banks, it may be necessary for the Registrar to revalidate the cheques previously issued.

Business Processes

- The Registrar will receive the requests for revalidation of cheques from the shareholders when the cheques have expired before being presented to the bank.
- The shareholder details, the cheque issue date, and the status of the cheque will be verified against the details maintained by the Registrar system.
- On successful validation, the Back Office user will stamp the cheque with a new valid date and not reissue a new cheque.
- The Registrar system will be updated with the new cheque issue date.
- The status in the inward register will be updated to 'Servicing Complete'.

Power of Attorney request

An authorized person can act on behalf of a shareholder or a minor under a Power of Attorney (POA).

The Registrar will require a valid evidence of the POA and the name and full address of the person so authorized.

Business Processes

- On receiving the request from a valid shareholder to grant the power of attorney to an authorized person, the full name and the address of the authorized person are captured in the system.

- The holder of a power of attorney can be given authority for the selected or all of the services provided to the shareholder (according to the terms of the POA).
- A power of attorney registration number will be generated by the system for the request.
- The authorization is valid in the system for a period with the start and the end dates specified. The authority will be revoked either on the authorization end date or on a request from the shareholder, whichever is earlier.

Change of shareholder details

- The registrar maintains the list of shareholders with their shareholdings. The details captured by the Registrar will be stored in the system with a unique Shareholder identification number (SIN) generated by the system. It will also contain the information on the history of holding by each shareholder

The shareholders can request for modifications in the following:

- Shareholder name
- Shareholder bank details
- Shareholder type
- Shareholder nationality

On receiving a request from the shareholder, the status of the shareholder will be checked. The request will be processed only if the shareholder is in 'Active' or 'To Delete' status.

Change of name

A shareholder can request for a change in name. The manual verification of an appropriate legal instrument regarding the name change will be undertaken. Certificates of the shareholder will be printed with the new name and the old certificates will be cancelled.

Business Processes

- The Back Office user will capture the new name of the shareholder.
- On successful verifications of the details provided, the name of the shareholder will be updated in the system.
- All the old certificates will be physically cancelled by the BOU and the record in the system also marked as cancelled and the new certificate details will be generated with the new name and the certificate number.
- The inward entry status will be updated to 'To Print'.
- On completion of the printing of the certificate by the Registrar system, the status of the entry in the inward register will be updated to 'Servicing Complete'.
- The Back Office user must verify the details of the new certificate issued in the outward register.
- The inward entry status will be updated to' Delivered' on the despatch of the certificates.

Change of bank details

Shareholders can request a change in the bank details. It can be a change in the bank name or the bank account number or both.

Business Processes

- The Back Office user will capture the new bank details of the shareholder
- On successful verifications, the shareholder bank details will be updated in the system
- The inward entry status will be updated to 'Servicing Complete'.

Change of shareholder type

Shareholders can request a change in the shareholder type.

Business Processes

- On receiving the request, details of the shareholder status will be manually verified.
- On successful verifications of the details provided, the type of the shareholder will be updated in the system.
- The status of the inward entry will be updated to 'Servicing Complete'.

Change of shareholder nationality

Shareholders can request a change in the nationality recorded.

Business Processes

- On successful verifications of the details provided, the nationality of the shareholder will be updated in the system.
- The status of the inward entry will be updated to 'Servicing Complete'.

Create a WBS diagram for the share registry services.

5

TIME MANAGEMENT: SOFTWARE MEASUREMENT

I often say that when you can measure what you are speaking about,
and express it in numbers, you know something about it;
but when you cannot measure it, when you cannot express it in numbers,
your knowledge is of a meagre and unsatisfactory kind
- Lord Kelvin, 1883

5.1 Learning objectives

In this chapter we will learn the following:

- What do we understand by metrics?
- Why are metrics important?
- How do we identify the right metrics?
- What are the major types of metrics?
- What are the popular metrics used in the software industry?
- How is a metrics program established?
- For which activities should the metric data be collected?

5.2 **Why measurement?**

Have you ever seen how the real estate promoters quote for their apartments? Do they talk about the large and the small flats? They talk in terms of sq.ft. So are the chemical plants, machinery, motors – all of them are characterized by some capacity measures, which are quantitative. Don't we need such a measure for software also? This chapter attempts to resolve this issue.

'What cannot be measured cannot be managed' is the adage we often hear in management.

Measurement is important for

- Estimation: Unless we know how much time each of the activities will take, a good estimate of the time that would be taken for the project is not possible. In a building construction project, with hundreds of years of experience and the standardization of the processes, a fairly accurate estimate is available for the low level activities. But in a software project, even after the breakdown to the lowest level of activities, the estimate of the duration is difficult and is widely divergent across organizations. For example, how much time will it take to develop ten lines of Java code? And for abstract activities such as analysis and design, the estimation becomes more difficult and divergent.

- Quality control: When we talk about the quality of the software, it needs to be described in terms of the size of the software. For example, the number of bugs could be one parameter for measuring the quality. But a statement such as 'the software has five bugs' by itself does not communicate the quality level of the software. Five bugs in a thousand line program and in a million line program do not represent the same level of quality.

- Productivity measurement: Each software organization employs thousands of software engineers. While as a team they may produce a software product, how do we know how productive each individual programmer is? Or for that matter, do we not want to know the productivity level of the team or the organization as a whole? In a factory, we measure the units produced by each workman / shift /

unit regularly. Should we not have a measure for the productivity in the software industry?

- Project control: We talked about the intangibility of a software product posing a challenge to the project manager in measuring the progress in Chapter 1. We saw that this challenge can be addressed to an extent through the work breakdown structure (Chapter 4). But WBS is only an imperfect measure for reporting the project progress, because we cannot be sure that all the WBS entries are of equal size and will demand equal effort. So we need a more accurate measure for use by the Project manager to assess how much has been completed and how much remains.

5.3 Metrics

Obviously, a universally accepted measure such as a foot cannot be identified for an abstract entity. Metrics are chosen instead for the software measurement. How are metrics different from measures? A measure is an amount or degree of something[24]. A sq.ft., for example, is a measure. On the other hand, metric is defined as a *quantitative measure of the degree to which a system, process possesses a given attribute*. The area in sq.ft. required to accommodate 100 people is a metric.

Two metrics are very important in software measurement:

- Productivity metric: measured in terms of the number of units – we are yet to identify the unit of measure - produced in unit time. Alternately the number of hrs. / days to produce one unit. The unit of task could be any of the development lifecycle activity including documentation, review and other associated activities.
- Quality metric: This measures the fitness for use. An appropriate measure could be the number of defects and a refined measure the number of defects categorized on the basis of severity (for which again some scale needs to be developed).

---

[24]   Merriam-Webster dictionary definition

The base data required for computing these metrics are collected from the existing processes and extrapolated for future use. For example the time sheets could be a source for collecting the effort data and the test reports for the defects data.

5.3.1 What do we want to measure?

While productivity and quality are important measures, let us identify the other parameters we want to measure in software.

Apart from the size and the defects, we would also like to measure the performance and the cost of the software. These are quantifiable measures. There could also be other measures not easily quantifiable such as functionality, quality. complexity, efficiency, reliability and maintainability.

While these and several other metrics may be intended to be collected, the means of the data collection for each of these may be quite taxing. So it is advisable to start with some simple but important measures and slowly increase the number of metrics.

5.3.2 Attributes of effective software metrics

- Simple: The easy-to-understand measures are always useful in effectively communicating the characteristic of a product such as sq.ft. for a building.
- Intuitively persuasive: It should not require an elaborate explanation as to how the metric is an appropriate measure for the parameter we intend to measure. For example, it does not require much labouring to convince that the number of defects is a measure of quality. Relating the number of menu options to user-friendliness may not be as direct.
- Consistent: The different measures collected for the same metric should be comparable at least in an ordinal scale. Bugs could be a good measure of comparing the quality levels of different programmers / processes. It may be reasonable to conclude that a program with ten bugs will take more time to correct than one with five bugs - with a

rider that some bugs may have a higher level of severity and a lower level of detectability.

- Objective: the measure should be independent of the person who is measuring it and thus need to be tangible and quantifiable. The number of lines and the number of bugs could be ideal examples.

5.3.3 Size-oriented metrics

Going back to the sq.ft. example, what could be the equivalent for software? Lines of code (LOC) emerges easily as a candidate size metric. It does not require much belabouring to prove that a thousand lines program is bigger than a five hundred lines program and requires more effort (with rare exceptions). All the other metric data collected may be related to LOC: effort in person days / KLOC (thousand LOC), defects / KLOC, cost / KLOC, pages of documentation / KLOC.

LOC is the most tangible aspect of software and is easy to measure and also a very appropriate measure applying the criteria of simplicity, consistency and objectivity. But

- LOC is dependent on the programming language. There is a vast difference between the expressiveness of different languages. A function that may require twenty lines to code in Cobol might require only five lines in C. Obviously the LOC metric is not applicable across languages and this may be overcome by specifying different LOC metrics for different language environments.

- with the same language, two programmers may code differently. Thus a functionality may be coded with five lines of code by one programmer, while another may do the same with ten lines. Using the LOC metric may lead to a conclusion that the second programmer is more productive. How does this anomaly arise? The right way of measuring efficiency is by measuring the output for a given input. LOC is not the output; it is just an intermediary in the process of developing software. The real output is functionality, for providing which the software is developed.

- the line itself is difficult to define. Look at the C code:

$$i++; j++$$

Is this one line? Or two lines? Then the questions such as whether the comment lines are included in counting arise. The Software Engineering Institute (SEI) resolves these issues by specifying the counts in terms of the logical instructions than the physical lines (Park, 1992).

- LOC may be an appropriate measure for coding. But how can this represent the other phases of the life cycle? In the LOC method, we take less than 25% of the effort of the software development life cycle – coding - to represent the entire life cycle.

- one of the main purposes of the size estimation is to prepare a time and cost estimate. And this is required at the beginning of the project when the client needs to be apprised of the cost and the time of delivery. Is it possible to get the line count from the Request for Proposal (RFP) obtained from the customer?

"the use of lines of code metrics for productivity and quality studies to be regarded as professional malpractice." - Capers Jones (Jones, 2013)

"Measuring software productivity by lines of code is like measuring progress on an airplane by how much it weighs." – Bill Gates

While LOC is still used as one of the size measures, the above-mentioned limitations have forced the industry to look beyond LOC – a functionality-oriented metric.

5.3.4 Function-oriented metrics

A language-independent software metric was developed by Allan Albrecht of IBM in 1979. This is called the function point, which is a measure of functionality and one level above source lines of code (SLOC).

The function point is derived from an empirical relationship of two parameters called the information domain and complexity.

5.3.4.1 Information domain

The information domain consists of five parameters:

- External Input (EI): an elementary process in which data crosses the automation boundary from outside to inside. This data may come from a data input screen or another application.
- External Output (EO): an elementary process in which the derived data moves across the automation boundary from inside to outside.
- External query (EQ): an elementary process with both the input and the output components that result in the data retrieval from one or more internal logical files and / or external interface files. To differentiate this from EI and EO, it is defined as a process without any arithmetic calculation. A mere listing is a query while a list with totals is an EO.
- Internal logical file (ILF): the user identifiable group of the logically related data that resides entirely within the application boundary and is maintained through the external inputs. These files / tables are created for the application on hand and so defining and altering this table are within the control of this application developer.
- External interface file (EIF): the user identifiable group of the logically related data that is maintained by another application. These files / tables have already been created for another application and thus are available for use by this application for reading and update.

The boundary referred to above is defined by the scope statement.

These parameters are then categorized as simple, average and complex. Albrecht himself did not define the basis for this categorization. The International Function Point User Group (IFPUG) (www.ifpug.org) has evolved the methods for this categorization. Based on the initial requirements gathered, a domain expert should be able to estimate the number of each of these information domains and also whether each of them is simple, average or complex.

5.3.4.2 Computing unadjusted function points

Albrecht gave a weightage table for each of these parameters.

Parameter	Count		Simple	Average	Complex		
EI		X	3	4	6	=	
EO		X	4	5	7	=	
EQ		X	3	4	6	=	
ILF		X	7	10	15	=	
EIF		X	5	7	10	=	
Total							

Table 5.1 Function point table

These values given by Albrecht in 1979 are used for function point calculation even today.

Based on the number of the information domains identified, the total weightage is calculated, which is the unadjusted function point.

5.3.4.3 Complexity adjustment

While the number of inputs, outputs and other factors might determine the size of the software application, the development effort could also depend on the complexity of the application. The unadjusted function point calculated has to be adjusted for complexity. The complexity is derived by answering fourteen questions on a scale of 0 (not applicable / not important) to 5 (most important):

1. Does the system require a reliable backup and recovery?
2. Are the data communications required?
3. Are there the distributed processing functions?
4. Is the performance critical?
5. Will the system run a heavily utilized operational environment?
6. Does the system require online data entry?
7. Does the online data entry require the input transaction over multiple screens?

8. Are the master files updated online?
9. Are the inputs, the outputs, the files or the queries complex?
10. Is the internal processing complex?
11. Is the code designed to be reusable?
12. Are the conversion and the installation included in the design?
13. Is the system designed for multiple installations?
14. Is the application designed to facilitate change and the ease of use by the user?

The total of the scores for these fourteen questions is the complexity adjustment factor.

5.3.4.4 Calculating function point

These two values obtained are plugged into the following empirical equation to obtain the function point:

FP = Count Total *{0.65+ (0.01 * Complexity Adjustment Factor)}

All the metric data will be related to FP: Effort in person days per FP, defects per FP, cost per FP, pages of documentation per FP.

5.3.5 Establishing a metrics program

The foregoing discussion would have made clear the need for a good metric program in an organization. Normally the Quality department is made responsible for this. It keeps collecting all the relevant data from different projects through an established procedure for the submission of the data and keeps analyzing them to arrive at the needed metrics.

An organization should start with a few metrics and expand them in number and scope. Again with a larger number of projects, the data may be collected domain-wise, technology-wise and unit-wise. With more and more data collected and averaged, the metric will represent the attribute more accurately.

SEI provides the following guidelines for establishing a metrics program:

1. Identify the business goals.
2. Identify what the organization would like to know / learn.
3. Formalize the measurement goals to realize this knowledge / learning.
4. Identify the data elements needed to calculate the indicators.
5. Define the measures for collecting these data elements.

The data collection for metrics should be automated, wherever possible.

5.3.5.1 Candidate Activities for Metrics Collection

For which activities should we collect the metrics data? Most of the organizations collect the data on the effort and the defects for programming only. Again the anomaly of collecting the data for only less than 25% of the effort of the project and extrapolating it to the rest! A good metrics program should encompass all the activities of the development life cycle and thus all the personnel in a software organization should be required to fill the time sheets with the project code, the activity code and the time spent on it. The higher levels of management would find this difficult because many of their activities could be directed to multiple projects, but still to the extent possible the project-wise, activity-wise data should be collected. A sample list of activities, by no means exhaustive, is provided:

1. Project Planning
2. Preliminary analysis
3. Requirements gathering
4. Architecture
5. High level design
6. Detailed design
7. Prototyping
8. Design review
9. Coding
10. Reusable code acquisition
11. Packaged software acquisition
12. Unit testing

13. Code inspection
14. Independent verification and validation
15. Configuration management
16. Integration
17. Integration testing
18. User documentation
19. System testing
20. Acceptance testing
21. Quality assurance
22. Installation and training
23. Project management

If data is collected for all these and more over a large number of projects, then the averaged data would represent the software size to a near perfect level.

Function Point – Case Example
Inventory System – Receipt Module

The consumables store of a manufacturing unit wants to develop a software solution to manage its receipts. The items are bar coded and packing notes, bills etc. from vendors are also bar coded.

Scope

The following functionalities are to be addressed by this system:

- Validation of the receipt of materials
- Computing the inventory value
- Sending acknowledgements to the vendor
- Information to Purchase and Manufacturing
- Inventory update
- Since most of the items are bar coded, the stores in-charge wants bar code reading and processing capability in the software.
- Inventory valuation is done at standard costing.
- Bill processing is not included as part of this exercise.
- P.O. Master, Item Master, Vendor Master, Stock Adjustment, Stock Transactions, Bar Code Master required for the new software have already been designed for other related systems.

- At the end of the day, the following reports are required:
  - Daily receipts with Purchase order no., Vendor, Item quantity and Value details.
  - Purchase order closure report: a list of the purchase orders that have been closed on account of the order fulfilment.

User Environment

- Users are not familiar with bar code and need training on its usage.
- Users are computer literate. An operation manual is good enough in addition to a system manual for reference.

Hardware and Software Platform

- The warehouse has ten desktop PCs and these are connected to a dedicated server in the Purchase department.
- The purchase order management and the financial accounting systems are in place and are integrated.
- The software is proposed to be developed in Oracle / Visual Basic environment.
- Barcode interface application to be developed.

Data Volumes

- Number of stock items: 26430
- Number of receipts: Average 300 per day
- Number of items per receipt: Average 2
- Number of Vendors: 2000

Performance Requirements

- Receipt acknowledgement within 10 seconds after the manual processing of the receipt
- Update of various records instantaneously after acknowledgement

Ease of Use

- Primary users to use the system with two hours of training and no further handholding sessions.
- Operations manual to be self-explanatory.

Table structure

- Purchase Order (PO) Master - PO number, Date, Vendor code, Item code, Quantity, Rate, Amount, Levies, Delivery instructions., PR (Purchase requisition) reference
- Receipts:– Receipt No., Date, Vendor code, Item code, Specification, Quantity

- Stock Adjustment: Document number, Date, Item code, Increase / Decrease, Remarks
- Stock Transactions: Item code, Document reference, Receipt / Issue, Quantity, Opening balance, Closing balance
- Item Master: Item code, Item name, Unit of measure, Specifications, Stock, Minimum level, Maximum level, Reorder level, Safety stock
- Vendor Master: Vendor code, Vendor name, Contact person, Address 1, Address 2, Address 3, City, Pin code, Phone number, Fax number, Email id
- Bar Code: Bar code, Item code.

FP – Calculation Worksheet

Step 1: Identify the project boundary and list the activities included in the scope:

1.

2.

3.

4.

5.

6.

7.

8.

9.

10.

Identify the ILFs and EIFs:

Table	ILF / EIF	RET*	DET**	Complexity	UFP	Remarks
Purchase Order Master						
Receipts						
Stock Adjustment						
Stock Transactions						
Item Master						
Vendor Master						
Bar Code						
Total UFP for Files						

*RET – Record Element Type –Type of records; in relational databases, RET will normally be 1.

**DET – Data Element Type – for all practical purposes, we can use field as a DET.

Complexity of Files:

DET / RET	<20	20-50	>50
1	Simple	Simple	Average
2-5	Simple	Average	Complex
>5	Average	Complex	Complex

Function Point weightage table:

Parameter	Simple	Average	Complex
Inputs	3	4	6
Outputs	4	5	7
Queries	3	4	6
Files	7	10	15
Interfaces	5	7	10

External Inputs (EI)

Identify the tables for which there will be inputs in the form of Add, Modify, Delete:

File	AMD	FTR*	DET	Complexity	UFP
	Add				
	Modify				
	Delete				
	Add				
	Modify				
	Delete				
	Add				
	Modify				
	Delete				
	Add				
	Modify				
	Delete				
Total UFP for EI					

*FTR – File type referenced – number of tables accessed in adding / modifying / deleting input

Complexity of Inputs:

DET FTR	<5	5-15	>15
0-1	Simple	Simple	Average
2	Simple	Average	Complex
>2	Average	Complex	Complex

External Outputs

File	FTR	DET	Complexity	UFP
Total UFP for EO				

Complexity of Outputs:

DET FTR	<6	6-19	>19
0-1	Simple	Simple	Average
2-3	Simple	Average	Complex
>3	Average	Complex	Complex

External Queries (EQ):

File	FTR	DET	Complexity	UFP
Total UFP for EQ				

Complexity of Query:

Count as if it were an input
Count as if it were an output
Take the higher score

Complexity Adjustment Factor:

General System Characteristic	Brief Description	Comment	Complexity Adjustment
1. Data Communications	How many communication facilities are there to aid in the transfer or the exchange of information with the application or system?		
2. Distributed data processing	How are the distributed data and processing functions handled?		

3. Performance	Was the response time or the throughput specified by the user?		
4. Heavily used configuration	How heavily used is the current hardware platform where the application will be executed?		
5. Transaction rate	How frequently are the transactions executed - daily, weekly, monthly etc.?		
6. Online data entry	What percentage of the information is entered online?		
7. End user efficiency	Was the application designed for end-user efficiency?		
8. Online update	How many ILF's are updated by online transactions?		
9. Complex processing	Does the application have an extensive logical or mathematical processing?		
10. Reusability	Was the application developed to meet one or many organizations' needs?		
11. Ease of Installation	How difficult are conversion and installation?		
12. Operational ease	How effective and / or automated are the start-up, the back-up, and the recovery procedures?		

13. Multiple sites	Was the application specifically designed, developed and supported to be installed at multiple sites for multiple organizations?		
14. Facilitate change	Was the application specifically designed, developed, and supported to facilitate change at the user end?		
	Total Complexity Adjustment factor		

Calculation of FP:

Count total   = UFP for (ILF+EIF+EI+EO+EQ)

Complexity Adjustment Factor   =

FP   = Count Total * {0.65 + (0.01 * Complexity Adjustment Factor)}

        =

Practice Questions

1. State whether true or false:

    a. The software metrics should be simple.
    b. Effort to develop a functionality will remain the same independent of the language used.
    c. Developing the reusable code requires less time than the non-reusable code of the same size.
    d. When you design a financial accounting system, the purchase system falls within the application boundary.
    e. An application cannot write on its external interface file.
    f. It is not rational to relate the pages of documentation to the number of lines of code.
    g. Function point is one level above SLOC.
    h. An external query has an input component.
    i. An external interface file is an internal logical file of another application.
    j. An internal logical file is always an external interface file of another application.
    k. Data communication requirement for a PC LAN is high.

2. Fill in the blanks with the appropriate terms.

    a. --- is the function which is responsible for metrics in an organization.
    b. --- is the source for collecting the production data in a software organization.
    c. ---- is the source for the quality data in a software organization.
    d. --- in the programs could be a good measure to arrive at the quality metrics.
    e. If an application can alter the structure of a table, the table will be an ------- for the application.
    f. For a core banking application, the score for reliability of back-up and recovery requirement is likely to be on the ----- (higher / lower) side.

3. Choose the most appropriate answer:

    a. What do you understand by metrics?
        i.   A subset of the quality function
        ii.   Means of measuring software
        iii. A measure followed by QA
        iv.   Unit of the software measurement

    b. Which is a good measure for effort?
        i.   Lines of code
        ii.   Hours
        iii. Persons
        iv.   Person hours

    c. Which of the following is a good metric to collect?
        i.   Functional richness of an application
        ii.   Number of lines in a program
        iii. Number of people in a team
        iv.   Number of person-hours to create ten pages of documentation

    d. Which of the following is the most important requirement of software?
        i.   Complexity
        ii.   Efficiency
        iii. Functionality
        iv.   Latency

    e. The software cost is directly related to
        i.   defects
        ii.   overheads
        iii. number of team members
        iv.   person-hours.

    f. Which of the following is an intuitively persuasive metric?
        i.   Attendance hrs. of programmers
        ii.   Length of a program
        iii. No of loop statements in a program
        iv.   Person hrs. required to develop a program

g. Response time is a measure of

    i. complexity

    ii. functionality

    iii. performance

    iv. quality

h. Demand for which resource is directly dependent on the size of the application?

    i. Hardware

    ii. Human resources

    iii. Networking components

    iv. Software

i. What causes complexity?

    i. Developer capability

    ii. Interconnections

    iii. Reliability

    iv. Size

j. The batch program efficiency is measured in terms of the

    i. frequency of run time aborts

    ii. accuracy of results

    iii. consistency of results

    iv. execution time

k. Maintainability is a function of

    i. functionality

    ii. modularity

    iii. size

    iv. testability

l. The customer bill preparation at a retail shop is a(n)

    i. external input

    ii. external output

    iii. external query

    iv. internal logical file

m. Why is it that the LOC method is found to penalize the efficient programming?

   i.   Efficient programmers produce less lines of code in unit time.
   ii. LOC is not the final output of a programmer.
   iii. LOC is inversely proportional to the functionality.
   iv. LOC does not affect the time to create it.

n. Which has the highest distributed processing requirement?

   i.   Email on an intranet
   ii. Inventory update at stores
   iii. Railway reservation application
   iv. Creating a text at a terminal

o. Why is performance a factor in the complexity adjustment?

   i.   Because it is not addressed as a part of the information domains.
   ii. Aggressive performance requirements need additional effort to design.
   iii. The performance improvement requires reduction in the number of files.
   iv. The performance increases the functional requirements.

p. An External Interface File

   i.   is not a file, but a device interacting with the application.
   ii. is data in motion.
   iii. resides outside the application boundary.
   iv. resides within the application boundary.

q. From the Function Point table, what can you infer about the external inputs and the external outputs?

   i.   At the same level of complexity, the EIs require more effort than the EOs.
   ii. At the same level of complexity, the EOs require more effort than the EIs.
   iii. The EOs are more complex than the EIs.
   iv. No inference is possible.

r.   Cash withdrawal from an ATM returns a message 'Insufficient balance'. This will be treated as an output if

    i.   the request triggers a process that does not access a database.

    ii.   it debits the balance and when found negative, reverses the entry.

    iii. the successful withdrawal is an output.

    iv.   the successful withdrawal is a query.

s.   Printing a master list of customers is an

    i.   external input

    ii.   external output

    iii. external query

    iv.   internal logical file

t.   Where is the algorithmic complexity addressed in the function point calculation?

    i.   As a part of the information domains

    ii.   As a part of the complexity adjustment factor

    iii. In calculating the unadjusted function point

    iv.   Algorithmic complexity is not addressed in the function point calculation.

u.   Which of the following is the correct calculation formula for FP?

    i.   Count Total + {0.65 + (0.01 * Complexity Adjustment Factor)}

    ii.   Count Total * {0.65 + (0.01 * Complexity Adjustment Factor)}

    iii. Count Total * {0.65* (0.01* Complexity Adjustment Factor)}

    iv.   Unadjusted Function Point * Complexity Adjustment Factor

v.   Which of the following will not affect the function point calculation of an application?

    i.   Information domain

    ii.   Computer language

    iii. Complexity adjustment factor

    iv.   Transactions

w. Which of the following is a transactional function?

   i.   Application boundary
   ii. External input
   iii. Internal logical file
   iv. Data at rest

4. How would you differentiate an application with a high data communication from the one with a high level of distributed data processing? Explain the difference with examples.

5. To assess the complexity of an application, two of the parameters are the requirement of reliable back-up and recovery and the extent of data communications. During requirement gathering, what information would you collect to assess these parameters?

6

SOFTWARE ESTIMATION

The art of prophecy is very difficult, especially with respect to the future. - Mark Twain

6.1 Learning objectives

This lesson defines the scope of the software estimation and the challenges therein.

Different approaches to the software estimation are explained

6.2 What is estimation?

Estimation is an attempt to determine how much money is required to develop a software application. The major cost of software is the cost of labour and so the effort estimation is an important driver in the cost estimation. Effort is measured in person-days.

In identifying the persons required and the duration for which they are required, the tasks that need to be performed by these persons need to be identified. Any omission in this will lead to an inaccuracy in the estimation. This point needs to be emphasized because even the experienced project managers tend to omit some activities (and regret later!).

The tasks are required to be identified not only for fulfilling the functional requirements of the software, but the non-functional requirements as well. While the functional requirements define what a system is proposed to do, the non-functional requirements define how the system should be or behave. Usability, reliability, interoperability are all the non-functional requirements.

Why would the non-functional requirements require an additional effort? In making the application screens to be user-friendly, the designer has to spend an additional time. Similarly for making the system fool-proof, the additional design, development and testing efforts may be required.

6.3 Challenges in Estimation

While several methods have been propounded for the software estimation, it has not reached the level of accuracy which many other disciplines have achieved. Your apartment promoters are able to price their product with enough protection for profit, because of their ability to estimate the cost fairly accurately. Ironically they use software for this estimation!

The software industry still suffers from imperfections in the estimation for the following reasons:

- Each project is unique that we are not able to extrapolate from the previous experience. How could we use the experience we have gained in designing and developing the processes in the banking domain to developing a supply chain management application? Is the experience gained in developing an ERP application useful in designing gaming software?
- The tools and technology keep changing in the software industry. The experiences gained in developing a financial application in COBOL may not be useful / relevant in developing the same application in Java. This is the reason why the software professionals associate their expertise with a tool – Java, VB and the like. Have you ever heard of a wrench specialist?
- Added to this are the changes in the methodology. Newer iterative methodologies make the experience in the waterfall method redundant, to a large extent.

- A lot more data on the project implementation experiences may be required before we evolve a formal process-product relationship. Seventy years is too short a period for this.

- Unlike in many other disciplines such as the civil construction, in which the lowest level processes have been simplified and standardized to such an extent that the variations in the effort required in these processes is minimal, coding still permits a wide variation across different programmers. Given the same coding requirement, different programmers might come up with widely varying estimates and the ratio of the lowest and the highest estimate could be as high as 1:16 (McConnell[25], 1998). In another study it has been shown to be 1:20 (Sackman, 1968)

- There are practical impediments too in the software estimation. Most of the time, the organizational pulls and pressures override the formal estimation. The market competition may force a business development manager to agree to a deadline and a price with the client before a formal estimation is done. The agreed price may restrict the resource availability to the project. So often the project managers find that these critical project parameters are handed down to them without allowing them to adopt any scientific approach to decide on the resource needs and the time of delivery. This reality should not make us turn cynical towards the formal methods. Even if all the trains come late, still we need a railway guide to tell us how late a train is. Similarly, even if the manpower availability and the duration have been pre-decided, a project manager should still insist on a formal estimation to understand how much (s)he is constrained for the resources and time, That would help him / her to decide how early (s)he would overwork the resources to achieve the desired result. The market forces cannot change the internal realities of organizational metrics!

- Many organizations are cynical about the formal methods and claim that they have developed their own thumb rules for the estimation. For the large projects, such informal methods may prove costly.

---

[25] Steve McConnell has the experience of working in and leading the software projects in highly demanding organizations such as Boeing and Microsoft..

6.4 **Can software be estimated at all?**

"The initial project estimate tends to be a target with only about a 10-20% chance of being met" said DeMarco (DeMarco, 1982). Over these years, with our knowledge of the software projects increasing, has the situation improved? As late as 1998, McConnell concluded that it was not only difficult to estimate a project in its early stages, it was theoretically impossible.(McConnell, 1998). Even after the requirements gathering phase, that is after the SRS is prepared, the effort estimation may have an error of 50%! (McConnell, 1998). Often the software organizations are asked to submit the quote much before the detailed requirements gathering starts.

In that case, is it worth attempting the software estimation? Or is the exercise a wild goose chase? The industry as well as the academics in this discipline is divided on this issue. Watts Humphrey[26], a thought leader in the software engineering area, believes that the software development is a set of processes and defining and complying with the processes will have a positive impact on the productivity and the quality of the software production. In the words of Humphrey, the industry process control concepts[27] "are just as applicable to software as they are to automobiles, cameras, wristwatches, and steel making" (Humphrey, 1987). Humphrey goes on to argue "A software development process, which is under the statistical control, will ... produce the desired results within the anticipated limits of cost, schedule and quality".

On the other hand, Bollinger holds a diametrically different viewpoint: "The creation of genuinely new software has far more in common with developing a new theory in physics than it does with producing cars or watches on an assembly line". (Bollinger, 1997)

Not only does the actual effort vary from the estimate; the gap between the actual and the estimated effort is about 75% in most of the projects (DeMarco,

---

[26]   Watts Humphrey was responsible for founding the software process program in the Software Engineering Institute (SEI) at the Carnegie Mellon University, which led to the development of the Capability Maturity Model (CMM).

[27]   The process control concepts Humphrey refer to are the rigorous statistical quality control techniques advocated by Edwards Deming.

1982). DeMarco asserts "An estimate is the most optimistic prediction that has a non-zero probability of coming true …or… what's-the-earliest-date-by-which-you-can't-prove-you-won't-be-finished?" (DeMarco, 1982).

6.5 Approaches to software estimation

This debate goes on; we may concede that there is an element of truth on both the sides. In real life, submission of quotation at the initial stage of the project is an inescapable reality, for which a reasonable estimate of the effort and the cost are required. To address this issue, some approaches are recommended, however crude or inexact they may be:

6.5.1 Delay

The more you buy time, the more you use the time to understand about the project, the more accurate will be your estimate. It is against an RFP from the prospect that your boss wants you to prepare the effort estimate. Most of the RFPs are quite sketchy and omit many details that are critical for preparing the estimate. Discussions with the customer and a preliminary systems study will improve your understanding of the project. The more intensive systems study your analysts are able to conduct, the more the estimate moves closer to accuracy and all this takes time.

The following figure shows how with the progress of time, the estimation accuracy improves. For example, at the Feasibility stage the uncertainty band is 16X (from 0.25 to 4.0), while at the Concept stage it has narrowed to 4X and by the Requirements Specification, it has reduced to 2.25X.

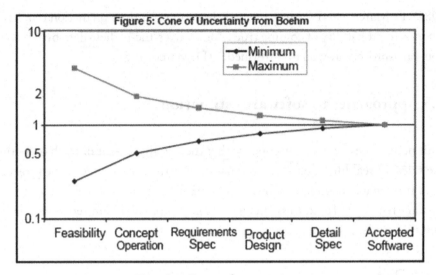

Fig. 6.1. Cone of uncertainty

(Source: Boehm, Barry W, Software Engineering Economics, Prentice-Hall, 1981)

This is the dilemma of the industry: the quotation for the software needs to be prepared at the beginning of the requirement specification stage, when the estimation uncertainty could hover anywhere between 0.5 times to twice the actual.

In some projects, where the requirement uncertainty is perceived to be of a high order, both the parties agree to have an initial estimate with a proviso that the quotation will be revisited at the end of the preparation of the SRS with a cap on the escalation permitted.

Delay is suggested as a tactical approach towards the estimation, but it is not a technique of estimation. The following three are the techniques of estimation:

6.5.2 Duplicate

A project completed in the past, very similar to the proposed one, is chosen and its estimate is taken as the basis for the current project. Whenever a project estimate is to be prepared, the first thing to do is to refer to the project repository[28]. When are two applications considered similar? When the domain and the requirements of both the application are the same. Not only that, the applications considered should be on the same hardware and software platforms and should be using the same development methodology.

Also known as the analogy method, this method is more favourable to the large organizations with a long track record than to the start-ups. Could the employees of a nascent organization use the data collected from some other organizations or their own previous organizations? No, the metrics of any organization are based on the learnings of that organization and these are not transferable to a new organization even if many of the employees of the first organization have migrated to the second one.

Some sites such as www.isbsg.org[29] give data on a large number[30] of projects. Again when this data is used for comparison, we need to be cautious that all the relevant parameters are identical between the compared projects.

6.5.3 Decompose

In this method, all the high level activities are broken down to tasks and this process is repeated till such time the lowest level of tasks can be estimated without an appreciable margin of error. The work breakdown structure is a popular technique for such decomposition. The technique has already been discussed in detail (Chapter 4).

---

[28]   It is a practice in the software organizations – particularly the large ones - to maintain an electronic repository of all the projects completed, with a record of their salient features and the important artefacts associated with each of the projects. The access rights are provided to the software team members based on their role and requirement.

[29]   The International Software Benchmarking Standards Group (ISBSG) is a not-for-profit organization that provides the data on the IT projects.

[30]   As of now ISBSG claims to have the data on 5600 projects.

6.5.4 Derive

Several empirical equations have been created based on an analysis of a large number of projects and these models help compute the effort from the count of the estimation variables (normally LOC or FP).

Two such equations are shown below:

- $E = 5.2 * (KLOC)^{0.91}$ Walston-Felix
- $E = -13.39 + 0.0545FP$ Albrecht & Gaffney

(on the right side are the names of the developers of these models.)

These models, however, are usable only in the environments similar to those from which the source data for these models have been extracted. For the same reason, the direct application of these models for the software estimation is not wide-spread in the industry.

6.6 Metrics for software estimation

6.6.1 Lines of code

The merits and demerits of this metric have already been discussed in the previous chapter.

6.6.2 Function points

Apart from being one level above SLOC, this metric permits the estimation by the non-technical members of the project team. The estimate is independent of the language and the methodology employed.

6.6.3 Expertise-based methods

In the areas, where the domain expertise is not available within the organization or the application itself is new, the assistance from an expert may be sought. The problem is in identifying the right expert.

6.6.3.1 Wideband Delphi approach

With a view to avoid the influence of the angularities of an expert in the estimate, this method advocates a consensus approach among the experts. In this method, instead of one expert, several experts discuss and arrive at an estimate. Originally developed by Rand Corporation in 1940s as a forecasting tool, this was fine-tuned for the software estimation by Barry Boehm (Boehm, 1981) and John Farquhar. The method has the following steps:

- The moderator issues the specifications to the experts.
- The experts discuss the scope of the product and the assumptions thereof.
- Each expert prepares a separate estimate.
- The moderator collates the estimates and prepares a summary form without mentioning the expert names against the estimate.
- A meeting is convened to discuss the differences in the estimates and the reasons for such differences.
- The experts rework their estimates individually.
- This process is continued till a consensus is reached.

Because of the repeated discussions, this method addresses all the issues comprehensively, but it may prove to be time-consuming and costly. Also it is not easy to assemble several experts in a specialized area.

6.7 Automation of estimation

If the other disciplines use software for estimation, why can the software industry not use it - can we have software for the software estimation? There are some attempts in this area, though with limited success.

There are more than fifty tools available in the market, majority of which are function point-based. These tools may be classified into three categories:

- Type 1 tools take the information domain and the complexity adjustment factors as the inputs and from these, the tools calculate the function points. Productivity Manager for Windows and S.M.A.R.T.

Counter fall into this category. This is the only class certified by IFPUG.

- Type 2 provides a large repository of projects to compare and arrive at an estimate. ANGEL is one such tool.
- Type 3 uses the artificial intelligence algorithms to estimate. This is still in the research domain and the estimate accuracy levels are uncertain.

The usage of tools is not widely prevalent in the industry. How does the buyer assess the estimation accuracy of the tool? No vendor is going to discuss the software logic with the buyer, as it is their trade secret. The best way to test is to put some completed projects through the tool and compare its results with the actual.

Practice Questions

1. State whether true or false:

   a. A formal estimation of software is impossible and so it is better to opt for the informal methods.
   b. As the project progresses, the accuracy of the estimate improves.
   c. An application takes the same time to develop, whether it is on mainframe or in the client-server environment.
   d. The knowledge of programming is a prerequisite for the FP estimation.
   e. Since the price and the duration of a software project are fixed by the senior management, the estimation is a wasteful effort.
   f. The FP estimation is an expertise-based technique.
   g. Once the effort is estimated, the resources can automatically be estimated.
   h. A neural network-based tool will provide a more accurate estimate than ANGEL.
   i. An AI based tool will not give the estimate in terms of the function points.
   j. ISBSG avoids the need for project estimation.

2. Fill in the blanks with the appropriate terms:

   a. FP is one level ------ (above / below) SLOC.
   b. According to the cone of uncertainty, the estimation accuracy may range form --- to --- at the end of the requirement gathering.

3. Choose the most appropriate answer:

   a. The project repository will be useful in estimating the software projects through the method of -----.
      i.   delay
      ii. duplication
      iii. decomposition
      iv. derivation

b. Maintaining the historical data in a project repository is very useful because with the historical data available,

    i.   most projects demand almost equal effort.

    ii. the estimation accuracy improves.

    iii. the estimation effort increases.

    iv. actual effort = estimated effort.

c. Why can the estimation not be postponed to the later part of the project?

    i.   The estimation can be done with certainty in the early phases.

    ii. The inaccuracies in the early phases of the estimation will not affect the project much.

    iii. The estimation-based cost-benefit analysis is important for a go - no go decision.

    iv. The estimation will be biased as the project progresses.

d. What is the advantage of the Delphi method?

    i.   Everybody in the group needs to be an expert.

    ii. The conclusion is reached fast.

    iii. Takes advantage of the individual expertise.

    iv. The issues are not overlooked.

e. A training set in an estimation tool is a(n)

    i.   algorithm

    ii. IFPUG certification

    iii. repository of the historical projects

    iv. user manual

f. If y-axis in cone of uncertainty is not logarithmic and if the shape of the graph remains the same, then the deviation of the actual effort from the estimated effort will be

    i.   less

    ii. more

    iii. the same

    iv. cannot say

g. The analogy-based tools use the method of
   i.   artificial intelligence
   ii. duplication
   iii. decomposition
   iv. derivation

h. The estimation tool vendors will not reveal their logic. How do you evaluate the tools in this context?
   i.   Talk to the existing users and get their feedback.
   ii. Feed past project data, use the tool to get the estimate, compare with the actual.
   iii. Go by the vendor reputation
   iv. Conduct a source code analysis to decode the logic

i. Data from the ISBSG site will help the organizations
   i.   understand the estimation techniques.
   ii. structure the WBS properly.
   iii. with data on projects.
   iv. develop algorithms for estimation.

j. WBS is a tool for
   i.   automated estimation
   ii. duplication
   iii. decomposition
   iv. computing FPs

k. What is most certain about the Delphi approach?
   i.   Most accurate
   ii. Possibility of bias
   iii. Non-iterative
   iv. Time consuming

l. What do you infer from the cone of uncertainty?
   i.   The actual effort could exceed the estimated effort by a factor of 2.
   ii. The estimation gets better as the project progresses.
   iii. The estimation improves with the availability of the historical data.
   iv. The estimate is as good as the expert's opinion.

m. Availability of similar project data helps in

    i. project estimation

    ii. risk analysis

    iii. productivity comparison

    iv. all the above

n. Which of the following is an expertise-based technique?

    i. Wide band Delphi approach

    ii. Decomposition technique

    iii. FP estimate

    iv. Work Breakdown Structure

o. Who are the participants in the wideband Delphi approach?

    i. Developers

    ii. Domain experts

    iii. FP counters

    iv. Project managers

p. Why is the software project estimation challenging?

    i. Homogeneity of the project experience

    ii. Poor knowledge of the project managers

    iii. Use of the sophisticated technology

    iv. Uniqueness of each project

4. An application, whether it is developed in Java or VB will have the same FP count, but the effort will vary – Explain how this is possible.

5. Because the accuracy of the software estimation techniques is still poor, it is better to provide a high buffer while preparing the quote – what could be the problems in adopting this approach?

7

PROJECT SCHEDULING AND TRACKING

The bearing of a child takes nine months, no matter how many women are assigned.
- Frederick P. Brooks, Jr. from 'The Mythical Man-month'

7.1 Learning objectives

In this lesson we will explain

- What is scheduling?
- What is the purpose of scheduling?

Different scheduling techniques are explained in detail.

7.2 Project scheduling

Now that we have estimated the effort in person months, we need to break it into the number of persons and months. It is not that during the entire project, the resources are demanded uniformly. Also it is not the same skills that are needed through the entire duration of the project. In the analysis phase, the business analysts will perform the elicitation of the requirements.

During coding, the business analysts may not have any role, but programmers and testers will take over and the number of members in the team will swell during this phase.

This exercise of identifying the tasks, sequencing them and assigning the skills required for each of these tasks is called scheduling.

It is unreasonable to expect that a perfect schedule will emerge in the first cut itself – more so in the large projects. This exercise goes through several iterations. Again, it is unreasonable to assume that the schedule will be followed to a tee in practice. With several imponderables, there will be slippages in the schedule and it may have to be reworked. The schedule evolves as the project progresses.

7.2.1 Scheduling – basic principles

- First the project is divided into the manageable tasks.
- A pre-requisite for sequencing the tasks is identifying the interdependencies among them.
- The effort for each of these tasks is measured in terms of person-days (described in the last two chapters).
- With the sequencing done, the start date / time and the end date / time of each task are identified.
- The role(s) responsible for the completion of each of these tasks is / are identified.
- Each task should have an identified outcome to confirm the completion of the task.
- Progress review points – milestones- are also identified.

7.2.2 Why scheduling?

- The skills required at different phases of the project are different. Scheduling helps determine the type of skills required and the time at which and the duration for which each of these skills is required.

- The scarce resources of an organization need to be utilized to the maximum extent. When two or more tasks compete for the same resource, the prioritization needs to be decided upfront.
- As the project progresses, the completed tasks are marked in the schedule such that the actual may be compared with the plan.
- It is also possible to mark the cash inflow and outflow points in the schedule. Many project management tools permit this.
- Deviation from the schedule, when it crosses a limit, may require redefining the scope, the deliveries etc. Such a mid-course review is very important particularly in the long duration projects.
- The first cut schedule may also be used for go-no go decision for a project. With the initial requirements, a gross schedule is prepared and the contention for the resources is analyzed in the context of the other projects in the organization. This helps in deciding on the capability of the organization to deliver the project on the specified due date.
- Schedule is a good communication mechanism, because it focuses on the highly relevant parameters of the project. Explicit display of the schedule helps the team understand the areas of shortfall and identify the remedies.
- Such a display also motivates the team, because the members can assess their own achievements and what and how much remain to be done. Some organizations even allow every team to view the schedule of all the teams, which introduces a healthy competition among them.

Scheduling Exercise

- It is your niece Jyotsna's second birthday next Wednesday. You have exactly one week to plan for a birthday party.
- About 50 children are expected to attend apart from the family, some friends and relatives.
- Gifts for each child need to be arranged. Some kids may need transportation to / and from the party venue.
- Rajasthan Royals is the preferred caterer for serving the dinner.
- Cake needs to be arranged for separately
- The apartment terrace will be the venue; The decorations will be done by a contractor.

- Games need to be arranged for the kids to keep them engaged.
- Your mother has asked you to download popular film songs on an iPod to play during the occasion.

Prepare a schedule.

7.2.3 Work Breakdown Structure (WBS)

The technique described in detail in the Chapter 4 is helpful in dividing a project into the tasks of reasonable size and assigning the resources. But interdependencies among tasks are not shown in a WBS.

7.2.4 Gantt[31] Chart

A bar chart representing the start and the end dates of tasks:

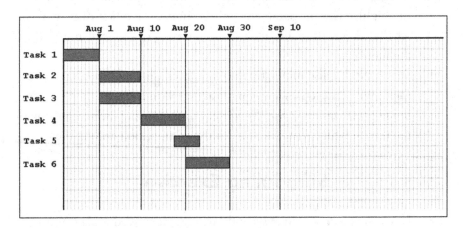

Fig. 7.1. Gantt Chart

---

31   Developed by Henry Gantt and hence the name.

An improved version of the Gantt chart includes dependencies also:

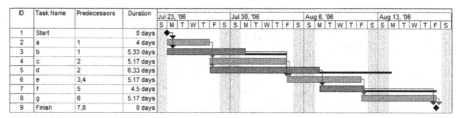

ID	Task Name	Predecessors	Duration
1	Start		0 days
2	a	1	4 days
3	b	1	5.33 days
4	c	2	5.17 days
5	d	2	6.33 days
6	e	3,4	5.17 days
7	f	5	4.5 days
8	g	6	5.17 days
9	Finish	7,8	0 days

Fig. 7.2. Gantt Chart (with dependencies)

Source: Wikipedia

However, complex dependencies are difficult to be depicted in a Gantt chart.

7.2.5 Network diagramming techniques

These techniques are very useful in depicting the interdependencies.

Critical Path Method (CPM) and Program Evaluation and Review Technique (PERT) are the popular network diagramming techniques.

7.2.5.1 PERT / CPM construction rules

- Only one start node and one end node for a project: This way the duration of the project is not left to any ambiguity.
- An arrow represents an activity and has a duration. The lengths of the arrows do not have any correlation to the duration.
- There is an alternate representation, in which the activity is shown on node. (We will follow the activity on arrow convention in this book).

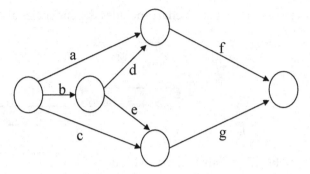

Fig. 7.3. Activities on arrow

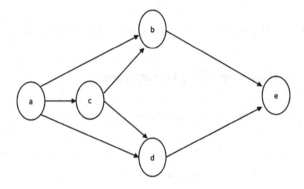

Fig 7.4. Activities on node

- All the activities except the first and the last, must have at least one activity entering and one activity leaving them.
- Predecessor activity: If an activity a1 must be completed before another activity a2 can begin or end then a1 is called the predecessor activity for a2.
- Successor activity: If an activity a2 must be started only after another activity a1 starts or ends, then a2 is called successor activity of a1.
- Time moves from left to right: this helps identify the chronological sequence of the activities.
- The nodes are numbered sequentially; this also helps in identifying the sequence.
- No loops: Loops are difficult to interpret in a network diagram, because the condition for the termination of the loop is not known and thus the duration of the activities in the loop cannot be ascertained. Loop

will also violate the rule of the time moving from left to right. But in real life there are loops such as programming – testing – debugging – testing – debugging and the loop continues till the program is certified by the tester to be bug-free. How does one represent this? Assuming that the coding takes three days and the testing two days and we know from our experience that on an average a program goes through three passes of testing and debugging, the total duration of programming and testing can be taken as fifteen days and may be represented as a single activity.

- No dangles: dangles are loosely hanging activities. For example, documentation may be a parallel activity right through the project. But it should not be represented like this

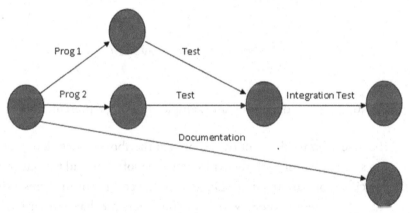

Fig. /.5 Network diagram with a dangle

It can easily be seen that this representation is fallacious, because it has two end nodes. Documentation has to be integrated with each of the activities and shown together.

- Dependency relationships: The predecessor – successor relationship was defined above. This relationship between two activities A and B could be
  o   Finish-to-Start (FS): When A finishes, B may start.
  o   Finish-to-Finish (FF): When A finishes, B may finish.
  o   Start-to-Start (SS): When A starts, B may start.
  o   Start-to-Finish (SF): When A starts, B may finish.

The dependencies could be mandatory, imposed by the very nature of the work; they could also be discretionary based on the preferences of the client or the project manager.

- Dummy activities: Look at the following example:

The software specification is a predecessor activity for preparing the RFP for software.

For preparing the RFP for hardware, the software and the hardware specifications are the pre-requisites. How do we represent this in a network diagram?

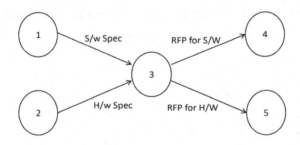

Fig. 7.6. Network diagram – an example of wrong representation

But the diagram does not truly represent the above description. It ends up saying that for both the RFPs, both the software and the hardware specifications are required. Do you see the constraint in representing the above requirement with the constructs we have discussed so far? To overcome this, we introduce a construct called the dummy activities. These do not have any real world significance, but are used for representation in the network diagrams.

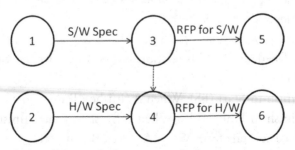

Fig. 7.7 Network diagram with dummy activity

The dummy activity (3-4) is represented with dotted lines. The dummy activities are required in PERT / CPM, because not more than one activity can have the same preceding and succeeding activity.

7.2.5.2 PERT / CPM – An exercise

Activity	Duration	Predecessor
a	14	
b	3	
c	7	
d	4	a,b
e	10	b,c

Did you get this answer? It has two dummies:

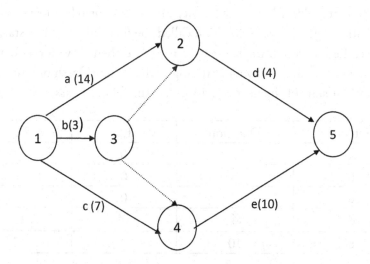

Fig. 7.8. Solution for the exercise

What is the duration of this project?

18? 7? 13? 17?

18 is the correct answer. How did you arrive at it?

7.2.5.3 Passes through the network

For every activity the earliest start (ES), the latest start (LS), the earliest finish (EF) and the latest finish (LF) have to be arrived at, which will help us know the slack in each activity.

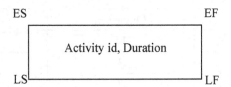

Fig 7.9. Representation of Activity with associated details

The slack is useful in prioritizing the jobs, when there is a contention for the resources. So each activity has to be embellished with these details:

The early start and finish for each activity can be computed by moving through the activities in the forward direction called the forward pass. The start node has the earliest start and the latest start as 0. And then move forward adding the duration of each activity and arriving at the earliest finish of that activity or the earliest start of the next activity. After the forward pass,

Activity	Duration	ES	EF
a	14	0	14
b	3	0	3
c	7	0	7
d	4	14	18
e	10	7	17

The latest start and finish can be computed through the backward pass, wherein we start with the end node. As with the start node, the end node will also have the same earliest and latest finish– in this case 18 (why not 17?); now move backwards subtracting the duration of each activity. After the backward pass,

Activity	Duration	LS	LF
e	10	8	18
d	4	14	18
c	7	1	8
b	3	5	8
a	14	0	14

Slack is defined as the difference between the earliest start and the latest start or the earliest finish and the latest finish of an activity.

With the earliest finish and the latest finish days plugged in the network except for the start node, the diagram looks like this:

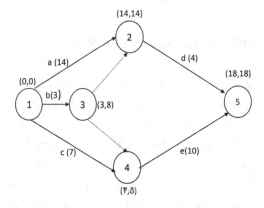

Fig. 7.10. Network diagram with LS and LF

7.2.5.4 Critical path

Any event with zero slack is known as a critical event. 1,2,5 are critical events in the above network.

There will at least be one path connecting the critical events and this path is called the critical path. a-d is the critical path in the above network.

Of the available paths, the critical path will have the maximum duration and hence it is the minimum time required to complete the project.

How many critical paths could be there in a project? There could be as many critical paths as the paths available in the network. For example, if the activity c has 8 days duration, then c-e is also a critical path. But in any project, there will at least be one critical path.

7.2.5.4.1 Significance of critical path

Since the slack is zero in a critical path, any delay in an activity in this path will affect the project schedule, which means that a project manager has to focus all his / her attention on the critical path activities. When there is a resource contention, the critical path activities will get priority.

Whenever the project duration has to be reduced, called 'crashing' of a project, it can only be done with the critical path activities.

7.2.5.5 How is PERT different from CPM?

PERT and CPM are always talked about together and the diagrams also look similar that the difference between these techniques gets blurred in the common parlance. In all the network examples shown above, we showed the activity durations. When we say that an activity a takes 14 days, how do we know this? Through our experience; but the experiences of different people are likely to be different. For any activity, there could be the optimistic and the pessimistic estimates and the realistic estimates will fall between these extremes. While in CPM, the realistic estimate is taken, PERT suggests giving due recognition to the extreme values as well. One third weightage is given to the optimistic and pessimistic estimates together and the two thirds to the realistic estimate:

$$\text{Activity duration} = (O+4M+P) / 6$$
$$O - \text{Optimistic; M- Most likely; P – Pessimistic}$$
$$\text{Standard deviation} = (O-P) / 6$$

The standard deviation is a measure of the confidence in the estimate.

It is possible to factor in risk in the activity estimation in PERT with the assignment of the probabilities to the different estimates.

7.2.6 Critical chain method

This method, developed by Dr. Eliyahu Goldratt, does not assign a buffer to each activity. Goldratt argues that with such an assignment, there will be a tendency to use up the buffer in the completion of the associated activity thus introducing complacency in the completion of the project. The buffers of all the activities are pooled and kept at the end of the critical chain for the common consumption by any activity that suffers delay. In the activity duration estimates and in the buffer pool, the method recommends only 50% of what is estimated and thus a tight schedule is created. There are already case examples available, wherein this method has significantly saved time over the traditional methods.

7.3 Assigning staff to activities

With the schedule prepared, activities with their start and end dates are known. The skills required for each of the activities are identified and the right persons are assigned to these activities.

7.3.1 Resource levelling

Based on the availability of the resources, the schedule may have to be reworked. In fact during the course of the project, the schedule will suffer several revisions depending on the availability of the resources.

7.4 Tracking the schedule

The preparation of the schedule is only one part of the job. The more important part is to monitor compliance to the schedule.

The project manager has to continuously update the schedule with the actual and take the remedial action on the slippages. The schedule acts as a quick feedback mechanism to address the delays as and when they happen.

For periodic reporting to the management and the client, the schedule and the actual performance are the inputs. The variances are discretely included in these reports.

Practice Questions

1. State whether true or false:

   a. Plan is at a macro level while scheduling is detailed.
   b. WBS is a scheduling technique.
   c. The schedule is prepared at the beginning of a project and is not changed afterwards..
   d. The purpose of a WBS is to break the project into the tasks, which are mutually independent.
   e. Monitoring the schedule will indicate the project delays.
   f. In the course of the project if the schedule is found unachievable, it may be changed.
   g. If a new project is found infeasible due to the existing load, one of the options available is to reschedule the existing project to accommodate the new project.
   h. A high slack may be disadvantageous to the project manager.
   i. Slack indicates a delay in an activity.
   j. An activity with zero slack will always be on the critical path.
   k. Highly critical projects have only one critical path.
   l. In a running race, when a person is given a handicap, this will result in two start nodes.
   m. The larger duration activities are difficult to accommodate in PERT / CPM because they occupy more space.
   n. A project manager should plan for a maximum number of activities with zero slack.
   o. Schedule could act as a communication tool.
   p. Gantt chart does not provide for showing the resources for each activity.
   q. When tasks are on node, the duration of the tasks is zero.
   r. A project can have only one start node.
   s. There may be multiple end nodes.
   t. A dangle is permitted in PERT / CPM only when an activity runs parallel to the entire length of the project.

u. Even if it is in the critical path, a delay in a non-critical event will not affect the project duration.

v. To reduce the project duration, crashing may be done in any path in the project.

w. All activity delays should be reported to the client.

x. Among the available paths, the shortest duration path is the critical path.

2. Fill in the blanks with appropriate terms:

a. Person-days is a unit of measure of -----.

b. Programming is a ----- (predecessor / successor) activity for testing.

c. The difference between the actual and the planned is called -----.

d. Duration of nodes in a critical path is ----.

e. ---- is the only node which does not have an activity leaving from it.

f. Early start of each activity is determined in the ---- pass.

g. Backward pass starts with ----..

h. Duration of the critical path is the ---- (minimum / maximum) time required to complete a project.

i. ---- is the networking technique that takes into account the risk in a project.

j. A delay is indicated when actual date - scheduled date is ----- (positive / negative).

3. Choose the most appropriate answer:

a. Which of these is not addressed by a WBS?
    i.   Bottom-up validation
    ii. Critical activities
    iii. Deliverables
    iv. Dependencies

b. Which cannot be shown in a WBS, but can be in a Gantt chart?
    i.   Hierarchy of activities
    ii. Project deliverables
    iii. Task duration
    iv. Parallel activities

c. Which of the following can never have a zero duration?

   i. Activity in non-critical path
   ii. Dummy activity
   iii. Milestone
   iv. Node

d. An organization displays the updated schedules of all the projects in its canteen. What could be the major purpose of this?

   i. Communication
   ii. Motivation
   iii. Education
   iv. Transparency

e. If loops are allowed in PERT / CPM, which of the following conditions will be violated?

   i. At least one activity must enter a node except the start node.
   ii. Nodes have no duration.
   iii. Nodes are numbered sequentially.
   iv. Time moves from left to right.

f. Milestone is a(n)

   i. activity
   ii. measure
   iii. review point
   iv. risk event

g. Which one is a network diagramming technique?

   i. CPM
   ii. Gantt Chart
   iii. LAN
   iv. WBS

h. The unique feature of the network techniques is their ability to show

   i. interdependencies
   ii. milestones
   iii. parallel activities
   iv. task sequences

i. In the network diagrams, tasks are shown on

    i. arrow only

    ii. node only

    iii. either

    iv. neither

j. The ratio of the combined optimistic and pessimistic estimate to the realistic estimate in PERT is

    i. 1:2

    ii. 1:3

    iii. 2:1

    iv. 2:3

k. The purpose of scheduling is

    i. measuring the actual against the plan.

    ii. mid-course review.

    iii. to plan for appropriate resources at the right time.

    iv. all the above.

l. A wall has to be painted 24 hrs after application of primer. So painting is a ------ activity to the primer application

    i. critical

    ii. milestone

    iii. predecessor

    iv. successor

m. A critical event is identified by

    i. its presence in the critical path.

    ii. its importance to the project.

    iii. the prioritized resource allocation.

    iv. zero slack.

n. Which of the following statements is true?

    i. A critical event has to be necessarily on the critical path.

    ii. A critical event may be on a non-critical path.

    iii. A non-critical event may be on the critical path.

    iv. There will be only non-critical events in a non-critical path.

4.

Activity	Optimistic	Most likely	Pessimistic
1-2	3	6	9
1-6	2	5	14
2-3	6	12	18
2-4	2	5	8
3-5	5	11	17
4-5	3	6	15
6-7	3	9	15
5-8	1	4	7
7-8	6	9	18

Draw a PERT network and calculate the estimated duration of the project with the standard deviation.

8

QUALITY MANAGEMENT

Quality is not an act, it is a habit. - Aristotle

8.1 Learning objectives

This lesson will

- define quality.
- describe the different parts of the software quality management.
- distinguish between the quality assurance and control.
- describe different factors that will define the software quality.
- describe the functions of the software quality assurance.
- and the techniques of quality control.

8.2 What is quality?

The definition of quality has evolved with time. Once it was defined only as 'fitness for use'. Its scope and meaning have expanded considerably since then.

Pressman talks about two aspects of quality (Pressman, 2001):

- Quality of design: the designer of a product specifies some characteristics for the product with the measure in which the characteristic should be available in the product and the tolerance.
  For example a component may have a specification of 2mm length ±.1 mm.
- Quality of conformance: the extent to which the product conforms to the design specifications.

While this may apply to software as well, the challenge in software is the identification of the characteristics and their measurement.

Another way is to define quality as the control of variation in the identified characteristic. Statistical quality control is built around the variation control.

Quality needs to be assured in the product as well as the process to make it. The issues that need to be addressed are:

- How does the software creation process affect the product quality?
- How do we manage the process to achieve the desired product quality?

Many thinkers in the software engineering area, chief among them Watts Humphrey, have postulated that the software process quality determines the product quality. The process management encompasses the process definition, the process measurement, the process control and the process improvement. Humphrey advocates the use of the statistical process control methods to understand the process behaviour and to bring stability, predictability and improvement to the software processes.

8.3 Quality management

Quality management consists of three parts:

- Quality planning
- Quality assurance
- Quality control

8.3.1 Quality planning

The quality plan is an important part of a project plan. Some organizations prepare this as a separate document, considering its importance.

The quality plan states the quality objectives of the project and details as to how the objectives are proposed to be achieved.

Inputs to determine the quality objectives and the action plan are:

- the environmental factors such as the regulatory guidelines applicable to the client industry; if the client is from a different geography, that country's regulations might also be an input to the quality plan.
  For example, if the software is proposed to be developed for a pharmaceutical manufacturer in the USA, the FDA[32] rules for the information systems need to be followed and the IPR regulations of the USA would also need to be taken into account. These need to be explicitly stated in the quality plan.
- the client organization's quality standards: these will override the standards of the development organization.

Quality plan will address

- the actions that will be taken to achieve the desired quality level such as the types of tests that will be conducted.
- the quality attributes that need to be monitored and the metrics that need to be collected.
- the measures that are proposed to be undertaken to improve the process.

These are the quality control and the quality assurance measures – the difference between the two is elaborated in the next paragraphs.

---

[32]   Food and Drug Administration of the US

8.3.2 Quality assurance

Quality assurance includes the implementation of the processes that ensure that they may be performed with the desired quality level and thus are preventive in nature. Quality audit, process analysis and the usage of tools will fall into this category.

8.3.3 Quality control

Quality control, on the other hand, includes the measures to ensure the compliance to a standard. Testing, reviews, templates and checklists are good examples of the quality control measures. These measures are detective and corrective in nature.

8.3.4 McCall's quality model

This model, presented by McCall et al (McCall, 1977), looks at quality from three different perspectives:

- Product operation: how well it runs.
- Product revision: how easily it can be changed.
- Product transition: how smoothly it can be moved across platforms

McCall et al went on to define 11 factors, which describe the external view of the software, as viewed by the users and 23 criteria, which describe the internal view of the software, as seen by the developers.

8.3.4.1 Quality factors

- Product operation
  - o Correctness: Does the software do what it is required to do and does not do what it is not supposed to do? (why is the second part necessary – think it over)
  - o Reliability: Does it provide the results with the same level of accuracy and run without failure?

    o   Efficiency: Does it use the hardware and software resources optimally? Does the software have an acceptable level of response time (online systems) and execution time (batch systems)?

    o   Integrity; Does the software have sufficient protection mechanisms in place to ensure that an unauthorized access will be prevented?

    o   Usability: How easy is it for the user to operate it? What is the skill level required to operate it?

- Product revision
  - o Maintainability: How easy is it to fix the problem in the software?
  - o Flexibility: How easy is it to modify the software?
  - o Testability: Are the requirements specified tangible enough to test it?

- Product transition
  - o Portability: Is it possible to move the software from one platform to another with ease?
  - o Reusability: How easy is it to use some part of the software in another system?
  - o Interoperability: How easily can this software be interfaced with another system?

8.3.4.2 Quality criteria

Quality factor	Quality criteria
Correctness	Traceability, consistency, completeness
Reliability	Error tolerance, consistency, accuracy, simplicity
Efficiency	Execution, storage efficiencies
Integrity	Access control, access audit
Usability	Operability, training, communicativeness
Maintainability	Consistency, simplicity, conciseness, modularity, self-descriptiveness
Testability	Simplicity, modularity, instrumentation, self-descriptiveness

Flexibility	Modularity, generality, expandability, self-descriptiveness
Portability	Modularity, self-descriptiveness, machine independence, software system independence
Reusability	Generality, modularity, software system independence, machine independence, self-descriptiveness
Interoperability	Modularity, communications commonality, data commonality

8.3.5 Metrics for software quality

The extent to which each of these factors exists in the software needs to be expressed in terms of some measures.

Any such measure chosen to express a factor should preferably be

- quantitative and capable of mathematical manipulation
  o for which the data collection is feasible
  o and should be capable of meaningful interpretation to gain an insight into the software quality
  o and capable of being corrected based on the interpretation

Some representative measures could be

- Correctness: errors/ KLOC
- Reliability: Mean time between failure (MTBF)
- Efficiency: average response time in seconds, the time required for the execution of the batch operations, the storage efficiency in terms of the size of the footprint in the hard disk
- Integrity: sum of the probabilities of repelling identified attacks
     integrity = $\Sigma[1\text{-threat} * (1\text{-security})]$
     threat – probability of an attack
     security – probability of repelling an attack(Gilb, 1988 as quoted in Pressman, 2001)

The problem in defining the metrics arises for the factors such as usability. In such cases, the proxy variables have to be defined for the metrics:

- Intellectual skill required for operating the software – this is often defined in terms of the academic requirement such as a person with eighth grade pass would be able to use this software. In the gaming software, this is defined in terms of age.
- Time required for learning the software and becoming fairly proficient in its operation - how much time does one require to become proficient in the use of the software? See how quickly a user is able to learn MS Office. That is why this suite of software is considered user-friendly.
- Productivity increase due to the software in terms of the increase in the quantum of tasks performed after its implementation. If a ticketing application improves the number of tickets issued per hour / shift then this could be taken as a measure of its usability.
- Measuring the usability through a questionnaire[33]:

  One of the popular and simple questionnaires used in the industry is the Systems Usability Scale (SUS)[34]. The SUS is a ten item questionnaire (box) measured on a 1 (strongly disagree) to 5 (strongly agree) scale (Brooke, 1996):

1. I think that I would like to use this system frequently.
2. I found the system unnecessarily complex.
3. I thought the system was easy to use.
4. I think that I would need the support of a technical person to be able to use this system.
5. I found that the various functions in this system were well integrated.
6. I thought there was too much inconsistency in this system.
7. I would imagine that most people would learn to use this system very quickly.
8. I found the system very cumbersome to use.
9. I felt very confident using the system.
10. I needed to learn a lot of things before I could get going with this system.

---

[33] The factors identified here have been adapted from 'Software Engineering – A Practitioner's Approach' by Pressman (Gilb, 1988 as quoted in Pressman, 2001)

[34] Developed by John Brooke, Digital Equipment Co, Reading, UK

8.3.5.1 FURPS

McCall's model of the quality factors might look intimidating for the small and medium size projects. In fact there have been additions to the factors identified in the McCall's model[35]. The FURPS model – standing for functionality, usability, reliability, performance and supportability – developed at HP - sums up the critical quality requirements of software.

8.3.6 ISO 9126

ISO is an acronym for International Organization for Standardization[36].

ISO 9126 is an international standard for the evaluation of software. This is an extension of McCall, Boehm[37] and FURPS models.

It defines the software quality with six characteristics and twenty sub-characteristics:

Characteristic	Sub characteristic
Functionality	Suitability Accuracy Interoperability Security
Reliability	Maturity Fault tolerance Recoverability

---

[35] Evans and Marciniak model adds two more factors (verifiability and expandability), while Deutsch and Willis model adds three more (safety, manageability and survivability) (Boukouchi, 2013).

[36] ISO was chosen instead of IOS, because iso in Greek means equal, and ISO wanted to convey the idea of equality - the idea that they develop standards to place organizations on an equal footing.

[37] Boehm model identifies seven factors: portability, reliability, efficiency, usability, testability, understandability, flexibility.

Usability	Understandability
	Learnability
	Operability
Efficiency	Time behaviour
	Resource utilization
Maintainability	Analyzability
	Changeability
	Stability
	Testability
Portability	Adaptability
	Installability
	Co-existence
	Replaceability

The standard defines the metrics for each of these characteristics.

ISO 25010, issued in 2011, supersedes ISO 9126 and has eight characteristics: functionality, efficiency, compatibility, usability, reliability, security, maintainability and portability.

8.3.7 Software Quality Assurance (SQA)

This function, independent of the project organization, will have a significant influence on the software projects.

8.3.7.1 Functions of SQA

- Quality management approach: SQA defines how the product and the process quality will be managed in the organization – the strategy and its implementation.
- A sub unit of SQA, called SEPG (Software Engineering Process Group), is responsible for the software process improvement tasks. This group recommends an appropriate software development model for each project. They keep track of the developments in the

software engineering filed and introduce newer approaches within the organization, if found suitable.

- Quality standards are defined by the SQA. These standards cover almost all the phases of the software development. More details about the quality standards are available in the next paragraph.

- Formal technical reviews (described in detail in a subsequent paragraph) are important activities in a project. The SQA gets involved in the design and code reviews and ensure that these reviews, conducted by the project manager along with the concerned technical staff, are done in compliance with the quality policy, standards and guidelines of the organization. The quality reviews, conducted primarily with an intent to review the project's overall compliance to the quality process – as detailed in the quality plan – are steered by the SQA.

- In case the client requires the compliance with their quality standards, it is the responsibility of the SQA to study those requirements and advise the project team of the steps for compliance.

- Different types of testing required for each project and the level of their rigour will again be advised by the SQA. While there will be mandatory tests for each development approach, there will be additional tests that are required depending on the project specifications. These will be advised, if necessary designed, by the SQA. For example, a banking application will require rigorous security testing; web sites may require the penetration test.

- With many documents for each project and each document undergoing several versions, control of the documentation is an important task in a project. While these documents will be maintained by configuration management (to be discussed in detail in chapter 17), the documentation control policies and checking their compliance fall in the realm of the SQA.

- The SQA conducts audit of the projects on a periodic basis and report to the management on the level of compliance to the prescribed quality process.

- Defining the metrics for each project and the collection and the analysis of the data for the same are also included in the responsibilities of the SQA.

8.3.7.2 Quality standards

The SQA defines the quality standards for the activities in the different phases of the software development. For example, the analysis checklists are provided to guide the business analysts in their interview such that no important point may be omitted. The coding standards may be prepared for different languages and these standards specify the details such as the naming conventions for the variables and the modules and the preferred syntax statements in case of options.

The quality standards, particularly the coding standards, become a thorny issue with the technical staff. The project manager is often torn between the quality department's insistence on the compliance to the specified standards and the resistance of the technical staff on the grounds that these standards promote sub-optimality or stifle creativity. Often the quick changes that take place in a particular technology environment / language are not reflected in the standards, losing out on the efficiency of the latest updates. To overcome this, it is suggested that the standards are reviewed at reasonably short intervals and the technical staff, who are hands-on in programming, are consulted in developing these standards. Once such reviews are done and a standard approved by the Quality function, the project manager should insist on its strict compliance. Tools and templates are the effective ways to ensure compliance.

The standards ensure uniformity in the software development and their importance cannot be overemphasized. Any compromise done to accommodate a programmer's convenience or a wizard's whim will lead to problems in the maintainability of the software.

8.3.7.3 Formal Technical Reviews (FTR)

Formal technical reviews have been found to be one of the most effective ways of removing defects from software. Hence a project manager should conduct these reviews periodically with diligence. Important among the technical reviews are:

- Design review: the technical architecture of the solution is reviewed by peer architects.
- Code review: This is done for the critical programs, which address a core functionality. The participants of this process will be, apart from the project manager and the programmer(s) who developed the code, the business analyst or the domain specialist, the technical specialists, the concerned team lead and the quality representative.
- Quality review: In addition, the project manager should convene the reviews to check that all the steps in the project meet the organization's / client's quality standards. The personnel from the quality department will play an important role in this review.

These reviews may be conducted as

- walk-throughs, in which a coder or designer explains the code / design step-by-step to one or more of his chosen peers or as
- small group assessments, as described above.

8.3.8 ISO approach

ISO is a generic model applicable across industries. It addresses the process quality requirements and thus complementary to the quality requirements specified for the product.

ISO 9001 defines a 'model for the quality assurance in the design, the development, the production, the installation and the servicing' (ISO, 1994) of a product or service.

It might at first instance look strange that the same set of quality standards would apply to manufacturing, independent of the product produced, service sector, utilities, educational institutions and any type of the organization you could think of. ISO defines only the requirements for the quality management system (QMS):

ISO 9001 QMS Requirements

a) Defined and documented quality policy; communication to all levels
b) Documented procedures
c) Contracts: mutually agreed requirements that the vendor is capable of delivering
d) Procedures to control and verify the design of the system to be supplied to the customer
e) Procedures to approve the design and other documentation
f) Third party-supplied components: procedure to check their quality
g) Traceability for individual products and the components
h) Planned and monitored process for the final product
i) Inspection during the development; also of the components supplied by third parties
j) Quality control of the equipment used for the production
k) Recording of the testing status of all the components and the systems
l) Ensuring that the items known to be defective are not used
m) Removal of an identified defective part and ensuring that it does not recur
n) Correct procedures for the handling, the storage, the packaging and the delivery of the product
o) Maintenance of the records for the working of the quality system
p) Regular audit of the quality system
q) Servicing and support activities
r) Establishment of appropriate statistical techniques to verify the acceptability of the final product

The underlying principle lies in asking an organization about the procedures they follow with the associated documentation, then audit the organization to check whether the documented procedures are complied with and seek the documentary evidence for the compliance.

To accommodate the unique processes of the software industry, an additional guidance ISO 9000-3 is available.

The deficiencies identified of the ISO approach are

- It forces a binary decision - whether a system is capable of being certified or not.
- It is perfectly possible for an organization to define an ineffective process, show the proof of its compliance and thus get certification.
- As a consequence, the organizations with the ISO certifications cannot be said to be of the same process quality level.
- Above all, a generic method, however well-defined, cannot be expected to provide a rigorous standard.

8.3.9 Capability Maturity Model (CMM)

The need for a specific standard for software led to the development of the CMM. The model is based on the process maturity framework prescribed by Watts Humphrey (Humphrey, 1987, 1988). It defines the increasing levels of process maturity.

A maturity model can be viewed as a set of structured levels that describes how well the behaviours, the practices and the processes of an organization can reliably and sustainably produce the required outcomes.(Wikipedia).

At each maturity level, the associated key process areas (KPA) are identified. Each KPA is defined by five characteristics: goals, commitments, abilities, the methods for monitoring the implementation and the methods for verifying the implementation.

CMM identifies the following levels:

1. Initial (Also known as Ad hoc or Chaotic)

   a. At this level there are no effective management procedures or project plans.
   b. Even if such procedures exist, there is no organizational mechanism to ensure that they are used consistently.
   c. The relationship between the process and the product is not established and so the product quality is unpredictable.

2. Repeatable

    a. Formal project management is in place.
    b. Organization capable of repeating the same type of projects.
    c. No formal process model
    d. Project success depends on individuals.
    e. Key process areas

        i.   Software configuration management
        ii.   Software quality assurance
        iii. Subcontract management
        iv.   Project tracking
        v.   Project planning
        vi.   Requirements management

3. Defined

    a. Processes are defined.
    b. Also procedures to ensure compliance with the defined processes are
        in place.
    c. Key Process Areas:

        i.   Peer reviews
        ii.   Intergroup coordination
        iii. Software product engineering
        iv.   Integrated software management
        v.   Training

4. Managed

    a. Product and processes are subject to measurement and control for
        which a quantitative data collection mechanism is put in place.
    b. Key Process Areas:

        i.   Software quality management
        ii. Metrics

5. Optimizing

    a. Now that the processes are fully understood and under control, at this level, the organizations attempt to improve the processes and optimize them for better returns.

    b. Key Process Areas:

        i. Process change management

        ii. Technology change management

        iii. Defect prevention – as against defect detection and control

8.3.9.1 CMMI

Over a period, several flavours of CMM were developed – CMM for the software development, CMM for the software acquisition, People CMM etc. CMMI was developed by SEI to integrate all these flavours.

8.4 Quality control

Quality control is responsible for

- deciding whether the product is of acceptable standard.
- giving inputs on the process adjustments for a good product delivery.

Tools for quality control

- Pareto analysis
- Quality control charts
- Seven run rule
- Six Sigma

8.4.1 Pareto analysis

Useful for identifying the vital few factors that cause a majority of the problems. It is also called the 80 – 20 rule meaning 80% of the problems are often due to 20% of the causes. Pareto diagrams can help in prioritizing the problem areas and addressing them such that the available scarce resources can be devoted to make the system functional to a maximum extent.

A bank in the Middle East was getting repeated complaints about the service level of its IT department. The CIO decided to take one week's complaints from the help desk to check the problems users were facing.

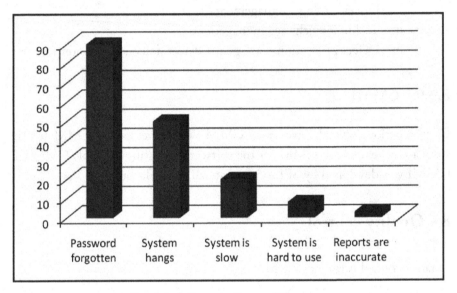

Fig 8.1 A Sample Pareto Diagram

It is clearly seen that more than 98% of the problems arise because of poor user training and the system overload. Remember the old dictum '*Spend your time on the things that really matter, but be sure that you understand what really matters*'.

8.4.2 Statistical process control

Sample data are collected periodically to check the average and variability are under control. Control charts are plotted to see that all the metrics fall within three standard deviations from the mean. A control chart is a graphic display of data that illustrates the results of a process over a period of time.

8.4.3 Seven run rule

This is associated with the quality control chart and addresses the process capability. In a chart, when seven points move in the same direction, the process needs to be checked for its stability.

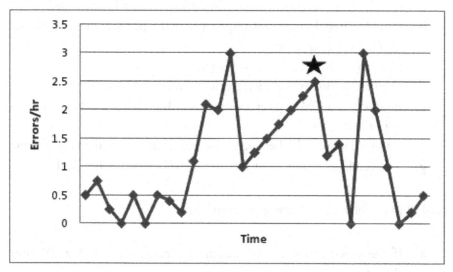

Fig 8.2 Seven run rule

Two bugs per hour is the upper control limit. When seven consecutive hours show an increasing trend in the number of bugs, a degradation in the process is suspected needing a process review.

8.4.4 Six sigma

Variation control is the underlying principle of six sigma, a set of processes and techniques for process improvement, developed by Motorola and popularized by Jack Welch. The method is to ensure that the number of bugs fall within six times the standard deviation. This is equivalent to 3.4 defects in a million opportunities – interpreted in software as 3.4 defects in a million lines of code.

Practice Questions

1. State whether true or false:

    a. Quality is an abstract measure and hence cannot be measured.
    b. CMM is based on the assumption that the process quality will lead to the product quality.
    c. MS Project is a quality control tool.
    d. Documentation is considered critical in the ISO standard.
    e. Products of a CMM level 5 company will not have any bugs and will not fail.
    f. Six sigma imposes higher quality control requirements than three sigma.
    g. The products produced at the initial level can never be good.

2. Fill in the blanks with the appropriate terms:

    a. If the specification of the length of a component is 5 ± .01 mm, then .01 is referred to as -----.
    b. ISO is a ---- (process / product) quality standard.
    c. Nested loops make an application ------ (simple / complex).
    d. Quality Assurance is ----- (detective / preventive), while Quality Control is ----(detective / preventive).
    e. When the quality policy of a client organization is at variance with that of the software organization, the policy of the ---- organization prevails.
    f. If the value of π is given as 2.14 in four places in a report, then it is ----, but not correct.
    g. The ability of a software package to perform without degradation with increase in the number of users is called ------.
    h. Monitoring compliance is a quality ----- (assurance / control) task.
    i. When a software application is said to have a small footprint, then it is high on ---- (execution / storage) efficiency.
    j. Walk-through is a method of ------
    k. ----- (CMM / ISO) is a standard specific to software.
    l. Green belt is a term associated with the ------ quality standard.
    m. The highest level in CMM a company can achieve is ----.

n.   ---- analysis is associated with the 80 / 20 rule.

o.   In statistics, sigma refers to ----.

p.   A sound quality control system will result in a ---- (low / high) standard deviation in the quality measures of the products.

q.   Six sigma is interpreted as ---- instances in a million opportunities.

r.   The quantitative measures for processes can be ensured by collecting ---- data.

s.   In the CMM level ----, the metrics collection will assume importance.

t.   When Microsoft created the first version of DOS, it could be said to have been at the level ----- as per the CMM standards.

u.   Reworking in manufacturing = ------ in software.

v.   The ability to track a problem reported by a customer to a deviation in the production environment is called -----

w.   Training is a ----- (preventive / detective) control measure in maintaining quality.

x.   At the CMM level ----, processes are defined

y.   Process optimization is feasible in the CMM level ----

z.   If an organization can execute a similar project with the same level of effort and accuracy, it is said to be in the CMM level ----.

aa. Training is a key process area in the CMM Level ----.

ab. Defect ---- is an important process area in the CMM level 5.

3.   Choose the most appropriate answer:

a.   Documentation within a program improves its
     i.   flexibility
     ii.   maintainability
     iii. portability
     iv.   reusability

b.   Which could be the most appropriate measure for the correctness of an application?
     i.   Defects
     ii.   Defects / KLOC
     iii. FP
     iv.   LOC

c.   Which quality factor is the most difficult to quantify?

    i.   Correctness

    ii. Efficiency

    iii. Reliability

    iv. Usability

d.   ISO audit is an activity in

    i.   product quality

    ii. quality assurance

    iii. quality control

    iv. quality planning

e.   Which is the most important requirement of a payroll application?

    i.   Universal access

    ii. Accuracy of results

    iii. Efficiency of execution

    iv. User-friendliness of interface

f.   Response time is a measure of

    i.   correctness

    ii. efficiency

    iii. integrity

    iv. reliability

g.   An organization developing an ATM application for a bank should ensure that it can integrate with the core banking application. This requirement is called

    i.   flexibility

    ii. interoperability

    iii. portability

    iv. reusability

h. A screen is designed with the PIN Code field permitting only 6 characters - neither more nor less. This ensures

    i. communicativeness

    ii. completeness

    iii. consistency

    iv. correctness

i. Response time is an important metric for

    i. batch applications

    ii. data storage

    iii. database update

    iv. online applications

j. If goods receipt number is referred to as xyz and account code as pqr in an application, which quality criterion is affected?

    i. Communicativeness

    ii. Confidentiality

    iii. Consistency

    iv. Correctness

k. Which of the following emphasizes on the variation control for quality?

    i. FTR

    ii. Pareto analysis

    iii. Six Sigma

    iv. SQA

l. The software that takes only two hours to learn and operate is

    i. accurate

    ii. consistent

    iii. reliable

    iv. user-friendly

m. Software maintainability is improved by

    i. improving the software integrity.

    ii. optimizing the code.

    iii. increasing the precision in calculations.

    iv. modularity of the application.

n. Modularity will increase the ------ of an application.

  i.   accuracy
  ii. consistency
  iii. testability
  iv. reliability

o. Which of the following is not a quality assurance task?

  i.   User interview checklists
  ii. CMM inspection
  iii. Metrics analysis
  iv. Approval of new process models

p. Which is the most important requirement of a B2C e-commerce application?

  i.   Ability to store terabytes of the customer data
  ii. Own payment gateway
  iii. Secure access to the catalogue
  iv. User-friendly interface

q. An important requirement of a mobile application is

  i.   ability to handle a large volume of input data
  ii. payment capability
  iii. portability
  iv. precision

r. Fault tolerance of an application is ensured by

  i.   coding standards
  ii. correctness
  iii. redundant facilities
  iv. reusability

s. The popularity of MS Office is due its

  i.   ease of use
  ii. efficiency of performance
  iii. security features
  iv. storage efficiency

t. The ability of identifying the cause-effect relationship is referred to as

    i. expandability

    ii. instrumentation

    iii. self-descriptiveness

    iv. simplicity

u. Which technique of the application development can improve the generality of software?

    i. Agile methodology

    ii. Modularity

    iii. Parameterization

    iv. Rapid prototyping

v. Which review is conducted more frequently during the course of the execution of the project?

    i. Design review

    ii. Progress review

    iii. Quality review

    iv. Technical review

w. Which quality factor addresses an unauthorized access control?

    i. Accessibility

    ii. Encryption

    iii. Hacking

    iv. Integrity

x. Traceability in code improves

    i. accessibility

    ii. portability

    iii. security

    iv. testability

y. Reliability is associated with

    i. accuracy

    ii. integrity

    iii. precision

    iv. security

z. If an application allows an easy modification, it is

    i.   compact

    ii. concise

    iii. flexible

    iv. precise

aa. A gaming software released for Windows and MacOS failed on Mac platform. The software is said to have failed in

    i.   interoperability

    ii. portability

    iii. reliability

    iv. reusability

ab. Organizations insist on the consistency of variable and module names. This will ensure

    i.   correctness

    ii. maintainability

    iii. reliability

    iv. reusability

ac. Machine independence will ensure the ----- of an application.

    i.   interoperability

    ii. portability

    iii. reliability

    iv. reusability

ad. Software usability is measured by

    i.   its durability.

    ii. the effort required to learn the software.

    iii. the number of concurrent users.

    iv. the fulfilment of user requirements.

ae. Which of the following is a quality criterion for software?

    i.   Integration testing

    ii. Low MTBF

    iii. Simplicity

    iv. Zero tolerance for error

af. Processes can be managed when there are / is

    i.   defined processes.

    ii. formal management.

    iii. formal procedures.

    iv. quantitative measures for processes.

ag. Pareto analysis helps in identifying the ----- causes.

    i.   insignificant few

    ii. insignificant many

    iii. significant few

    iv. significant many

ah. Unstable metrics data will have a high -----.

    i.   mean

    ii. median

    iii. mode

    iv. standard deviation

ai. Which of the following is a key process area in the CMM level 2?

    i.   Process change management

    ii. Software configuration management

    iii. Peer reviews

    iv. Software quality management

aj. Which of these statements truly reflects the basis of Pareto analysis?

    i.   20% causes are responsible for 20% of the consequences

    ii. 20% causes are responsible for 80% of the consequences

    iii. 80% causes are responsible for 20% of the consequences

    iv. 80% causes are responsible for 80% of the consequences

ak. Which of the following standards measures the process maturity?

    i.   CMM

    ii. Coding standards

    iii. ISO

    iv. Six sigma

4. Processes are constraints in the software development– comment.

5. Why is contract review considered an important quality process in ISO?

9

RISK MANAGEMENT

If trouble comes when you least expect it then maybe the thing to do is to always expect it –Cormac McCarthy

9.1 Learning objectives

In this lesson we understand the following:

- What is risk?
- What are the different activities in the risk management?
- How are the risks identified, assessed and mitigated?

9.2 Risk defined

The uncertainties in a project are referred to as risks. Their outcomes could be positive – yes, the uncertain events with the positive outcomes are also called risks – or negative, though we will focus on the negative consequences for control and management. If something is uncertain, about which we do not know anything, how do we manage it? Based on his / her experience, a project manager should anticipate what could go wrong and to what extent and plan for the remedial actions.

9.3 **Risk management life-cycle – Phases**

There are four major phases under risk management:

- Risk identification
- Risk assessment
- Risk mitigation
- Risk monitoring and control

9.3.1 Risk identification

PMBOK identifies the project risks in several classes, of which four cover majority of the risks. These classes are

- Technical
- Project management
- Organizational
- External

9.3.1.1 Technical risks

This category of risks relate to the technology of the product. These may arise due to the deficiencies in the suitability and / or the reliability of the chosen technology and / or the support availability for the same. Choice of the technology, though ideally should be dictated by the application requirements, is also influenced by the other factors such as the current technology used by the organization for other applications.

One such classic example was the choice of Fortran for the passenger reservation system by the Indian Railways, guided by the VAX[38] hardware and the VMS[39] operating system they were using. We are all aware that Fortran is better

---

[38] VAX was the mid-range computer manufactured by the Digital Equipment Corporation (DEC), since discontinued.

[39] The operating system proprietary to the VAX hardware

suited for the scientific and the engineering applications and here was a large commercial application for which Fortran was chosen.

Both obsolete technologies, with poor support and documentation and the leading edge technologies – the term 'bleeding edge' is also used to refer to the latest technologies in the industry - because of their limited usage and field test prove to be risky.

Some technologies are inherently complex and could introduce an element of risk in their usage. In a team particularly, every member cannot be expected to have the same level of competence in such technologies.

Choice of an inappropriate methodology proved to be a risk in the De Beers case (Chapter 3).

9.3.1.2 Project management risks

Project management is critical for the success of a project (a point we have been labouring all along in this book!) and the project management has multiple facets and some of them get overlooked due to the exigencies of the day-to-day management of the project. Due to lack of knowledge and competence, young project managers may miss out on some important aspects of the project management. The knowledgeable, experienced managers too err due to complacency. Some of the usually encountered omissions are

- Poor organizational structure
- Poor planning
- Poor definition of the roles and the responsibilities
- Poor allocation of the resources
- Not matching the right skill with the right task
- Poor monitoring

The constraints in the budget and other resources could lead to risks (Revisit chapter 3 to understand the distinction between constraints and risks). Poor management control could result in the cost and the schedule overrun of a project.

9.3.1.3 Organizational risks

Some projects suffer because of poor organizational support – this could happen either on the side of the client organization or the development organization. The reasons could be many:

- The project does not fit into the strategy of the organization anymore.
- The project is considered of low priority compared to the other projects.
- The project gets poor budgetary support, maybe because of the reasons stated above.
- Poor management structure and policies – while the management deficiencies specific to the project management are covered under the project management risks, the poor management style of the organization will be covered here.
- Politics within the organization impeding the project progress

An extreme and rare example is the collapse of the Indian software behemoth Satyam Computer Services[40], which put many of their ongoing projects in jeopardy.

9.3.1.4 External risks

This covers all the factors which are outside the control of the participating organizations:

- Change in the legal or the regulatory environment: a change in the taxation rules could make a project unviable.
- Change in the foreign exchange rates
- Supplier's failures, for example the hardware not arriving in time, the outsourced contractor not delivering their part in time
- Even an employee strike in the organization is considered a factor outside its control and this is included in what is called the force-majeure clause in the legal contract.
- Natural disasters are also covered in this clause, also referred to as the acts of God.

---

[40] Due to the Chairman's confession of falsification of accounts, the company collapsed suddenly in 2009.

9.3.1.5 A typical list of risks

- Tight schedule
- Constrained fund allocation
- Poorly drafted contract
- New technology
- Erroneous estimation
- Unsuitable development model
- Unfamiliar hardware
- Poorly defined requirements
- Volatile business environment
- Staff talent not matching to the requirements of the project
- Frequently changing requirements
- Poor project planning
- Poor compliance with the standards
- Unsupported technology
- Poor management support for the project
- Low user involvement
- Resignation of a critical team member
- Vendor failure
- Market disinterest in the product

Can you classify these risks? It is also important to set early warning indicators for the risks relevant to your project, so that they can be addressed quite early before affecting the project.

Risks could be generic, which are applicable to all the projects in the organization or specific to a project. Risks identified should be independent of each other and the interdependent risks should be clubbed together.

9.3.2 Risk assessment

Each of the identified risks is assessed on the basis of the likelihood of its happening (probability) and the monetary loss that it could cause (impact). The probability will range from 0 to 1 and the impact will be assessed in monetary terms, so that a quantified estimate of the risk is available. The impact could be in terms of extending the schedule, cost overrun, deterioration in the deliverable quality, non-fulfilment of the committed deliverables, levy of penalty, inability to realize the full benefits of the software or deleterious fall-out on the human resources.

It is also important when the risk is likely to surface and when its impact will accentuate. This will help on focusing on the risks which will have an immediate effect.

Risk exposure = Probability of risk X Risk impact

The risks are organized in the descending order of the risk exposure and only those risks above a specified cut-off exposure will be chosen for the remedial actions. This ensures that the risks that matter more in terms of likelihood or impact or both are addressed on priority. While working on a mature technology familiar to the team, the technical issues would be solved quickly because of the competence of the team. So a control measure for this risk may not be necessary.

An example:

There is a possibility that 25% of the programming staff in the team might leave the organization before the end of the project.

Induction and training of the new staff in the team might extend the schedule by three months. On a committed schedule of 12 months, this means 25% additional commitment of resources.

Since the cost of the project is INR 10 million, this loss could be estimated as 2.5 million.

Probability of the attrition = 0.7

Risk exposure = 2.5 X 0.7 = 1.75 million

In real life, the challenge will be on the quantification of the probability and the impact.

To overcome this, the probability could be estimated as high, medium or low and the impact could be categorized as catastrophic, critical, marginal, and negligible[41]. An organization may evolve a guideline - probability could be categorized based on the frequency of the occurrence of the event and impact on the extent of loss.

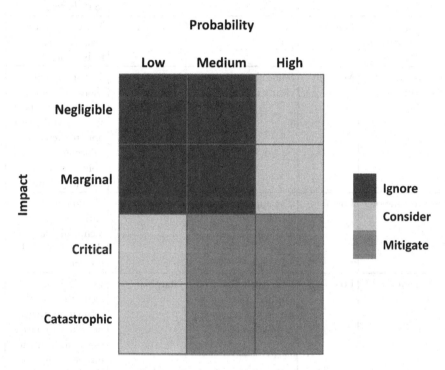

Fig 9.1 Risk assessment matrix

Risk assessment should neither be conducted with complacency that nothing will go wrong nor with a paranoid attitude of seeing danger everywhere. An objective analysis should result in a list of five to ten risks selected for the mitigation action. Even after a balanced analysis, if the number of risks addressed is too high, then the project feasibility needs a relook.

---

[41]   These terms are used in the army for the risk assessment. The impact categorization of catastrophic, critical, marginal and negligible is based respectively on the consequences of death, permanent disability, injury resulting in more than one day of absence and injury resulting in less than one day absence.

For a specific project let us attempt a risk analysis:

Risk	Probability		Impact	
	Range	Explanation	Category	Explanation
Tight schedule	Low	Proper estimate has been done and an adequate time provided.	Marginal	Even if there is a delay, it is expected to be marginal and so is the loss.
Constrained fund allocation	Low	Sufficient budget provided.	Marginal	The cost control measures are not fully in place.
Poorly drafted contract	Medium	Some clauses are not clearly defined.	Negligible	The ambiguous clauses are not expected to impact the project delivery nor are they likely to become the points of dispute with the client.
New technology	Low	The application is developed in Java and our staff are quite familiar with it.	Negligible	We do not anticipate any technical issue that could stall the project.
Erroneous estimation	Low	This is a domain very familiar to us and so we do not expect any estimation error.	Marginal	Even if there are some errors in the estimation, they are not likely to have a substantive impact on the duration of the project.
Unsuitable development model	Medium	There has been some debate whether we should have chosen the agile model instead of the waterfall.	Marginal	Since we are familiar with the domain, our choice of the waterfall will not affect the project significantly.
Unfamiliar hardware	Medium	The application will be hosted on a mainframe. We are developing the application in an emulation mode.	Critical	We are not sure of the shortcomings of the emulation mode and this is the first time we are using this emulation.

Poorly defined requirements	Medium	SRS is quite exhaustive; previous experience with the client shows some interim changes in the requirements.	Critical	We may expect many change requests based on our prior experience
Volatile business environment	High	The telecom industry is subject to a high level of volatility.	Critical	The billing application is expected to be volatile because of the market conditions.
Staff talent not matching with the requirements of the project	Medium	Our staff are quite experienced in the domain and Java. Only two members are quite adept in the backend DB2 environment.	Marginal	Since the staff are quite familiar with the client level technology, no problem is anticipated on this count.
Frequently changing requirements	High	Based on our previous experience with this client, we could anticipate many change requests.	Critical	This could impact the project deliveries seriously.
Poor project planning	Low	A good plan has been put in place. The project manager is quite experienced in handling similar projects.	Critical	The volatility of the requirements will cause frequent modifications in the plan.
Poor compliance with the standards	Low	The organization has a clear set of standards. The project manager is known for his strict compliance with the standards.	Critical	There are some parts of the standards we have adopted from the client. Compliance with these standards needs to be ensured.
Unsupported technology	Low	DB2, Java are all well established technologies.	Negligible	The technology issues are not likely to affect the project.

Poor management support for the project	Low	The application is quite critical to the client's business. The management is quite committed to the project.	Negligible	The project will remain a top priority of the client management.
Low user involvement	Medium	This problem has been encountered with this client in the past.	Marginal	Since the domain is familiar to our team, low user involvement is unlikely to affect the project.
Resignation of a critical team member	Medium	Due to the emergence of a new company in the same domain and technology with a higher salary level, we anticipate some attrition.	Critical	The attrition could affect the schedule of the project.
Vendor failure	Low	No part of the software outsourced. Nor are we dependent on any vendor for the other facilities.	Negligible	Since none of the major components is dependent on any vendor, no impact on the project.
Market disinterest in the product	Low	This product is created for a specific client.	Negligible	This product is created for a specific client.

Table 9.1. Risk analysis – an example
(Risks chosen for mitigation are highlighted)

9.3.2.1 Risk refinement

As the project progresses, our understanding of the risks will improve. To have a better control over a risk, we may identify the causative factors for each risk and monitor these factors.

Example continued:

Risk: There is a possibility that 25% of the programming staff in the team might leave the organization before the end of the project.

Factor 1: A new company, which is in the same domain and technology, has commenced its operations in our city and it offers a salary 30% higher than ours.

Factor 2: H1 visas have been processed for three engineers in the team.

Factor 3: Our salary level is 20% below the industry average.

Factor 4: We are just adequately staffed in the telecom domain with Java expertise.

9.3.3 Risk mitigation

Risk can never reach a zero level; in other words, one can never be sure that a particular risk will not occur at all; its probability may become very low, but never zero. What is the probability that your data centre will be bombed by terrorists? Zero? Had you asked anybody working in the WTC a day before 09/11 attack, that is what (s)he would have said. That is the reason why we talk about risk mitigation and not elimination. Sherlock Holmes would have said *"when you have excluded the impossible, whatever remains, however improbable, must be the truth"*[42].

Risk mitigation would mean reducing the probability of a risk or its consequential impact or both to an acceptable level. This acceptable level again is not a uniform standard across individuals or organizations. Each individual or organization has a level of risk acceptance and this is called the risk appetite. Inasmuch as you find different people have their own different investment preferences – some dabble in shares, some thrive in the penny stocks to the other end of the spectrum, wherein the long term low yield government bonds would satisfy some others – organizations have their own risk appetites.

---

[42]   This quote appears in more than one instance in Sherlock Holmes novels – as quoted in Wiki quotes.

There are four ways in which risks can be addressed:

- Terminate – Risk avoidance: While risks cannot be eliminated, the project itself may not be accepted due to the risks associated with it. We did mention earlier that a project, after due analysis, if found to have too many risks, this is an option, but an option that should be exercised rarely. If you have vertigo, don't attempt bungee jumping! But a person with a high risk appetite such as Marc Zuckerberg would say "The biggest risk is not taking any risk... In a world that is changing really quickly, the only strategy that is guaranteed to fail is not taking risks."[43]

- Transfer – move the onus to somebody else. Outsourcing is often cited as one such remedy. When the organization does not have the required skills, outsourcing could be an option, but we need to remember that this protects the organization only to the extent of the skill availability and not beyond. Still the contractual commitment of the deliveries will remain with the organization. Insurance is another transfer mechanism, through which not the risk likelihood, but the impact - cost of the risk – is reduced.

- Treat: This is what the mitigation is all about. For example, by taking a good training in driving, the probability of accidents may be reduced and by wearing a seat belt or having an airbag, we may reduce the impact of an accident.

- Tolerate – accept the risk: normally this is recommended for the residual risk after all the treatments, because the residual risk can never be zero. Protective measures such as a helmet and cautious driving all do not leave a motor cycle rider with zero probability of accidents. This residual risk with the reduced probability and impact may have to be accepted. To what extent the probability and the impact need to be reduced depends on the risk appetite of the individual / organization.

How may the risks identified earlier for the staff leaving the project be addressed? Which mitigation measures could be useful?

- Revise the team's salary, if you can convince your management and the HR department.

---

[43]   From BrainyQuotewww.brainyquote.com/quotes/quotes/m/markzucker453450.html

- Defer the US trip of the engineers with H1 visas.
- Announce an attractive incentive plan for the team – 'On completion of the project, the team will get one week vacation in Singapore with spouses', provided your management and the budgets are favourable!
- Recruit staff – create a 20% bench[44], so that any attrition does not affect the project adversely.
- Through training, create the back-up resources for the critical functions.
- Ensure documentation.

A point of caution: a step in the risk mitigation could introduce a new risk. If to retain some critical staff, a salary increase is offered to them, this could demotivate others in the team and the result could be a net decrease in productivity!

9.3.3.1 Cost of risk mitigation

Is a decision to mitigate a risk taken on the basis of the cost-benefit analysis? Or should the risks be mitigated at any cost?

Cost-benefit analysis forms the basis of all the business decisions. Unless the benefits accruing out of the risk mitigation overwhelm the costs associated with it, the mitigation measure is not undertaken.

Take the example of wearing a helmet as a safety measure:

The probability of a motor cycle rider meeting with an accident = 0.1 (say)

Without a helmet, in the case of an accident, the skull injury would require INR 200000/ for the medical expenses.

With a helmet, the injury is expected to be less serious and the medical expenses could be INR 20000.

Risk exposure before wearing a helmet = INR 20000

Risk exposure after wearing a helmet = INR 2000

---

[44] Staff not allocated to any project

Imagine the cost of a helmet to be INR 50000, would you buy it? Or rather take an insurance cover and risk an accident?

We define a measure called the risk reduction leverage (RRL) in this context:

$$RRL = \frac{RE \ (before) - RE \ (after)}{Risk \ Reduction \ cost}$$

Ideally RRL should at least be 1. Higher the RRL, more worthwhile the plan.

For our helmet example, assuming the price of helmet to be INR 600,

$$RRL = (20000-2000) / 600 = 30$$

9.3.3.2 Contingency plan

The plans that are put in place to address the consequences, in case the risk becomes a reality despite the mitigation measures, are called the contingency plans.

(e.g.) Dedicate the last week of the resigned employee only for the knowledge transfer.

9.3.4 Risk monitoring and control

The project manager creates a risk log with the following format:

Risk id#	Risk description	Probability	Impact	Risk owner	Action to be taken	Result

Table 9.2. Format of risk log

The project manager should monitor the consequences of the mitigation actions – to what extent have the risk probability and impact reduced.

And this log will go through several revisions as the project progresses, because of the changes in the nature of the risks encountered in the project. In case the mitigation actions do not produce the desired result, the project manager has to plan for the alternate actions.

9.3.4.1 Risk referent level

The project manager has to continuously monitor some critical variables in a project delivery. These normally form the most important commitments to the customer. In case even after repeated attempts, the project fails to achieve these targets, then the project manager may have to take crucial decisions on the continuance of the project.

Risk referent level is the level beyond which if a risk exceeds, the project may have to be terminated.

Some good examples could be:

- A bank ATM application is specified to have 3 seconds response time. But repeated architectural and coding changes fail to achieve this.
- Cost overrun beyond an acceptable limit (See Table 9.3).
- Schedule overrun beyond an acceptable limit (See Table 9.3).

Boehm et al (Boehm, 2000) list several high profile projects that had to be aborted because they crossed the risk referent level:

Project	Initial and final estimates		Cancelled at month
	Cost ($M)	Schedule (months)	
PROMS (Royalty collections)	12: 21	22;46	28
London Ambulance	1.5:6+	7;17+	17
London Stock Exchange	60-75;150	19;70	36
Confirm (Travel Reservations)	56:160+	45;60+	48
Master Net (Banking)	22;80+	9;48+	48

Table 9.3. Some examples of aborted software projects

Blessed is the project manager who never had to use the risk referent level!

Practice Questions

1. State whether true or false:

    a. We should always choose projects with zero risks.
    b. Technology can be a source of risk.
    c. Old technologies, since they are proven, can never be risky.
    d. A risk will result in a loss.
    e. Risks should be treated at any cost.
    f. Leading edge technologies are less risky than proven technologies.
    g. Training is a risk mitigation measure.
    h. Risks with negligible loss are not treated.
    i. Risk plan should contain exhaustively all the risks identified.
    j. A risk treatment may introduce a new risk.

2. Fill in the blanks with the appropriate terms:

    a. Architectural complexity leads to a ----- risk.
    b. A few team members were not familiar with the domain. So the project failed. What type of risk is this? -----
    c. The financial problems of the development organization affected the deliveries. This is a(n) ---- risk.
    d. The chief executive of a C2C site was arrested because contraband stuff was traded on the site. This is a(n) ----- risk.
    e. Employee attrition is a ----- (generic / specific) risk.
    f. Risk exposure is expressed in ----- (monetary / probability) terms.
    g. When you switch to driving a car to avoid motor cycle accidents, what type of risk treatment is this? ------
    h. Insurance is a risk ------ (control / transfer) method.
    i. A tight schedule could be treated as a(n) ------- risk.
    j. Because an outsourced component was not delivered in time, a project got delayed. This is a(n)----- risk.
    k. If a project was suffering from the funds constraint, it may be called a ----- (generic / specific) risk.

l. Mitigation plans are worked out for the risks with ---- (high / low) exposure.

m. ----- is a point at which the decision to abort a project is taken.

n. Natural disasters are covered under ----- risks.

o. The administrative procedures of the development organization affected the working of a project. This is a(n) ----- risk.

p. Risks with ----- probability and ---- loss will certainly be picked up for risk mitigation.

3. Choose the most appropriate answer:

a. Which of the following could be a good definition of risk?
    i. Constraint
    ii. Danger
    iii. High return
    iv. Uncertainty

b. Which of the following could be a reasonable probability estimate for a risk?
    i. -0.5
    ii. 0.5
    iii. 2
    iv. 100%

c. Which of the following could be a consequence of a risk?
    i. Cost overrun
    ii. Deterioration in the quality of the deliverables
    iii. Schedule overrun
    iv. All the above

d. A project was aborted because of high cost overrun. Which class of risk was responsible for its failure?
    i. External
    ii. Financial
    iii. Project management
    iv. Schedule

e. Which project parameter will get impacted by deficient requirement gathering?

    i. Cost

    ii. Human resources

    iii. Scope

    iv. Time

f. Which dimension of a project is most likely to get affected by the poor allocation of the human resources to the project?

    i. Benefits

    ii. Cost

    iii. Schedule

    iv. Scope

g. Pick up the risk that should be treated on priority:

    i. High probability high loss

    ii. Low probability low loss

    iii. Medium probability low loss

    iv. Medium probability medium loss

h. Fire in the data centre could be a risk. What could be a contingency plan?

    i. Identify an alternate site from which the services may be continued.

    ii. Provide fire extinguishers.

    iii. Use fire-proof materials in the data centre.

    iv. Train the staff on using the fire extinguishers.

i. A continuous process manufacturing company chose an ERP software designed for discrete manufacturing. Which risk is it exposed to?

    i. External

    ii. Project management

    iii. Software

    iv. Technical

j. Risk likelihood is expressed in terms of

   i.   dollars
   ii. impact
   iii. loss
   iv. probability

k. Which of the following is a part of the risk management cycle?

   i.   Cost and schedule overrun
   ii. Risk funding
   iii. Risk identification
   iv. Risk planning

l. Which order is correct in the risk management?

   i.   Assessment, identification, control
   ii. Assessment, identification, mitigation
   iii. Assessment, control, identification
   iv. Identification, assessment, mitigation

m. Which of the following may lead to a project management risk?

   i.   Your company has decided not to be in the domain of your project.
   ii. Inadequate progress review meetings
   iii. Failure of an application to meet the targeted response time
   iv. The new rules by the Government have rendered the roll-out of the application unviable.

n. Which of the following is not a force majeure risk?

   i.   Collapse of the country's economy
   ii. Flooding of the data centre
   iii. Failure of the hardware vendor to supply in time
   iv. Employee strike

o. Prioritization of risk is done on the basis of

   i.   risk exposure
   ii. impact
   iii. loss
   iv. probability

p. Causative factors are identified as a part of the risk ----- process.

    i.   assessment

    ii. identification

    iii. mitigation

    iv. refinement

q. When you treat a risk, you ---- the risk.

    i.   mitigate

    ii. terminate

    iii. tolerate

    iv. transfer

r. Residual risk is

    i.   normally higher than original risk.

    ii. tolerated

    iii. treated

    iv. zero

s. When the risk management plan fails, we invoke

    i.   contingency plan

    ii. risk referent level

    iii. risk refinement

    iv. no action; accept the risk.

t. Which of the following is covered under the technology risk?

    i.   Cost overrun

    ii. Poor allocation of the project resources

    iii. Performance standards

    iv. Poor organizational support

4. What are the possible risks in the introduction of a new banking / telecom application?

5. The project manager's experience with the internal risk management team has not been very good. They will conduct an elaborate exercise and come up with a big list of risks and will insist on monitoring at least 50% of them. To avoid this, the project manager decided to engage a consultant with a mandate that within 15 days he has to identify five major risks. Internal risk management team would subsequently be asked to identify mitigation measures for these risks. Comment on this strategy.

6. Risk response changes with culture – comment.

10

PROJECT COST MANAGEMENT

*A wise man should have money in his head, but
not in his heart* – Jonathan Swift

10.1 Lesson objectives

In this lesson we will learn the following:

- What is cost management?
- Why is it important for a project manager?
- What are the different types of the cost estimates prepared in a project?
- How are projects priced?
- How is a budget prepared and what is the importance of a budget?

With this chapter we come to the conclusion of the planning module. A template of the project plan is presented at the end.

10.2 Importance of project cost management

IT projects are known for poor cost management and thus suffer a high cost overrun. A joint study by McKinsey and Oxford University found that the large software projects on an average run 66 percent over budget and 33 percent over schedule; as many as 17 percent of projects go so bad that they can threaten the very existence of the company (Bloch, 2012). A study of 1471 projects (Flyvbjerg 2011) reveals that one sixth of the projects have a cost overrun of 200%. The additional cost burden could render an organization unviable, as in the case of Kmart (Flyvbjerg 2011). A large number of projects get cancelled. A sample list of cancelled projects may be viewed at http://spectrum.ieee.org/computing/software/why-software-fails (Charlette, 2005).

Most project managers, with their technical backgrounds, find the cost management difficult to understand and thus try not to focus on it. Going back to the scope triangle (Chapter 1), it may be reiterated that cost is one of the major areas that requires a project manager's continuous attention. The project manager should not be under the misguided notion that the cost management is the job of an accountant. Inasmuch as the quality function will facilitate, but not manage quality in a project, cost will also need to be monitored and managed by the project manager.

The senior management will always prefer reporting in monetary terms – another reason why a project manager should develop a good understanding of costing and competence in managing the costs.

10.3 Project cost management processes

The major processes under the knowledge area of cost management are

- cost estimation
- budgeting
- cost control

10.3.1 Cost estimation

Through the project life cycle, the cost estimation is done several times – three major points are identified here:

10.3.1.1 ROM (Rough Order Magnitude) estimate

This is a very approximate estimate, prepared immediately on the receipt of the RFP – for a first level decision whether to undertake the project or not. It provides the cost range in which the project falls and hence the accuracy level could be between -25% and 75% or -50% to +50% (PMBOK).. At this point of time, the understanding about the project is minimal and so a substantial buffer is built into the estimate.

10.3.1.2 Budgetary estimate

This estimate is prepared by the CIO of the client organization or by the software organization to aid the CIO in preparing his / her budget. Normally prepared before the beginning of the financial year, the objective of this estimate is to get the monetary approval from the management for a project to be undertaken during the coming year. In this estimate the variation is between -10% to 25%. It is advisable to have some extra provision in this estimate, as the supplementary budgetary demands are normally resented by the senior management. However, the buffer should not be high, lest the management might reject the proposal.

10.3.1.3 Definitive estimate

This is the basis for preparing the quotation and thus has to be of high accuracy. The variation could be in the range of -5% to 10%. This estimate is prepared based on the effort estimate (discussed in detail in Chapter 5).

10.3.1.4 Tools for cost estimation

The methods of the effort estimation will be the basis for the cost estimate, because the software project cost depends primarily on the cost of labour. The methods are

10.3.1.4.1 Top-down or analogous approach

This is what we called the duplication method in the effort estimation. The cost of a similar project done in the past is used as a basis in this estimate. It might be worthwhile recalling the parameters considered to call two projects similar (Chapter 5).

10.3.1.4.2 Bottom-up method

The project is broken down into its components and the cost is estimated as the sum of costs of the components. A WBS could be used for the decomposition. Each of the components is sized on some factor such as LOC or FP and then the cost is estimated.

This method is also called the activity based costing.[45]

10.3.1.4.3 Parametric method

These are the mathematical models derived from a study of a large number of projects and each of them provides an equation to compute effort / cost from a set of project characteristics. Some sample equations were shown as part of the effort estimation in Chapter 6. Constructive Cost Model (COCOMO) is one such model we will discuss in detail, not so much for its use in estimation, but more for understanding the factors that influence the software development effort and the extent to which they impact the effort.

10.3.1.4.3.1 COCOMO

Developed by Barry Boehm, COCOMO is a regression model. It was first published in his book 'Software Engineering Economics' (Boehm, 1981) in 1981. The model was useful in estimating the effort of the projects in the second and the third generation languages using the waterfall model, which was widely prevalent at that time. In 1995, Boehm released COCOMO II to address the

---

[45]   Popularly referred to as ABC, this was defined by Robert Kaplan and W. Bruns in their book Accounting and Management: A Field Study Perspective in 1987

requirements of the modern practices. COCOMO II is available on the web (http://csse.usc.edu/csse/research/COCOMOII/cocomo_downloads.htm).

COCOMO consists of a hierarchy of three increasingly detailed and accurate estimates - Basic,. Intermediate and Detailed. The model calculates the effort taking the SLOC as an input.

Basic COCOMO is a simple equation computing the effort only from the software size. Intermediate COCOMO takes into account several other relevant parameters to compute the effort and takes the form

$$Effort = C*EAF*(KSLOC)^E$$

Effort is calculated in person-months.

C is a constant co-efficient, defined for each class of projects (Boehm classifies the projects as organic, semi-detached and embedded. These may be viewed as projects of increasing complexity and hence will have different coefficients in an increasing order.)

EAF – Effort Adjustment Factor derived from a set of factors called the cost drivers

E – An exponentiation factor derived from five scale factors

From the form of the equation, we may infer that the scale factors will have a higher influence on the effort than the cost drivers.

The five scale factors are

- Precedentedness (how much is the organization familiar with this type of the project?)
- Development flexibility: how many different options are available to achieve the desired result?
- Architecture / risk
- Team cohesion
- Process maturity

The scale factors are given a rating on the basis of a six point scale from very low to very high and the product of all these factors is taken as the exponent in the equation.

Fifteen cost drivers are identified in the intermediate COCOMO and each of them given a rating on a six point scale from very low to extra high in importance. The product of all the effort multipliers results in the Effort Adjustment Factor (EAF).

Cost Drivers	Ratings					
	Very Low	Low	Nominal	High	Very High	Extra High
Product attributes						
Required software reliability	0.75	0.88	1.00	1.15	1.40	
Size of application database		0.94	1.00	1.08	1.16	
Complexity of the product	0.70	0.85	1.00	1.15	1.30	1.65
Hardware attributes						
Run-time performance constraints			1.00	1.11	1.30	1.66
Memory constraints			1.00	1.06	1.21	1.56
Volatility of the virtual machine environment		0.87	1.00	1.15	1.30	
Required turnaround time		0.87	1.00	1.07	1.15	.
Personnel attributes						
Analyst capability	1.46	1.19	1.00	0.86	0.71	
Applications experience	1.29	1.13	1.00	0.91	0.82	
Software engineer capability	1.42	1.17	1.00	0.86	0.70	
Virtual machine experience	1.21	1.10	1.00	0.90		
Programming language experience	1.14	1.07	1.00	0.95		
Project attributes						
Application of software engineering methods	1.24	1.10	1.00	0.91	0.82	
Use of software tools	1.24	1.10	1.00	0.91	0.83	
Required development schedule	1.23	1.08	1.00	1.04	1.10	

(Source: Wikipedia)

Detailed COCOMO calculates the effort for each phase of the lifecycle.

10.3.1.5 Parkinson's law[46]

In a few cases, practical constraints dictate the effort estimate. 'Customer wants the delivery in 12 months and we have 5 people. 60 person-months is what we can afford.'

10.3.1.6 Other factors in cost estimation

While effort is the main contributor to the cost, there are other factors that need to be reckoned in the detailed costing.

These other factors include the cost of hardware, software, travel and training. Depending on the contractual requirements, some of these costs could have a substantial influence on the final product cost. For example, if the installation is required in hundreds of branches all over the country, the travel and the training expenses could be very high. We will get into a detailed list of the cost elements, when we discuss budgeting.

10.3.2 Project pricing

Costing is an input for pricing. While the costs directly associated with the project such as staff cost are easily assignable to the product, there are several indirect costs such as rent, utilities, senior management salary, a portion of each of which should be included in the product cost. If these costs are not assigned to any project, then how do we recover them? These are referred to as overheads and an allocation basis is decided by the cost accountant to apportion each of these costs to the different projects. After adding the direct cost and the apportioned overhead, a profit margin is added and the price is determined.

The prevalent method in the software industry is to arrive at a person-month cost (also referred to as person-month rate) based on the average staff salary, overheads and profit margin. An easy and quick method to arrive at the price is provided by multiplying the effort estimate in person-months by the

---

[46]   Parkinson's law is the adage that "work expands so as to fill the time available for its completion".

person-month rate. While this is the normal pricing method, there could be other factors which influence the pricing in some special cases:

- Market opportunity: An organization may decide to price their offering aggressively to enter a new market. For example, if a company decides to enter the BFSI (Banking and Financial Services Industry) segment, they may decide to quote for the first project in this segment at a deep discount. The company may look at this as an investment to enter into the market and may decide to amortize the cost over the next few projects they may get by virtue of this experience.

- Cost estimate uncertainty: If the confidence level of the estimate is not high, then sufficient buffer should be added to the price. The incomplete initial information is usually the reason for the low confidence level of the estimate.

- Contractual terms: If the contract with the customer imposes binding conditions, the consequent opportunity loss needs to be factored in the pricing. For example, if the customer demands the source code ownership, the transfer of the intellectual property should be done at an added cost. Where the customer is committing on the maintenance contract for a fixed period, the initial price may be negotiated at a lower level.

- Requirements volatility: If the demands of an industry or an application are known to be changing frequently, then the price should be appropriately increased.

- Financial health of the service organization: When the software development organization is under cash constraint, it is not uncommon for them to quote an overall reduced price for a higher initial payment for a higher advance would help them tide over their immediate cash constraint.

- Pricing to win: Competition is an important factor in deciding the price. On an order which you want to win at any cost – in reality many projects will fall in this category – it is the market that will decide the price.

10.3.2.1 Time and materials method

An alternate to the fixed price bid is what is known as the time and materials method. In this method the client makes periodic payments based on the effort input at a pre-agreed rate. The development organization submits the time sheets of the team members and on that basis the payment is made by the client. Where the requirements are highly volatile, this method may be useful. Agile projects, wherein the number of iterations cannot be pre-specified also fall in this category. Software maintenance projects may also be on a time and materials basis.

Obviously this approach puts less pressure on the project team for the completion of the project and to that extent the clients are at a disadvantage.

10.3.3 Budgeting

A budget is prepared by identifying the different cost elements and the expected expenses under each of these heads. A detailed budget will show these amounts split month-wise. A budget is prepared based on some assumptions and these assumptions need to be spelt out clearly. During the course of the project, the budget will be reviewed against the actual expense under each head and the variances – particularly the adverse ones - will need to be explained by the project manager.

Budget – An Example		
Budget Head	Amount (INR in millions)	Basis
Staff cost	14.46	10 programmers @ INR 500000 p.a. for 14 months, 5 testers @ INR 330000 p.a. for 14 months, 1 business analyst @ INR 1 million p.a. for 4 months, 2 administrators @ INR 440000 p.a. for 14 months, 2 team leads @ INR 960000 p.a. for 14 months and one project manager @ INR 1.6 millions p.a. for 18 months. 10% increment is factored into annual salary.
Hardware depreciation	0.33	1 server @ INR 200000 and 18 terminals @INR 25000 It is assumed that in 18 months, 50% of the hardware will be depreciated.
Training	0.30	Tool training for programmers for 15 days @ INR 20000 per day
Travel	1.79	2 trips to client site for 15 days each by two business analysts, 4 staff for on-site implementation for 15 days Rs. 150000 for each round trip and $ 100 per diem is assumed. An exchange rate of INR 65 per dollar is assumed.
Communication	0.18	at an average rate of INR 10000 p.m.
Supplies	0.05	Stationery, CDs and tapes for back-up
Contingencies @ 15%	2.57	
Total	19.68	

These are the most important heads. In the budget prepared by the project manager, staff salaries and depreciation may not be shown and their variances will also not be discussed during every review, because they are not under his / her control. However the senior management will monitor these two closely.

10.3.4 Cost control

Will be discussed in detail in Project Execution and Control module.

10.4 Project Plan

With this we come to the end of the planning module. A project plan is prepared documenting all the activities during planning.

Contents of the project plan are

- Synopsis
- Client organization details
- Project overview: what is proposed to be done as a part of the project?
- Planning approach: methodology adopted to develop the planning document and reasons thereof.
- Assumptions: any assumption about the project needs to be stated explicitly here.
- Pre-requisites: any condition that needs to be fulfilled or any facility that is required for the project. Any special hardware / software / skill requirement required for this project needs to be stated here.
- External dependencies: Does the project depend on any outside factor for its completion?
- Scope of the project
- Process model to be adopted
- Work breakdown structure
- Schedule – in the form of Gantt chart or a network diagram
- Resource requirements with assignments to tasks
- Time: total time required for the project with the final deadline with tolerance specified.
- Milestones with dates

- Customer's quality expectations, acceptance criteria
- Quality management plan
  o Standards
  o Stage wise test plans
- Major risks identified and mitigation plans
- Project cost with tolerance
- Budgets
  (Cost and budget details may not be available in the client's copy)
- Communication management plan: Mode of communication to the different stakeholders and its contents and periodicity (We will discuss this in detail in Execution module – Chapter 15).
- Lessons from earlier projects that have been incorporated

This plan is submitted to the managements of the software organization and the client organization for their approval. A formal presentation of the salient aspects of the plan may be necessary in many cases. The plan, after the incorporation of the changes suggested by the managements, is formally approved.

The approved plan is the version 1.0 of the project plan and this document will undergo revisions with major changes in the project and it is mandatory that all such changes are duly approved by the software organization as well as the client management.. It is imperative that all the team members and the other stakeholders are aware of the current version of the project plan - this is the guiding document for all those involved in the project. For any new joinee in the team, this document will act as a training input.

Practice Questions

1. State whether true or false:

    a. Cost control is the sole responsibility of the accountants and not of a project manager.
    b. The person-month rate is used to arrive at the price of a software project.
    c. The staff pay increase will not affect the cost of the software.
    d. The source code should never be handed over to the client.
    e. A ROM estimate will always be higher than the budgetary estimate.
    f. Budgeting is a cost control mechanism.
    g. COCOMO is a parametric model.
    h. The entire cost of the software is charged to the expense account in the year of the purchase itself.
    i. Fixed bid approach will impose higher levels of efficiency on the staff.

2. Fill in the blanks with the appropriate terms:

    a. What a development organization charges to the customer is ---- (cost / price).
    b. The person-month rate is expressed in the ----- (money / time) dimension.
    c. Normally the price of a project will be ---- (higher / lower) than its cost.
    d. The ---- estimate will have the lowest buffer.
    e. Common expenses across all the projects are known as --------.
    f. Between the EAF and the scale drivers, which will have a higher impact on the effort? -----
    g. Effort is ----- (directly / inversely) related to the response time requirement.
    h. Mathematical models are used in the ------- method of cost estimation.
    i. Depreciation is calculated by distributing the cost of the hardware over its ------- life.
    j. The cost accounting process of arriving at the rental cost associated with a project is called ------.
    k. COCOMO stands for -------.

l. COCOMO takes the software size in terms of ------ (FP/SLOC) to compute the effort.

m. Higher the software reliability requirement, -----, (higher / lower) is the effort.

n. The projects with tight schedules require a ----- (higher / lower) effort.

o. The price of the product may have to be ----- (increased / lowered) to explore a market opportunity.

p. When the customer keeps on changing the requirements, the requirements are said to be ------ (volatile / non-volatile).

q. The cost plus pricing model is referred to as the ------- approach in the software industry.

r. The ------ pricing approach is the most suitable for the R & D type of projects.

s. Given an option, a customers will prefer ------ (fixed bid / time and materials) pricing.

3. Choose the most appropriate answer:

a. Which of the following forms the highest proportion of the software cost?

    i.   Consultancy fee
    ii. Cost of hardware
    iii. Staff salary
    iv. Travel expenses

b. Parkinson's law is based on

    i.   FP
    ii. LOC
    iii. regression
    iv. none of these

c. Barry Boehm was responsible for enunciating

    i.   cone of uncertainty
    ii. FP
    iii. ISBSG
    iv. WBS

d. If a quotation is based on ROM, what could be the consequence?

    i.   Possibility of loss to the software organization

    ii. Possibility of rejection of the proposal by the customer

    iii. Either of the above

    iv. Neither of the above

e. A regression model is based on

    i.   bottom up estimation

    ii. historical data

    iii. a set of equations

    iv. heuristics

f. The Back-step software company has been asked to provide a cost estimate for a software project. To do the project, the firm has to borrow money to pay the salaries. What is the most important part of the cost planning of the company?

    i.   Accurate activity duration estimates

    ii. Cheap hardware

    iii. Low cost of resources

    iv. Low interest rate for the loan

g. Effort is measured in terms of

    i.   FP

    ii. SLOC

    iii. team size

    iv. person-months

h. What is the purpose of a budgetary estimate?

    i.   Project cost control

    ii. Helping the client allocate funds

    iii. Decision on go-no go

    iv. Basis for quotation

i. The analogy method of cost estimation uses the same basis as the ------ method of size estimation
    i.   decomposition
    ii. duplication
    iii. parametric
    iv. none of the above

j. The decomposition method may also be called the ----- method.
    i.   analogy
    ii. bottom-up
    iii. top-down
    iv. parametric

k. Which technique will be useful in the activity based costing?
    i.   COCOMO
    ii. Comparing with historical data
    iii. PERT
    iv. WBS

l. What could be a good basis for allocating the premises rent to a project?
    i.   Duration of the project
    ii. Number of concurrent projects
    iii. Revenue from the project
    iv. Team size

m. Which of the following will not be included in the software cost?
    i.   Communication expenses
    ii. Hardware depreciation
    iii. Revenue from the project
    iv. Cost of training

n. Under 'pricing to win' approach, price is determined on the basis of
    i.   competitor price
    ii. fixed cost
    iii. total cost
    iv. variable cost

o. Which of the following can have an impact on the budget?

    i. Use of CPM to control the schedule

    ii. Realization of a risk

    iii. Increase in the size of the company

    iv. Variance analysis

p. The objective of budgeting is

    i. cost control

    ii. cost reduction

    iii. shifting the capital expenditure to the revenue expenditure wherever feasible

    iv. defining the scope

11

PROJECT EXECUTION

Plans are only good intentions unless they immediately degenerate into hard work – Peter Drucker

11.1 Learning objectives

From this chapter we start the Execution module. In this chapter we discuss the activities during the execution phase.

The chapter also identifies the different stakeholders in a project and explains their roles.

11.2 Launching the project

With the plan approved by the managements of both the software and the client organizations, it is now time to execute the project. The phases of execution and control will run concurrently from now onwards. In a project life cycle, this is the longest phase in terms of its duration.

The major activities during project execution:

- Identifying all the stakeholders of the project
- Identifying the skills required for the project and forming the project team
- Finalizing the project schedule
- Establishing the operating rules for the team
- Establishing the rules for communication within the team and with the management and the client
- Establishing the scope management process
- Maintenance of versions

11.3 Stakeholders of a project

- Who is providing the funds for the project? – this is an important role called the sponsor or the champion of the project. The entire financial requirements of the project come from the budget of this function. So any change in the scope or the schedule of the project needs the approval of this role. For example, for the computerization of the inventory system of an organization, the head of materials function would be the champion. For the organization-wide mission-critical systems such as the ERP implementation, the CEO of the organization will be the sponsor.
- Who will specify the requirements? It is the users who specify the requirements, but the users are large in number and there has to be somebody or a set of people, who should be responsible for finalizing the requirements and act as a point of contact for the business analyst / project manager / development team.
- Who will authorize the change requests? This role is critical for effective change control. While the scope changes could be requested by different users, there has to be some authority – normally a role at the business head level – which would evaluate these requests from the business point of view and approve / reject them. The scope changes could result in the schedule / cost changes and so this role should be of such a high level in the hierarchy to approve these changes.

These three roles are from the client / user side. The following roles are from the side of the software development organization:

- Who will provide the human resources? Different skills are required for each project. Unlike in a traditional organization, where a staff member is attached permanently to a department, projects are temporary organizational units and have to draw the resources from a common pool. There could be pools for different skill types such as coding, business analysis etc.

- Who will manage the projects? Project manager obviously. But it should also be decided as to who would discharge this role in the absence of the project manager? – this responsibility may be assigned to more than one person - one each for the decision-making in the different areas such as technical, commercial etc. Also when the teams are distributed in different locations or different shifts, a leadership role needs to be defined for each of these. In the cases where the project manager is located off-shore, the on-site team should have a defined leadership role for the client to interact on a day-to-day basis.

- Team members: On the basis of the activities identified in the project, the required skills are identified (This flow was discussed in Chapter 7 – 7.3. Assigning staff to activities). Some organizations prepare what is called the Resource Breakdown Structure (RBS), in which the count of each skill required with the schedule as to when they are required are prepared and the available persons with the required skill(s) are allocated to the project by the business unit head / human resource head in consultation with the project manager.

- Who will maintain the quality standards? While the quality function will be responsible for developing the quality standards for the organization, within a project one or more persons need to be identified to ensure the conformance with the standards specified in the quality plan. This / these team member(s) will also be responsible for the ISO / CMM audit coordination.

- Who will maintain the custody of the developed products? While a large number of programs are developed simultaneously and they go through several iterations of coding, testing and debugging, there have to be a clear segregation of programs under development, those under testing and those that have been cleared after testing. The developed products need to be in a protected directory under the custody of a specified individual, so that they are not tampered with.

- Who will maintain the versions? Documents, programs, test plans and many such artefacts undergo several changes during the course of the project and the trail of these changes need to be maintained.. The number of artefacts and the number of revisions each one of them undergoes will make this job challenging and thus require a dedicated role for maintaining and managing these. This role is known as the configuration manager (To be discussed in detail in Chapter 16).
- Who will maintain the documents? The current versions of the plan, the SRS, the design document and such other documents should be available in a specified location under the custody of an identified individual.
- Roles within the project team: There will be a hierarchy of roles and the specialist skills within the project team. We will dwell on them in detail when we discuss the project organization (Chapter 12).
- Limits of authority: It is also important to define the limits of the financial authority of the project manager. This should delineate which decisions with financial impact can be taken by the project manager and to what extent. This may involve many day-to-day decisions such as the taxi travel and food for the employees staying late, where these are not explicitly defined by the policies of the company.

Practice Questions

1. Fill in the blanks with the appropriate terms:

   a. The ------ function is responsible for maintaining the standards in a software organization.
   b. Responsibilities are associated with -----.
   c. Authority is delegated to a ----- (higher / lower) level.
   d. The role providing the funds is called the ------- of the project.
   e. Scope changes need the approval of -------.
   f. Version control is the responsibility of ------.

12

PROJECT STAFFING

Identify the person who could do the job with the resources required thereof and assign the responsibility to him. – Thiruvalluvar

12.1 Lesson objectives

This lesson addresses the following:

- What are the traits required of a staff member to be in a project team?
- How are these staff members chosen?
- What are the procedural options available to induct a staff member in a team?
- How are the staff organized in a team?
- What are the different roles in a project?
- How are the responsibilities assigned to the different staff?
- What is the function of the project management office?

12.2 Project staffing

Throughout the project execution module, we will emphasize on the human resource management - people will make a significant difference in the execution and the delivery of the project. This is perhaps the least understood part of the software project management. There are many grey areas in the people management that we will not be able to pinpoint or prescribe one unique method of management.

The following criteria should be applied in choosing the staff for a project:

- Eligibility and suitability: The eligibility criteria would be the minimal requirements for the task such as the competence and the experience in a particular platform / domain. Graduates with four years experience in Java could be an eligibility criterion. Mostly such criteria are the facts available in the curriculum-vitae (CV) of a person.

  Suitability, on the other hand, is defined by the additional factors that a member should possess to be successful in a project. These are mostly the behavioural criteria and are specified taking into account the client and the location characteristics. Knowing the sensitivities of a client, we may prefer an on-site lead with more public relations capability. For an assignment in a cold country, we would avoid the staff with bronchial complaints.

- Non-discriminatory: This is a needed qualification of any professional that he / she should not show any favouritism or prejudice in the choice / rejection of any member. The code of ethics of PMI clearly states "*We do not discriminate against others based on, but not limited to, gender, race, age, religion, disability, nationality, or sexual orientation*" (PMI Code of Ethics and Professional Conduct, Clause 4.3.4). The project managers sometimes make statements such as "this task requires extended working hours and may not be suitable for the female staff members". Well-intentioned these may be, such viewpoints may be viewed as discriminatory.

- Educational background:
  o The level of the competence required for executing each project may determine the needed educational qualification.
  o The client approves the consultants on the basis of their CVs and the educational background, being the most tangible parameter, becomes an important criterion in the approval.
  o For an on-site work in a country like the USA, the visa requirements specify the number of years of education.

- Experience: The experience in the domain and the technology need to be assessed. For instance, the requirement is specified as four years in BFSI and Java. The criteria of choice may further be refined as the experience in the large banks and / or in JavaScript. Experience in the tools used in the project could also be a criterion. Prior experience with a client or a country could be an added positive factor in favour of a staff member to be inducted in a team. Proficiency in the language spoken in the client environment could be another consideration, particularly for the non- English speaking regions.

- Behavioural traits: The frameworks, process standardization, coding standards have all made programming increasingly simpler. Thus when a project manager chooses a team member, (s)he need not have to take rigorous tests to check the technical capabilities of a programmer. But what is of paramount importance is the ability of the programmer to be effective within a team. Several of the 'soft' skills required for the project execution need to be assessed:

  o Communication capability: With the software services being offered for many countries across the globe, a major proportion of which being for the USA, it has become important that the team members are capable of expressing their thoughts adequately and appropriately in the English language. That many such conversations are over telephone makes it more challenging to understand the accented expressions without the lip reading or the body language. Ability to communicate to the client in an accent-neutral fashion is an important requirement. For the business analysts, the team leads and the on-site team members, the communication requirements are very important.

  While communicating across cultures, the sensitivities of those cultures need to be understood and respected. The difference becomes obvious even when you ask a simple question "would you have a cup of coffee?" While the western cultures tend to be direct in their responses, oriental cultures are more circumspect. As the issues involved become more complex, the differences turn starker. It is not just the oral communication, but the capabilities in the written communication also need to be judged. From simple emails to the formal reports, the team keeps communicating with the client all through the project. (See Box)

Effective presentation skill is required at least for the business analysts and the lead levels.

Can communication turn lethal?

The project was unduly delayed and the client had shot out a severe reprimand.

The Vice-President asked the project manager to draft a suitable letter of apology.

The project manager compiled the reasons for the delay and sent them with a covering letter which started "Please apologize for the delay in the project"!

That one sentence was sufficient to bring the project to the brink of disaster.

---

o   Commitment: Invariably, every project goes through difficult phases, when the team tends to get demotivated. Unless the team members show a commitment towards the completion of the project, the successful execution might not be possible, more so at the client site, where the project resources are limited.

o   Flexibility: While the roles define an organization's working, they should not become the constraints in the performance. There are times when the staff are needed to rise to the occasion and should be willing to exceed beyond their brief to fulfil the successful completion of the project. It is the staff who are willing to put in the extra hours and take the extra load, who can pull the project to success.

o   Team member: There are the wizards, who can work alone and create wonders, but in a team they fail. Projects are team efforts which can run with many averagers, but can be spoilt by a single wizard. It is not just the individual achievement that counts in a team, but a spirit of accommodation is important for its success. Helping the laggards to complete the tasks to achieve the overall success of the project is not just the responsibility of the project manager, but every team member.

o   Willingness to learn: Every project is a learning opportunity – to learn new things in a business domain, a technology or about a client or a culture in a region. An open mind to assimilate new learnings is an important requirement of a project team member. Know-alls, who resist learning new things become an irritant in a team.

The behavioural traits can be assessed only by talking to the project managers under whom these staff worked previously. The data on the other aspects may be obtained from the CV and the interview of the candidate.

12.2.1 Staff Outsourcing

If the requirement is temporary, an organization may opt for taking staff on a contract basis from a staff outsourcing organization instead of recruiting.

Such contract labour may be needed for the specific skills also. Cost could also be a driving factor for the outsourcing.

While such a facility may be useful for replenishing the staff without a long term commitment, the approach is beset with its own demerits:

• The commitment of the contract staff is questionable, particularly when there is a significant difference in the salary levels of the permanent and the contract employees.
• The contract staff may not be fully familiar with the quality processes of the organization that take their services and this can have an adverse impact on the quality of the deliveries.

However it should be noted that many large and established organizations have entered into the staff outsourcing business[47] and these companies have

---

[47]   Many large Indian organizations such as TCS, Infosys, Wipro and HCL are into the outsourcing business

established quality processes and quite a few of them even have the CMM level 5 certifications and this has made outsourcing a popular option.

12.3 Project organization structure

12.3.1 Projectized organization

Most of the large software organizations adopt this structure: the organization is divided into verticals (domains) and horizontals (technology). Thus there will be a group dedicated to BFSI and Java; another for retail and Microsoft technologies and so on. Each of these matrix cells will have its own business analysts, programmers and testers. The specialized services such as the technical architecture and the system administration may be unique to the cell or drawn from a common pool of services.

This structure is quite appropriate for developing the expertise within the organization. Repeated exposure to the same domain and technology improves the staff competence.

The resource utilization may not be optimal in this structure, because the staff are not interchanged across the cells depending on the project needs.

12.3.2 Matrix organization

In a matrix organization, the staff are grouped in terms of skills and competencies. Thus the business analysts form one group; the programmers are classified into groups based on their language proficiency; the technical specialists such as architects and the database administrators are also grouped separately, with each group having its own head called the functional manager. For each project, the required resources are loaned from these functions / departments and once their contribution to the project is over, the resources return to the parent function. Each of the resources is assessed by the functional head for his / her functional competence and by the project manager(s) for his / her contribution to the project and other behavioural traits.

After the completion of a project, the resources are always anxious where they would go next. This uncertainty is removed in a matrix structure with an established parent organization for each resource. The common pool of resources helps monitor their utilization better.

Dual reporting is the biggest problem with this structure. The employee is often torn between two bosses and their expectations. The project manager too experiences a limited authority over the team members. For many professionals, the traditional unity of command principle[48], which has worked well in the organizations like army, is a better form.

12.3.3 Roles in a project

- Project manager: Responsible for the delivery of the scope with the required quality within the planned time and cost.
- Business analyst: Responsible for eliciting the requirements from the users and creating a document (SRS) for the development team.
- Module lead / Team lead: Module is a subset of a project. Each of these modules will be headed by a module / team lead.
- Programmer: The staff who converts the specifications into code.
- Tester: Tests the programs for bugs and clear them.
- Database administrator: One who manages the data at the server level.
- Domain expert: For the specialized domains, this role may be important to appraise the team of the specific requirements of the domain. The business analyst may take his / her assistance in the requirement gathering interviews.
- Technical writer: To create the documentation for the project, particularly the user manual. In the absence of a technical writer, the programmer will be responsible for the documentation.

---

[48]   Unity of command principle states that each employee is responsible to only one supervisor.

12.3.4 RACI matrix

For each of the activities identified in a project, the persons responsible need to be identified. The assignment of the responsibility could be at different levels, which also need to be clearly documented. These assignments are abbreviated as RACI:

- R – Responsible; this person is responsible for the completion of the task; every activity should necessarily have an R.
- A – Accountable; this person approves the task and thus is one level above the R person and takes the overall responsibility for the task.
- C – Consulted; advice of this person is sought on the issue; mostly this person is an expert in a particular area.
- I –Informed; needs to be kept informed of the status.

	Pramod	Betty	Tamal
Gather requirements	A	R	
Prepare scope document	A	R	
Prepare project plan	R		
Draft functional requirements	A	R	
Develop acceptance criteria	A	R	
Design a solution	A	C	R

Table 12.1 RACI Matrix

12.4 Project Management Office (PMO)

PMO is a common organizational unit across several projects with a responsibility to maintain the standards, collect the data and create the documentation about the projects, report the progress and such staff responsibilities. PMO's role is supportive. Normally, the project teams with a deadline commitment fail to ensure a proper documentation and accurate reporting. PMOs with no pressure of the project targets help maintain the continuity and the integrity of the documentation.

Practice Questions

1. State whether true or false:

    a. If the processes are properly defined, the people are unimportant for the success of a project.
    b. A project manager has the total control over shifting a staff from one project to another.
    c. In the software industry, the technologies are also referred to as platforms.
    d. The educational qualification is not taken into account in selecting staff for a project.
    e. Soft skills are the important requirements for a software engineer.
    f. One of the important requirements for a software engineer is his / her ability to work in a team.
    g. MS Project may be termed as a project management tool.
    h. All the eligible candidates may not be suitable for a project.
    i. A service provider organization normally has a higher level of quality standards than the outsourcing organization.
    j. Horizontals and verticals are found in the matrix organizations only.
    k. Assigning the staff to horizontals and verticals improve their expertise in the domain and / or the technology.
    l. Matrix organizations may be referred to as non-functional organizations.
    m. A common bench for the staff not engaged will optimize the labour utilization.
    n. Unity of command is the underlying principle of the matrix organization.
    o. Where there is a functioning PMO, a project manager may not be required.
    p. PMO may be used for creating the user manual.
    q. PMO has the cost and the schedule targets.

2. Fill in the blanks with the appropriate terms:

    a. The business domains are referred to as ------- (horizontals / verticals) in the software industry.

    b. A project manager fears the safety of girls on-site and does not recommend them for the same. Is it an acceptable project management practice? ----- (Yes / No)

    c. Table 12.1: If there are discrepancies in the documented customer requirements, whom should the manager hold responsible? ----

    d. In a RACI matrix, for each activity ---- (I / R) is a must.

    e. Dual reporting is a feature of the ------ organizations.

    f. An adequately staffed bench ensures ----- (effectiveness / efficiency) of the project delivery.

    g. In a matrix organization, a business analyst will report ------ (administratively / functionally) to a project manager.

    h. ----- is the most competent person to create the user manual for an application.

    i. While PM is a ---- function, PMO is a ---- function (line / staff).

3. Choose the most appropriate answer:

    a. What could be the best source for getting the information on the behavioural attributes of a staff member?

        i. CV

        ii. Friends of the candidate

        iii. Interview

        iv. The project manager(s) under whom the candidate has worked previously

    b. Which of the following is not a reason for outsourcing the software development?

        i. Higher commitment of the contract staff

        ii. Lower cost

        iii. Shortage of skills

        iv. Shortage of staff

c.   Whom does a team lead report to?

  i.   Business analyst
  ii.   Database administrator
  iii.   Domain expert
  iv.   Project manager

d.   Who creates the SRS document?

  i.   Business analyst
  ii.   Project manager
  iii.   Requirement engineer
  iv.   System administrator

e.   Who can certify a program to be bug free?

  i.   Programmer
  ii.   Project leader
  iii.   QA head
  iv.   Tester

f.   Which function is most likely to use MS Project?

  i.   DBA
  ii.   Programming team using Microsoft technologies
  iii.   PMO
  iv.   QA

g.   As per RACI matrix, who may not be required for a meeting?

  i.   R
  ii.   A
  iii.   R & A
  iv.   I

h.   Which of the following is not a reason why the roles are defined in an organization?

  i.   They ensure accountability.
  ii.   They separate the powerful from the powerless.
  iii.   They define responsibility.
  iv.   They define the reporting relationships.

4. Match the role with certifications:

Role	Certification
DBA	.Net
Domain specialist	APIC certification
Programmer	DB2
Project manager	PMP

13

PROCUREMENT MANAGEMENT

If you deprive yourself of outsourcing and your competitors do not, you're putting yourself out of business. – Lee Kuan Yew

13.1 Lesson objectives

This lesson covers the processes required in outsourcing a project:

- How is an outsourcing proposal sought?
- How is a vendor selected?
- What are the clauses to be covered in the contract?
- What are the processes during the execution of the project by the outsourced vendor?

13.2 Growing importance of Outsourcing

Either the whole or a part of a project is outsourced to an outside vendor due to the cost considerations or the non-availability of skill. With the cost-effective communication facilities available across the globe, outsourcing has evolved into a robust business model. The global IT outsourcing market is about $ 315 billion and is expected to reach by $ 480 billion by 2022[49].

Procurement management as a knowledge area is of importance in obtaining the services from an outsourced vendor. The projects in the countries like the USA are outsourced to the countries like India. So a project manager in the USA will look at procurement from the customer perspective, while the project managers in the service provider nations need to understand the processes from the vendor angle.

13.3 Request for Proposal (RFP)

For the software development outsourcing, the SRS or the design document is the starting point. An RFP is prepared and circulated among the prospective vendors. A typical RFP contains the following:

- Background information: an introduction of the company, existing systems, hardware and software infrastructure, overview of the proposed project
- Project purpose and description: Why this project was necessitated and a detailed description of the project, how it fits into the overall application architecture of the organization
- Project scope: what is proposed to be outsourced, broad functional specifications.
- Criteria of success: how the project delivery will be judged.
- Project timeline: expected date of delivery; if different deliverables are identified or if a phased delivery is planned, all or at least some of the delivery dates need to be indicated. The final delivery date should necessarily be mentioned.
- Budget: An indicative upper limit of the financial allocation for the project; Some RFPs exclude this to extract the best price from the vendor.

---

[49] http://www.reportlinker.com/p03659143/IT-Outsourcing-Global-Market-Outlook.html

- Terms and conditions: payment terms, performance bank guarantee, if needed to be executed, penalty clauses, incentives, escrow required, if any. Third party inspection, if part of the project, is also mentioned here.
- Bidder qualification: This may be in terms of the annual revenue of the vendor, prior experience in the domain or the location. In case of the large projects, running for a long duration, to avoid the fly-by-night operators, a minimum turn-over for the bidding companies is specified.
- Standards and tools: The client-specified standards, if any, need to be mentioned here. Specific tool requirements, if any, will also find a mention here. For example, some RFPs may specify the CASE tool to be used.
- Proposal evaluation criteria: These criteria need to be decided upfront and shared with the prospective bidders. Any further step involved in the evaluation process such as the vendor presentation needs to be mentioned here.
- Award process: how the award of the contract will be communicated. The likely date of the announcement of the award and the likely date of the commencement of the project.
- Contact details: The entire SRS / design document may not be shared with the prospective bidders – only an overview of the project is provided. The contact details are provided so that the bidders may seek any further information / clarification.

13.4 Vendor evaluation

The bids are evaluated on the basis of some pre-specified criteria. In some cases, a two stage process is undertaken – first the technical evaluation of the bids and the selected ones will be subjected to a commercial evaluation. A shortlist of the vendors is prepared, who are then called for the presentations. While the vendor presentation is not a mandatory step in all the evaluation processes, the step is useful in checking the vendor's understanding of the project. The customer organization will identify a project manager to liaise with the vendor during the software development and installation.

13.5 Contract preparation

With the selected vendor, a final negotiation is conducted on the price and the other commercial terms. A legal contract is prepared delineating the responsibilities of the vendor and the customer with the aid of legal experts.

A Statement of Work (SOW) is an attachment to the contract and is legally enforceable.

The contract should specify the following:

- Deliverables with the schedule
- Non-functional requirements
- Change control procedure
- Price with the payment terms
- Entitlements and disentitlements of the contractor: For example, if an on-site team works within the premises of the outsourcing organization, what are their entitlements? Would they be covered by an accident insurance, for instance? Laws may differ across countries and an understanding of the laws of the country, in which the services are created / rendered is important in drafting the contract.
- Intellectual property rights: This is important in a software project and the contract should clearly define that the contractor does not have any right over the software and should not reuse the code in part or whole in any of the future projects.
- Force majeure clause: This clause is generally included in the contract to cover the events that are not under the control of the service provider; any non-performance of the contract due to these clauses will not warrant any liability on the part of the service provider. Also referred to as the 'acts of God', these include the natural calamities, terrorism, the economic collapse, the employee strike etc.
- Non-compete clause: The service provider may be prohibited from taking up projects from the competing entities during the project period.
- Non- disclosure clause: By virtue of the close working during the project period, the service provider may become privy to some trade,

process secrets of the outsourcing organization and thus the former needs to give an assurance to protect all such secrets from being leaked out.

- Non-poaching clause: Through this clause, the vendor organization protects its interests by stipulating that their staff may not be recruited by the customer organization not only during the project period, but also for an extended period with a limit specified.

- Warranties: This clause specifies the service provider's obligation to correct the bugs found after the delivery free of cost for a stipulated period.

- Indemnification: The service provider indemnifies the buyer from any claims that may arise due to the former's infringement of the intellectual property or any such violation. The customer too needs to indemnify the vendor of any liability arising due to the usage of the software by the customer for any purpose violative of the legal requirements.

- Termination: On what grounds could either of the parties terminate the contract, the notice period, the penalties involved, the return of the properties are all covered in this clause.

- Jurisdiction: Both the parties have to agree on the jurisdiction under which any legal dispute between them will fall. For example, when a US organization outsources the software development to an Indian company, will the disputes fall under the jurisdiction of the US courts or the Indian courts? The applicable laws being different across countries, this clause assumes importance when disputes arise.

13.6 Vendor Management

During the course of the software development, the customer side project manager has to maintain a continuous contact with the service provider. The service provider organization will also identify a project manager from its side. These two project managers will interact frequently during the execution of the outsourcing contact. It is the responsibility of the project manager on the buyer side to ensure that the service provider delivers within the specified cost, time and quality levels. The important tasks in this phase are:

13.6.1 Setting vendor expectations

It needs to be clearly specified as to what is expected of the vendor. The quality and the commercial processes of the buying organization need to be communicated to the service provider in terms of

- the tests needed to be conducted.
- the associated documentation needed to be provided.
- the interim inspections / audits that will be conducted by the buyer.
- the phases of the software delivery.
- how the success of the delivery will be communicated to the vendor.
- the phases and the modes of payment.
- the documentations required for the payment.

13.6.2 Monitoring progress and performance

The type, format and frequency of the progress reports should be communicated to the service provider and any deviation in the progress needs to be discussed with the vendor. Any mid-course correction needed should be advised to the vendor organization.

13.6.3 User Acceptance Testing (UAT)

UAT should be conducted on the buyer side. This becomes the bottleneck in the progress of many projects and so the project managers from both the sides should ensure that these are expeditiously completed.

13.6.4 Transition

Overseeing the movement of the software from the service provider to the buyer is the responsibility of the project managers from both the sides. This is all the more challenging, when the development and the target platforms are different.

Practice Questions

1. State whether true or false:

    a. The client may specify the testing tool that should be used by the vendor.

    b. The outsourcing organization should ensure that the service provider organization fulfils all the statutory obligations towards its employees.

    c. A buyer organization can deny access to the SRS document for the outsourced entity under the non-disclosure clause.

    d. There is no scope for termination of a project before delivering all the commitments.

    e. Vendor payment is not the responsibility of the project manager.

    f. Soft copy reports are not acceptable in the outsourcing arrangements.

2. Fill in the blanks with the appropriate terms:

    a. On-site presentations by the vendors may be requested ----- (after / before) the submission of bids.

    b. The service provider organization protects its interest against the customer making job offers to the on-site project manager by the --------- (non-compete / non-poaching) clause.

    c. A project manager ----- (may / may not) insist on the periodic progress reports from the vendor.

3. Choose the most appropriate answer:

    a. Which could be an input that needs to be handed over to a vendor for the software development?
       i. CPM diagram
       ii. Project plan
       iii. Programs
       iv. SRS

b.   Which of the following may not be a criterion for vendor evaluation?

   i.   Cost of development

   ii. Delivery time

   iii. Quality of the software

   iv. Price for the services

c.   To facilitate the responses to the bidder's questions, RFP should include

   i.   contact details

   ii. contract terms

   iii. FAQs

   iv. SRS

d.   Which of the following sequence is appropriate?

   i.   Evaluation of bids, submission of bids, RFP, Vendor selection

   ii. submission of bids, RFP, vendor selection, contract preparation

   iii. RFP, submission of bids, evaluation of bids, vendor selection

   iv. Vendor selection, RFP, submission of bids, evaluation of bids

e.   What could be the activity between vendor selection and contracting?

   i.   Bid evaluation

   ii. Monitoring the vendor performance

   iii. Negotiation

   iv. Transition from the vendor to the client

f.   In which phase of the procurement management cycle is the setting vendor expectations an activity?

   i.   Vendor evaluation

   ii. Vendor management

   iii. RFP release

   iv. Vendor selection

g.   Which of the following is optional in an RFP?

   i.   Bidder qualification

   ii. Budget

   iii. Delivery deadline

   iv. Terms and conditions

h. Which of the following steps is optional?

   i.   Vendor evaluation

   ii. Vendor payment

   iii. Vendor presentation

   iv. User acceptance test

i. Two-stage bid evaluation ensures that

   i.   Only the bid that is the best is selected.

   ii. Only the most cost-effective bid is selected.

   iii. A poor technical bid does not get selected because of the low price.

   iv. A sound technical bid is not disqualified because of the high price.

j. In a contract, scope is described in

   i.   RFP

   ii. SOW

   iii. SRS

   iv. UAT

k. Which of the following will be covered under the force-majeure clause?

   i.   Death of a critical employee

   ii. Customer dissatisfaction with the deliveries

   iii. The country of the service provider severs diplomatic and trade relations with the country of the buyer organization

   iv. Virus break-out affecting a large number of computers in the service provider organization

l. The jurisdiction clause will assume importance during

   i.   arbitration

   ii. bidding

   iii. contracting

   iv. deliveries

m. Which among the following is chronologically the last in the development life cycle?

    i.   Code review

    ii. Integration test

    iii. Unit test

    iv. UAT

n. An application that is proposed to be installed on a mainframe is developed using a PC emulation software. In which stage could this become challenging?

    i.   Business analysis

    ii. Coding

    iii. Testing

    iv. Transition

4. In a six month outsourcing contract, after one month you realize that the vendor is not in the right direction. You have two options: continue with the current vendor or choose a vendor totally new to the organization.

a. If you decide to stay with the current vendor, what steps will you undertake to bring the project on track?

b. If you choose a new vendor, what would be the considerations in choosing and what are the steps needed to ensure the success of the project?

5. Of the five proposals that have been submitted for a project, the prices of four are within a range of 10% difference. Only one vendor has quoted 50% less. As a buyer how would you handle this situation?

14

PROFILE OF A PROJECT MANAGER

He is a genius, a philosopher, an abstract thinker – he sits motionless, like a spider in the centre of the web, but that web has thousand radiations, and he knows well every quiver of each of them[50].–
Nicholas Meyer in The Seven Percent Solution

14.1 Lesson objectives

In this lesson we are not going to discuss the technical requirements of a project manager. Our emphasis here is on the behavioural traits that would distinguish a good project manager.

To equip the project manager with these skills, some techniques are introduced.

14.2 Skills required of a project manager

What makes a good project manager? He has to demonstrate good leadership qualities. Now that brings us to the next question: what constitutes good leadership?

---

[50] The description by the protagonist of the novel is about a presumed villainous character. But this fits in well here. Sorry folks!

A good leader is expected to be a

- problem solver
- decision maker
- conflict manager
- motivator
- team builder
- communicator

While there is no one way of defining each of these skills, we will attempt to deal with some aspects of these skills and the ways of acquiring and practicing them.

14.2.1 Problem solving

We will use a case example to illustrate problem solving:

Case of the Haunted House

When John was transferred to the new city, he did not anticipate the acute housing problem there. At last he managed to find a house in the outskirts near the aerodrome. The house had not been occupied for quite some time because it was believed to be a haunted one. It was rumoured that a Formula 1 racer, who was staying there, had committed suicide.

John did not have any option and took the house. He had an eerie experience from the day one. The garage door was found opening and closing at random on its own and this continued through the day and the night on and off.

John experienced a strange feeling: Did he take the right decision? Or has he bargained for the worst?

Steps in problem solving:

- Recognize the problem: One of the important requirements for the problem solving is to understand what the problem is. We have already discussed how people often confuse the symptoms with the problems

(Chapter 2). Because of this, we end up treating the symptoms, leaving the problem unaddressed.

How do we define a problem? A problem is a deviation from the normal.

How do you state the above problem? A door is not supposed to open and close without a trigger; so we recognize a deviation here and thus identify the problem.

- Define the problem: This is a step of narrowing the problem to more defined limits. This process is asking the right questions and getting the data to answer these questions. The questions are
  o What is the problem and what is not the problem?
    Opening and closing of the garage door without any trigger is the problem. No other unusual phenomenon is observed..
  o When does the problem occur? When does it not?
  o Seeking the answers to these questions, John finds that it occurs throughout the day, but not at 12 noon – 2 pm and 12 midnight – 2 am.
  o Where does the problem occur? Where does the problem not occur?
  o The problem is with the garage door only; not with the other doors in the house.
  o What is the extent of the problem? What are the limits of the problem – meaning beyond which limit does the problem not occur?
    The frequency is high in the early mornings and in the evenings to the late nights; it is less during the day.

Normally we tend to define a problem only by what it is. The emphasis here is to delineate the problem by defining what it is not also and thus the problem is defined in a more focused manner.

- Identify the causes: with this definition of the problem, we try to trace what could be the causes. List them; check how much the causes fit with the observations:
  o Is the door hinge loose?
  o Are the winds too strong?
  o Is it due to rats, cats or dogs?

o Is the sensor fitted on the door for the remote operation malfunctioning?

o Or is there a ghost?

Check for the facts to answer each of these questions.

o Based on the observations, the first three causes are eliminated. The presence of an aerodrome nearby suggests that the sensor could be a cause: The sensor may be responding to the signals from the aeroplanes taking off from the nearby aerodrome. Now check if the other observations on the timing and the extent fit in with this cause.

• Design a solution: Having identified the most likely cause, design a solution to address the cause. There could be more than one solution and none of them may address the problem wholly. It is important to identify which part of the problem has to be addressed necessarily and which part can be lived with. Identify the criteria of evaluation and applying the criteria, arrive at the optimal solution.

What could be the possible alternatives available to John?
• Remove the door, in which case the safety of the car cannot be assured.
• Remove the sensor, in which case the remote operation is not possible.
• Live with the problem.

The criteria for evaluation could be cost, the ease of implementation, user acceptance and / or any other.

• Implement the solution: In implementing the solution there could be side-effects and these need to be anticipated. The fall-outs about which we are certain should be separated from the ones that are probable. The probability of each of these consequences with the extent of seriousness need to be assessed. Sometimes the solution may be more problematic and thus it may be better to live with the problem!

- Contingency plan: Sometimes the identified solution may not work, in which case we need to have a Plan B in place[51]

14.2.1.1 Techniques of problem solving

14.2.1.1.1 **Brainstorming**

Whenever the situation does not present itself with a direct solution, the brainstorming technique is used to generate many ideas and options. It has been found that in many cases, brainstorming is useful in arriving at an innovative solution.

The technique involves the participation of a group of 8 -10 people familiar with the problem, with a moderator. For the first twenty minutes, the participants will be allowed to express the possible solutions. The participants need not worry about the practicality of the solutions and the implementation issues. In fact they are encouraged to articulate wild ideas because such ideas may lead to the out-of-the-box solutions. The rule of the game is that nobody should criticize or comment on any idea expressed and so no participant needs to feel intimidated. The moderator will keep writing all the ideas on a board.

The next twenty minutes will be spent on evaluating the ideas on the basis of some agreed-upon criteria. In this process some ideas may be dropped and some may be combined and on an evaluation, a list of ideas will be selected for implementation.

14.2.1.1.2 **Fishbone diagram**

Also known as Ishikawa[52] diagram, this depicts for each effect the causes and for each cause further causes and so on.

Causes are usually grouped into major categories such as personnel, method, material, equipment etc.

---

[51]   The steps have been adopted from The New Rational Manager (Kepner, 1981).
[52]   Named after its creator Kaoru Ishikawa

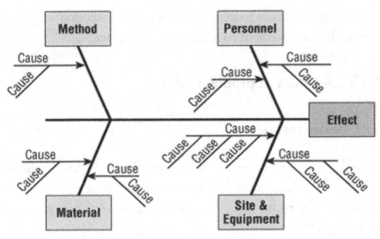

Fig. 14.1. Fishbone diagram

The idea is to dig deep into each of the causes to the level of the root cause. If all the root causes are addressed, the problem is solved.

14.2.1.1.3 Five whys

This method encourages the practitioner to seek the cause for each symptom five times. By this way, the root cause is likely to be reached. The method is similar to the fishbone diagram.

14.2.2 Decision making

There are several ways of decision making:

- Rational: Normally a manager adopts this method, wherein (s)he uses the available data to arrive at an optimal decision. Managers, in their academic and professional trainings, are exposed to different optimization techniques.
- Satisficing: An optimal decision may be acceptable to many, but may dissatisfy a few. The satisficing approach aims at ensuring a minimum level of satisfaction to all. In this attempt to build a consensus, optimality may be sacrificed.
- Intuition: While it may sound odd, the role of intuition in the managerial decision-making cannot be deemphasized. This is why

after a strenuous perusal of a problem, when the solution is still not in sight, we prefer to "sleep over it". It is recognized that some managers emphasize more on intuition than others (Myers, 1995). Intuition has the capability to provide amazing insights into a problem (Myers, 2004). On the flip side, it may also mislead the decision-maker dangerously (Myers, 2004).

- Heuristics: All of us have some thumb rules developed over a period of time with our experience, even though they cannot be explained or proven rationally. The deep-rooted opinions such as 'the teachers' wards have a high value orientation' or 'handsome persons perform well in sales' may not have any scientific basis, but they tend to influence our decisions sub-consciously. Recognizing this is important to ward off any prejudice arising out of such beliefs.

- Expert advice: In the areas where we do not have sufficient knowledge, we tend to seek the opinion of an expert in that area. For example, an organization may be asked to quote for an avionics system and the company may not have any exposure to that area, in which case it is necessary to seek the advice of an expert to prepare a proposal. We did discuss the role of experts in the software estimation in Chapter 6.

- Group decision-making: In some instances, the project managers, instead of arrogating all the decision-making to themselves, may adopt a team-based decision-making. On the issues looking intractable or where the solution requires the team's commitment to implement, this approach is useful. Brainstorming is a group decision-making technique that helps identify out-of-the-box solutions for complex issues.

14.2.2.1 Tolerance for ambiguity:

This is considered to be one of the important requirements in the managerial decision-making. Most of the project managers with a background in science and technology tend to expect all the data needed for arriving at a conclusion and use the sequential logic for the decision-making. But the real life problems do not come with all the data presented cogently. Decisions need to be made based on incomplete data by making reasonable assumptions, using both the divergent and the convergent thinking.

14.2.2.2 Decision-making styles

In the following inventory, several situations have been given wherein the relative importance of quality and acceptance could vary. The style of decision-making varies depending on whether the optimal returns (quality) or the acceptance by the stakeholders is more important. There could be situations when both are equally important and there could also be situations where neither is important.

Decision making Style Inventory

Below each question mark your weightage against Q (Quality) and A (acceptance) on a scale of 1 (no importance) to 7 (very important). It is not necessary that the scores need to add up to 7. For example, you may score both Q and A for a situation as 7, both as 1 or any other combination.

While giving the weightage, assume the role of the protagonist in each instance– for example, in situation 1 as the University Dean (Academics).

1. The University is planning a sandwich program, in which the students will be required to spend alternate terms in the university and the industry. Past experience indicates that the graduates from such a program get better jobs. But this has ramifications for the professors: There will be several changes in the teaching schedule and the professors will be required to interact continuously with the industry.

   Q: A:

2. A firm has developed a new product. The Managing Director is concerned about the correct pricing of the product.

   Q: A:

3. A confectionary company has decided to reward its sales staff for a superb year by holding a dinner. This has to be a surprise for the sales staff. Two of the best restaurants have quoted approximately equally.

   Q: A:

4. As the Head of Administration, you are required to decide on the seating arrangement of the staff in the new office.

      Q: A:

5. Sridhar, Head of Personnel, is a strong believer in the participatory management style and the group decision making. But in his company, all the managers are so busy that they do not want to attend meetings and keep telling Sridhar that they trust his decisions. In this context, how should Sridhar make decisions?

      Q: A:

6. Printed Circuit Ltd. manufactures micro-circuitry for the electronic instruments. This system uses an etching process and molten copper in place of wires to join the electronic components. Salim Ali is a research scientist in charge of the circuit development. Highly respected, he is one of the few people with the knowledge and the experience necessary for his position. He supervises ten bright, but less experienced researchers. The team has developed a new alloy apparently superior to copper. Although not tested for a long period, it has passed most of the required standards. Ali has just received a request to make a recommendation on the process. The prospective buyers will arrive the next morning. It is already 4.55 pm.

      Q: A:

7. Bharat is the foreman of a group of thirty women, who operate looms for a weaving firm. Although the looms are automated, the output has to be watched continuously for flaws. If they fail to notice a flaw, hundreds of feet of the material might be spoilt. Some looms seem to produce a better material than the others. Unfortunately, the looms that produce a somewhat inferior product are easier to operate. Recently a new series of looms has been developed and the management has asked Bharat to appraise these looms.

      Q: A:

8. The Managing Director of World International has a problem. The firm specializes in imports and exports. With the increasing globalization trend, the company has to reassess whether it should set up the warehousing and distribution facilities in Africa.

Q: A:

9. Serena is in charge of a diving crew working from an offshore drilling rig. She is an experienced diver. Since diving is a dangerous task, divers tend to feel rather independent of authority. Their attitude is "I would rather depend on myself for my life than on anybody else." It is Serena's opinion that the most suitable apparel for the divers is the 'wet suit'. This is made of porous rubber. It allows the diver a greater flexibility. Some divers however prefer the 'dry suit'. Dry suits are made of non-porous wool-lined rubber. One danger of these suits is that a sudden increase in the air pressure can turn them into 'balloons', the diver being turned upside down, unable to right himself without outside help. The morale and the cooperation in the group have been excellent.

Q: A:

10. As the creative director of a small advertising agency, Ram Pendse develops the dreams of other people. The success of the firm is attributed to its ability to act quickly and innovatively. Pendse feels that the group brainstorming approach used to generate ideas is the key factor for the firm's achievement. Every decision made is a group decision. One morning, as Pendse arrives in the office, he receives a call from a client for developing a radio commercial by that afternoon.

Q: A:

(Adapted from the inventory developed by Rick Roskin)

Source: The 1975 Annual Handbook for Group Facilitators, University Associates Publishers)

- Command: This is a purely rational decision-making situation, when the manager considers the available facts and arrives at an optimal decision. Many decisions relating to the quality of the delivery or the pricing of the product are taken in this way, wherein it is expected that the team members will accept the manager's decision. The quality standards, for example, may be imposed on the team and no choice is allowed for the team in its adoption. These are cases, where the quality assumes more importance than the acceptance. Managers, who have earned the trust of the team, tend to adopt this approach more successfully.

- Consensus: In these cases, the acceptance by the team members is more important than the quality of the outcome. Implementation of a dress code in an organization might fall in this category.

- Consultation: There are instances where both the quality and the acceptance assume equal importance. A decision to increase the working hours of the staff may be a critical requirement for the completion of a project. The right quality of the output in the extended hours can be ensured only if there is a buy-in from the staff. In such situations, the manager meets the team in small groups so that (s)he is not overwhelmed by the resistance from the team. It makes sense to identify the advocates (who accept the decision), the adversaries and the neutral people and to meet a judicious mix of these in several groups such that the adversaries can be neutralized through the advocates in each session.

- Convenience: Here neither the quality nor the acceptance matters. If the manager decides to have a party for the completion of a milestone, (s)he should go ahead immediately without too much of analysis or worrying about taking everybody's opinion into account. The timing and the enjoyment of the event are more important.

14.2.3 Conflict management

In a project team, conflicts are unavoidable. Conflicts may arise because of any one or more of the following:

- Technology: In the information technology world, technology is almost like religion; you could often come across strong advocates / detractors of one technology or another. A mainframe programmer will look at a PC programmer with contempt and the latter will treat the former as an outdated dinosaur. These create differences in a team, much more so when there is a problem with some technology. We need not only have to resolve the technical issues, but also the negative attitude of the detractors.

- Cost: Cost overruns create a strain on a project and consequent expense cuts may demotivate the team, more so when the muscle is cut in an attempt to reduce the fat.

- Schedule: Delay in a project is a thorny issue. The clients and the managements do not take the schedule and the cost overruns of a project lightly. The manager of a delayed project is pulled from different directions to achieve the result and the things turn worse if the team fails to live up to the demands of higher work output. We saw how conflicts aggravate in a delayed project (De Beers case study (Chapter 3)).

- Resource: Availability of the right resource at the right time may not be assured all the time. A concurrent project with a higher level of priority may deprive a project of the needed resources. Delays may render the original schedule and the resource allocation redundant and the resources may not be available to suit the altered schedule. Attrition too takes its toll on the resource availability.

- Priorities: Software projects aim to satisfy different requirements from multiple users. With different users having different priorities, conflicts are a natural consequence. Sometimes the client priorities may also change. Such changes affect the resource allocation adversely.

- Personality conflicts: The technical staff are personalities with strong opinions and the differences in the opinions tend to create conflicts. Human biases play a big role in affecting the team cohesion.

- Administrative procedures: The purpose of the administrative procedures is control and that is what is resisted by the technical staff. The bureaucratic procedures put a spoke in the progress of a project. These irritants become more acute when the teams are on-site and the accounts department back home applies the standard rules without sensitivity to the locational constraints of the on-site team.

How do we manage the conflicts? Fearing and avoiding conflicts is a natural tendency exhibited by many managers. Brushing the conflicts under the carpet may only aggravate them. We need to face the reality that no project / organization will be absolutely free of conflicts. When so many individuals with diverse backgrounds participate in a project, it is unnatural to expect that there will be no conflict.

Conflicts are good as far as they are within control. Conflicts help confront issues and generate new ideas and new thinking. The teams that avoid conflicts tend to encourage 'group think'. On the other hand, the teams that have learnt to handle the differences encourage innovation. Controlled conflicts strengthen relationships unlike the conflict-free teams, wherein the differences keep simmering under the surface and explode suddenly.

14.2.3.1 Conflict resolution

There are different approaches to the conflict resolution. Since every conflict involves humans, one has to be concerned not only about the resolution of the problem, but also should be sensitive to how the process of the resolution and the final result impact the people involved.

14.2.3.1.1 Problem solving

This is the most rational way of resolving a conflict. Earlier we discussed about how to approach a problem rationally and this approach is expected to provide an optimal solution to the problem to the satisfaction of all the stakeholders. This is the ideal way of resolution of conflicts. But real life is not so ideal to permit such resolutions to all the conflicts.

14.2.3.1.2 **Smoothing**

This technique is used in the negotiation processes. First the problem is split into the areas of agreement and disagreement. The areas of agreement are emphasized and it is attempted progressively to minimize the areas of disagreement. But in this case the acceptance of the solution is given a higher importance than its comprehensiveness to addresses all parts of the problem.

14.2.3.1.3 **Compromising**

This is a give and take approach. Both the parties agree to give up something in return of some gain. In this case, the problem may or may not be fully addressed. The involved parties also have only a partial satisfaction, because of the sacrifices they have made.

14.2.3.1.4 **Withdrawal**

This is more of an escapist approach and thus the problem is not solved nor does it ensure the satisfaction of the involved parties. This approach is adopted with the hope that by postponing, the intensity of the conflict might cool down. This is an approach which has to be adopted in rare occasions. This should not become an alibi for a project manager not to confront conflict.

14.2.3.1.5 **Forcing**

This is an autocratic approach. The manager decides what is good for all and forces the decision down the throats of his team members. The problem might be solved, but might leave the parties unhappy, which could itself become a source of another conflict. When persistent persuasion does not make the team see the reality in a crisis situation, the project manager may use this approach; again to be used sparingly.

14.2.4 Motivation

First a review of the popular theories of motivation:

- Taylorist model: Frederick Taylor[53] was one of the earliest to theorize on the issue of motivating workers to produce more. Based on his experience with the factory workers, he postulated that men work for money. The design of the financial incentives for productivity was the consequence of this model.
- Theory X vs. Theory Y: This was developed by Douglas McGregor at MIT Sloan School of Management in the sixties. In his book 'The Human Side of Enterprise', McGregor differentiates between two management styles, which he calls the Type X and the Type Y. The type X managers believe that men normally do not like to work and are insincere in discharging their duties and so need continuous supervision. The type Y managers, on the other hand, believe that men are self-motivated and given the proper conditions will achieve the results on their own. As a consequence, the type X managers adopt a more autocratic or directive style and the type Y managers believe in creating a climate of trust and allowing the employees autonomy and freedom. While in general the type Y may seem a preferred managerial style, there are situations, where the X style may be necessary..
- Maslow's hierarchy of needs: In the year 1943, Abraham Maslow, an American psychologist, proposed that humans progressively pass thorough the fulfilment of different needs.

---

[53] Frederick Winslow Taylor (1856 – 1915) was a mechanical engineer, who after twenty six years of industry experience occupied a professorial position in the Tuck School of Business. Taylor was the president of the 'American Society of Mechanical Engineers' (1906 – 07). He is recognized as one of the earliest contributors to the scientific management. His book 'Principles of Scientific Management' is considered a classic in management science and is a harbinger to view management more as a science than as an art.

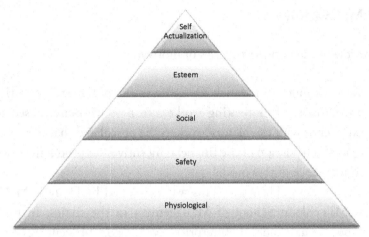

Fig. 14.2. Maslow's hierarchy of needs

An understanding of this hierarchy helps structure the rewards to the employees to suit their needs. While money may still incentivize an employee, whose basic needs have not been fulfilled, at higher levels, status and recognition matter more than mere monetary incentives.

- Hygiene vs. motivators: Also known as the two factor theory, this was developed by Frederick Herzberg, an American psychologist. Herzberg classified the factors affecting the performance of workers into two – hygiene and motivators. The hygiene factors are those, the presence of which may not enhance the productivity of a person, but the absence of which will cause dissatisfaction among the employees. Salary, the working conditions and the company policies will all fall into this category. On the other hand, the motivators contribute to the enhancement of productivity. Recognition, job challenge and the career growth prospects fall in this category.

- Expectancy theory: Proposed by Vroom in 1964, this theory postulates that humans are motivated to choose a course of action depending on the expected outcome due to a particular course of action, which he called the instrumentality and the perceived value of the outcome. As a consequence, organizations need to structure their incentives in such a way that the employees are able to relate them to their performance and also these incentives are viewed by them as substantive.

- Oldham – Hackman model: This model talks about three characteristics that should be built into a job to motivate a person:

o   Providing meaning to the work

o   Autonomy: how much of independence and discretion an employee experiences in his / her job.

o   Feedback: Is the employee made aware of how well (s)he is performing to achieve the desired goals?

o   Meaning to the work may be ensured by the following three factors:

  ▪   Skill variety

  ▪   Task identity: ability of an employee to identify his / her contribution as holistic. Tasks such as those in an assembly line have a limited task identity.

  ▪   Task significance: ability of an employee to see his / her work contributing to a larger purpose. A soldier in a battalion may not have high task identity, but the task significance in such roles is high.

In a software environment, with a large number of programmers engaged in the tasks very similar, the skill variety, the task identity and the task significance are difficult to provide. To compensate for this, the software organizations encourage many activities beyond what is demanded by the work such as the cultural events and the social outreach programs to bring out the organizational and the leadership skills of the staff. The product organizations are better equipped in making their staff identify with the final product they are making and normally in such teams, the motivational levels are high.

14.2.4.1 Motivating geeks[54]:

Programmers seem to be of a different type that the traditional methods of motivating the staff may not apply to them. The motivational lectures, for example, rarely inspire programmers. The job of a programmer is problem solving and (s)he is conscious of the intellectual component of his / her job – a typical case of (s)he knows and knows that (s)he knows. With this in mind we need to structure effective motivational measures for them.

---

[54]   The title was inspired by the title of a chapter in the book 'Leading Geeks' by Paul Glen.

In this context, the differentiation proposed by the Harvard Business School professor Teresa Amabile is relevant (Amabile, 1993). She talks about two types of motivation: intrinsic and extrinsic. People are *intrinsically motivated* when they seek enjoyment, interest, the satisfaction of curiosity, self-expression, or the personal challenge in their work. People are *extrinsically motivated* when they engage in the work in order to obtain some goal that is apart from the work itself.

Managers have a control over the extrinsic motivators. They may not have a direct control over the intrinsic motivators, but they can create an environment that encourages intrinsic motivation. Since the software job involves creative problem solving, the managers need to focus more on the intrinsic motivators. The challenge for the manager is to make the people interested in the problem they are handling. Once this is done, the motivational level of the team will be high. This is the reason why the teams engaged in the development of challenging products are found to have a higher level of motivation.

The software professionals are also motivated to work in the projects which offer them the career enhancement, an opportunity to network with professionals, an exposure to new technologies and marketable skills. But the project requirements may not always synchronize with these expectations of the software professionals. In such cases, the project managers should employ alternate strategies such as increasing the responsibility of the team members or providing an in-depth exposure to a technology. Even the extraneous activities such as a membership in the professional bodies or the participation in seminars motivate geeks.

Glen (Glen, 2003) talks about providing a larger meaning of the project to the team by communicating to them the significance of the product to the client or to the development organization or to the society at large.

Some of the common demotivators Glen identifies are

- Exclusion from decision-making; This is the reason why we discussed the methods of group decision making earlier.
- Inconsistency in decision-making; Teams resist unfairness in decisions.

- Excessive monitoring: Micro managing is a trap the project managers should avoid; this trait is particularly found in the managers, who have spent long years in programming and more so are proud about their programming skills. The managers, who breathe down the necks of the team members, end up extracting less output from their teams. A more desirable style of management is to set the targets for each staff member and leave the tasks to them.
- Misaligned reward system: While the rewards not commensurate with the performance of a staff member being the cause for demotivation is understandable, a disproportionately high reward also has a negative consequence. Such rewards end up impairing the productivity because of the cognitive dissonance.
- Artificial deadlines: Project managers, who set unrealistic targets in an apparent effort to introduce challenges in the job might end up demotivating the staff. A successful project manager understands the thin line of difference between the challenging and the unrealistic targets.

14.2.5 Communication management

With multiple stakeholders, communication plays an important role in a project. Poor communication has been responsible for many a misunderstanding and failure of projects. The case of Scheme Annalakshmi discussed later in the chapter is one such example.

14.2.5.1 Communication choices for a project manager

A project manager has to formalize the communication mechanism, which includes

- when a communication should take place.
- what should be communicated
- who should communicate: This is particularly important with respect to the client communication: The Project manager should define a protocol as to who from the team may communicate with the different stakeholders.

- where should the communication take place: Some communications need the privacy of a cabin and several others could happen in public.
- what should be the medium: there are many options available today and a proper choice needs to be made.
  - Face-to-face: This is the most effective medium, but may not be possible in all the cases, particularly when the stakeholders are in different locations. But sensitive private communications such as the performance appraisal should be conducted face-to-face.
  - Video-conferencing: This is the next most effective option. For the weekly reviews with the on-site teams and the discussions with the client in a remote site, this could be a good option. Ability to rope in the participants form different locations is an added advantage in the video-conferencing. Body language is an important part of any communication and video-conferencing is able to capture this at least partially and thus a more effective option than audio-conferencing. Bandwidth and cost could restrict the number and frequency of the video-conferences.
  - Telephonic: good for one-to-one communication; could be extended to a small group. Reviews and discussions over conference calls are widely popular in the software industry.
  - Email: This is the most frequently used communication channel due to its economy, the ease of access and use and speed. Ability to reach a large number of people fast is the biggest advantage of email. Its popularity itself could be its weakness as sometimes important messages could be lost in a deluge of mails. Setting priority and marking urgent and important in the subject line could be a solution. There is a possibility of misinterpretation of emotions in an email.
  - Oral vs. written: For urgent messages, oral communication may be preferred. Formal communication has always to be in the written form. Extensive discussions could be conducted on issues, but the action plan has to be documented for the follow-up. The written communication ensures the trail required for a project, which involves several people and spans over an extended duration.
- how the communication should be tracked: recording of the minutes is one method of tracking.

14.2.5.2 Meetings

Meetings are an integral part of the organizational life. For the same reason, a manager has to manage meetings properly, lest too many of them would impair the productivity of the organization. Remember an unnecessary meeting is a time-waster for not one, but many staff members.

So before every meeting, the question that should be asked is whether this meeting is necessary and whether there are alternate ways the same purpose can be achieved. If a meeting is necessary, an additional question that should be answered is who should attend. Only those people, who can directly contribute to the discussions or who would be required to take actions based on the discussions, need to be invited to the meeting. In the RACI matrix, the I people could be kept away from the meeting. They need to be only informed of what transpired in the meeting subsequently through the minutes. Restricting the number of attendees to 8 – 10 is useful; a larger number affects the participation level and could turn out to be a one way communication or pandemonium with no productive decisions and action plan.

14.2.5.2.1 Planning for the meeting

Every meeting should have a purpose, clearly identified and communicated ahead to all the attendees. The formal meetings should also have an agenda written down and communicated to all.

A good practice is to define the duration of the meeting as well ahead as otherwise meetings tend to prolong. The meeting invitation itself should contain the start and the end time.

The project manager should fix the frequency for different meetings and the timing and the duration also. There are some meetings such as the progress review meetings that need to be conducted frequently.

It is also a desirable practice that each meeting should have minutes, as otherwise the points discussed remain at the same level without any follow-up action. The project manager should fix the responsibility of preparing the minutes to an identified individual.

If a formal presentation is to be made in a meeting, it should be rehearsed beforehand.

14.2.5.2.2 Conducting a meeting

Every meeting should have a chair, who has the authority to frame the rules of the meeting and to moderate the discussion. (S)he is the final authority on what is allowed and what is not in a meeting. For most of the project team meetings, the project manager will act as the chair. It is the responsibility of the chair to ensure that

- the meeting starts in time.
- the objectives and the expectations are set explicitly and clearly.
- the participants do not get stuck at a point: in case of a stalemate, the chair decides on the course of action.
- the discussion points are summarized periodically to check that everybody in the meeting is on the same page and also to progress further based on these.
- the action items are assigned to the identified members.

Whenever any item needs explanation / elaboration, the visual aids are useful.

14.2.5.2.3 After the meeting

The preparation of the minutes is an important post-meeting activity. For effectiveness, the minutes should be circulated within three days. To ensure the accuracy of the minutes, the draft is circulated among the attendees and then taking the relevant inputs from them, a final version is made and circulated.

The minutes, tagged with the date, the time, and the venue of the meeting should name all the attendees and should list each discussion item with a number, record the salient points of the discussion with reference to the persons, who raised each point and the action item identified with the person(s) responsible for each of them.

The minutes may contain the next (tentative) date for the follow-up meeting.

14.2.5.2.4 Type of meetings

Of the several meetings conducted by a project team, the following are the most important:

14.2.5.2.4.1 Daily status meetings

This is conducted by the team leader / project manager to assess the team's progress on a daily basis. This is a stand-up meeting, wherein all the attendees stand to make it quick and fast. Normally this is of less than fifteen minutes duration. Every one reports on the status briefly as "on schedule" or "delayed by so many days / hours". The people who are behind the schedule need to add whether they can manage by themselves or they need any help. The team lead identifies the resources who are ahead of the schedule and who are capable of helping others who are late.

14.2.5.2.4.2 Progress review meetings

This is normally conducted by the project manager towards the end of every week. From the schedule, the activities that should have been started and completed last week should be picked up and their status reviewed. In case of delay in any of the activities, the reasons need to be discussed. The delay could either be due to the project team or because of the non-availability of the resources from the client. The problems and the remedial actions need to be identified. It should also be ascertained whether the delay will affect the project schedule.

14.2.5.2.4.3 Quality review

Periodically the SQA will conduct a review of the quality process in a project. Apart from the select project members, the quality staff will also participate in such meetings.

14.2.5.2.4.4 Technical problem resolution

Whenever the team is stuck in a technical issue, this meeting is called for. The experts in the technology in question from the general pool will participate in this meeting along with the team members who are involved in the problem.

14.2.5.2.4.5 General problem resolution

These meetings are intended for issues other than the technical issues. The nature of the problem could be the staff issues to the delay in the project. The team as a group tries to find a solution to these problems. Techniques such as brainstorming, useful for such meetings, have already been discussed.

14.2.5.2.4.6 Project status review with management

Periodically presentations on the status of the project need to be made to the management and to the client management as well. These are formal presentations made by the project manager and a few senior members of the team may be invited.

Case Study: Scheme Annalakshmi

Scene 1   Venue: Chamber of the Minister for Food and Agriculture

Minister Krishna Prasad was restless on seeing the report brought by his secretary.

"Another spate of farmer suicides. In this quarter alone 489 are dead. It isn't going to be easy to face the Parliament."

"It is more than a year since we announced the Annlakshmi scheme (Details in Exhibit I) and we are seeing no let up in the farmer suicides."

"Bhaiyaji is planning a farmer rally in Delhi and in the state capitals later this month" the secretary's information did not come as any comfort to the minister. The social activist Lakshmipathy – popularly known as Bhaiyaji – was leading a movement called Kisan Bachao Aandolan (KBA) – literally meaning Save Farmer Movement - and was a vocal critic of the implementation of Annalakshmi. With a large number of complaints on the loan disbursement by MFDB, the movement was gaining support from several social service organizations and the political parties.

With just six months for the elections, these are some of the things that Krishna Prasad would have loved to avoid.

"Call Hegde" roared the minister.

Scene 2   Venue: MFDB Chairman's office

With the minister at the other end, Shashikant Hegde, Chairman of the MFDB knew it was not going to be a pleasant call. This has been the routine for the last six months – only things have been turning from bad to worse.

"I expect things would be corrected by next month. The core part of the software is functional." Hegde said hesitantly.

"What functional? 125000 loan applications are pending. The report is not coming from you. Bhiyaji has put up a website and is updating the daily status. Did you see the posting of the complaints in his site?"

"Yes sir. Bhiyaji sends a weekly extract to me also."

"You should be ashamed of telling this, Hegde. Your dashboard is out of date and inaccurate. Farmers are complaining that when they are applying for a second loan, again you are asking for the same documents. When a farmer calls you for a loan status, your customer support is quite tentative about the status."

"The CRM module is not fully functional. What we propose to do is…."

"Stop this nonsense, Hegde. Junk the software. We asked the Top4 Consultants to study the business process and advise. They are well known for such type of work and the PM is also happy with their previous assignments. The software needs to be redeveloped according to their specifications without any deviation."

"Yes sir. I have given their report to Calculus."

"Calculus?"

"Calculus software is the company developing the software. But they feel that it is too difficult to redesign now. If the changes are insisted upon, they need another one year to complete."

"In one year all of us will be gone. If they cannot implement the redesigned processes by March, they may as well go". The minister slammed the phone.

Shashikanth called for an urgent meeting of GM, IT Head and Calculus project manager Mohan.

Scene 3:   MFDB Conference room

"Mohan, There is not much time left. In the next forty five days, you have to implement the business processes recommended by Top4 in toto" Shashikanth directly plunged into the matter.

"Sir. Please understand. The project is near completion. Help desk process also has been corrected with the inputs from the users." (To get an overview of the processes involved in the project, see Exhibit II)

"But we cannot trust your software anymore. It is three months since you people have been fixing the bugs. Integration of the workflow with the help desk has taken so much time that the customers are totally unhappy with it. Now newspapers have also started talking about this" intervened the Manager – IT, Hari Krishna.

"With the ministry also backing Top4, we have to necessarily adopt the processes recommended by them only" Sahashikanth was clear about his priorities.

"Sir. The controls introduced by Top4 will make the workflow longer and time consuming. Changing the design at a point when 90% of the coding is complete will upset everything". Mohan was trying to reason out.

"This has been taking us nowhere. We need to serve the ultimatum. Call Prof. Kautilya"

Scene 4   Venue: Calculus Software

After a long experience in academics, Prof. Kautilya had started the Calculus software in Pune. An expert in the computational algorithms, Kautilya was a respected figure in the academic and the industry circles. He did not expect that the first e-governance project they had undertaken will enter into hot waters. Worse was the adverse publicity in the media about the software being responsible for the delay in the disbursement of loans.

"Where did we go wrong?" Kautilya asked Mohan as he was browsing through the project performance reports (an extract available in Exhibit III) from the PMO.

"The initial specifications were not clear. For the MFDB management also the processes were new. We evolved the specifications as we went along."

"Mohan. You are one of our senior project managers. When you prepared the proposal, did you not know all these?"

"Anyway we have crossed most of the hurdles. The last UAT reported very few bugs. Helpdesk which has the largest number of users is happy with the software now."

"What is the use, Mohan?. The customer is now changing the basic design itself. Whatever work has been done so far is down the drain."

Mohan was obviously offended. "We should not allow them to do that. They want the software to be redeveloped, tested and ready in forty five days. It is impossible. Somehow we have to dissuade them."

"Somehow?" Kautilya smiled sarcastically. "I thought it was the project manager's job. The project has had a heavy schedule and cost overrun. That is bad enough. The bad publicity is affecting the organization. Do you have any concrete plan to salvage the project, Mr. Mohan?" The formal address showed that Kautilya was angry.

"We should not accept the redesign. Too many controls have been introduced by Top4, which will make the workflow time-consuming and cumbersome. The customer complaint capture goes through three screens with several validations, because Top4 believes a lot of complaints are not genuine."

"Then why are they swearing by the new processes?" Kautilya asked with disbelief.

"Nobody in the top management has reviewed the processes. They are just going by the image of Top4. The IT Head is upset with the new help desk process, but nobody listens to him."

"All that leads to what?" Kautilya was impatient

"We have to collectively think of a strategy" Mohan fumbled. That he did not have a clear plan was clear.

"If you do not have a plan, Mohan, I have. You are being replaced. Sorry, but you forced the situation. Naren will take over from you with immediate effect. Next week - please use it for the transition".

Mohan was too shocked for any response. A sound technical hand with an MBA from a premier school and a PMP, he had fifteen years of experience under his belt – eight years as a project manager. Not only has he had a major setback, he is being replaced by a junior, who is more known for his public relations and political skills than technical knowledge.

Questions:

1. Do you think Mohan was at fault? If so what were his mistakes? If you had been in Mohan's position, how would you have handled this better?

2. What should Naren do now?

Exhibit I
Scheme Annalakshmi

The scheme was started with a goal to alleviate the financial strain of the small and medium farmers in the country under the aegis of the Food and Agriculture department with an initial corpus of INR 1000 million. The scheme provides for seed loan, well / bore loan, working capital loan and harvest loan at low interest rates and also aids farmers for crop insurance. To deliver the end-to-end comprehensive services to the small and medium farmers, a special agency called the Marginal Farmer Development Bank (MFDB) was started with the headquarters in Mumbai and the branches in all the state capitals.

With the initial infrastructure not extending to the Tier II and III towns, the farmer has to travel to the state capital for the loan disbursement. While the bank has a web site with the regional language interfaces, with facilities for all the interactions with the bank, many farmers did not find it easy to use.

In the first year of operation, the bank had disbursed only 27% of the targeted amount as loans and the recovery record has also been poor because of poor tracking of loan.

Exhibit II

Loan sanctioning process

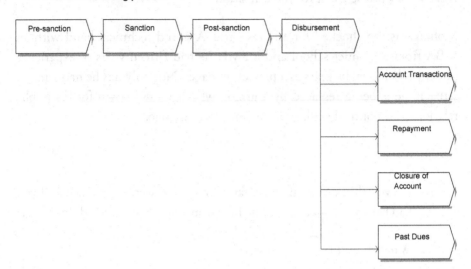

Loan sanctioning workflow

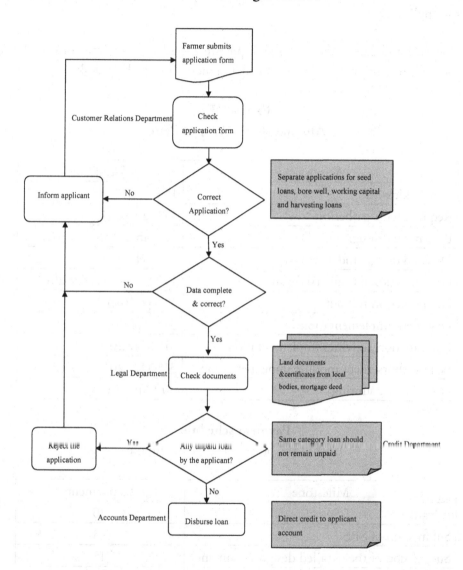

Help Desk module:

This is part of the CRM subsystem.

The customer requests for information / complaints may come through phone to the call centre or through the web. Each of the customer input is provided a number called the request number. On the basis of the application number provided by the customer, the help desk is required to provide the status of the application.

The time and date of the customer input are logged and the time of the reply too. The resolution cycle is monitored as a metric for the help desk.

Exhibit III
Annalakshmi – Project Plan

Activity	Deadline
Project kick-off	1st Dec 2012
Requirements gathering	15th Jan 2013
Preliminary design	31st Jan 2013
Detailed design and approval	15th Feb 2013
Loan sanction module trial run	15th Feb – 31st Mar 2013
Loan sanction roll out	1st Apr 2013
Help desk implementation	30th Apr 2013
Post sanction activities implementation	31st May 2013
Loan disbursement module implementation	31st May 2013
Financial accounting	30th Jun 2013

Payment schedule
Cost of the project: INR 120 million

Milestone	% payment
Advance	20
Submission of SRS	15
Submission of the detailed design document	15
Loan sanction module roll out	15
Help desk module roll out	15
Disbursement module roll out	10
Sign off	10

October review highlights:

Loan sanction and Help desk module UATs have again thrown out some bugs.

Post sanction and disbursements have been developed in parallel and testing still not complete.

The project is delayed by 5 months.

The customer has made only 45% of the payment.

Cost overrun of the project 20%.

14.2.5.3 Why does communication fail?

- Poor linguistic ability is one of the major reasons for the communication gap. But this is not the only reason.   ·
- Two individuals with perfect knowledge of English may still have a misunderstanding because of their assumptions. The assumptions, in turn are influenced by the background of the individuals (See box: communication: check your assumptions),
- Poor listening is another reason for the communication failure. Communication is not just about talking; it is about listening also; in fact more about listening. It is said that we have two ears and one mouth to emphasize that communication is 67% listening and 33% speaking.

Communications: Check your assumptions

The famous painter was approached by the celebrity actress of the times. She asked him "Would you please paint me in the nude?"
The painter was hesitant. The actress said "I will pay 1000 gold coins".
This was too much for the painter to resist. He said "Ok madam. But please allow me to wear socks. Where else do I keep my brush?"

14.2.5.4 Methods of improving communication

- Reduce misunderstanding:
  - o Understand the background of the person you are interacting with.
  - o Empathize with him / her.
  - o Modify your communication to suit him / her.
  - o Paraphrase periodically what (s)he said and check your understanding is correct.

- Reduce ambiguity
  - o Improve the clarity of expression.
  - o Periodically check that the other person has understood what you have said.

- Trust is an important pre-requisite for communication. In the absence of trust, whatever you communicate will not have the desired impact on the listener.

Communications Exercise

You assign the job of the preparation of a report to an employee and tell him that it must be done by the end of the week. Your employee accepts the job, asks no questions and goes off to do the job.

On Friday morning, you ask the employee about the job. He seems surprised, saying it is not done yet. You insist that you need it for a meeting at 2 o'clock and want to see what is done. You find the data is not what you wanted – the employee has missed some of the steps in the data gathering. The report is not in the format you wanted.

You are angry. You are going to look bad in the meeting. You ask him to hurry and finish the job by 1.30.

What is the problem?

What is your assessment of the situation?

If you were in the position of the manager, how would you have handled the situation?

If you were in the position of the employee, how would you have behaved?

14.2.5.5 Communicating for improving team performance

Steps involved:

14.2.5.5.1 Setting expectations:

Tell the staff

- what should be done.
- who will do it.
- when will it be done
- where is it to be done
- why is it done
- how well should it be done

14.2.5.5.2 Observe

- Periodically check the progress the employee is making.
- Observe in a non-intrusive manner.
- Counsel the employee to put him / her on the right path.

14.2.5.5.3 Train

In case the employee has not understood the job still,

- show him how to do it.
- ask him / her to do it.
- review his / her performance.

14.2.5.5.4 Providing feedback

Providing a feedback is a sensitive issue. Many managers do not find this comfortable, particularly when a negative feedback is to be given. We have already discussed that the employees expect a feedback and it is a motivational tool.

Feedback should be

- specific, not general.
- descriptive, not evaluative.
- focused on the performance.
- data based and not impressionistic.
- reinforcing the positive aspects of the performance.
- based on the verified data.
- focused on the factors, on which the employee has control.
- helpful to the employee and not destructive.

The timing of the feedback is important. It has to be immediate and it has to be provided in private. As the old saying goes "Praise in public, criticize in private"[55]. However there are exceptions to this rule, when a team member may have to be criticized in public (Schwarz, 2013).

14.2.6 Team building

Not all cultures are easily amenable to team work. Indians, for example, are generally known to be individualistic, which makes them poor team players. On the other hand the Japanese and the Chinese show a tremendous capability for team work. The biggest challenge before a project manager is that (s)he has not only to build a team, but sustain it through the ups and downs of the team.

14.2.6.1 Optimizing team productivity

It is usually said that a battalion works for the captain, not for the country. This shows the importance of a team leader / project manager. A team's performance rises or falls to the expectations of the team leader. This is referred to as the 'Pygmalion[56] effect' in the management literature.

It is a misconceived notion that the managers, who are lax in their supervision, are popular among the employees. The demanding managers

---

[55] This adage is attributed to Publilius Syrus, ancient Latin writer
[56] Named after a sculptor in Greek mythology, who fell in love with the statue he carved and prayed that it come to life and the statue did come alive!

not only achieve high results, but are also remembered by the teams as their best bosses ever.

Only the managers, who elicit trust, are able to set such a high benchmark for the achievement by their team members.

An effective team is one in which

- the task allocation is done as per the skills and the capabilities of the team members.
- there are defined roles and each member knows what is expected of him / her.
- the members feel that there is no favouritism and all enjoy equal importance.
- the procedures and the processes are defined clearly.

Managers often demand the best talents be allocated to their projects. While the talent level appropriate to the problem at hand is desirable, wizards often prove to be counter-productive in a team. The Japanese have shown to the world how the teams with ordinary men can produce extraordinary results.

14.2.6.2 What can affect a team performance?

The factors that are said to create the team toxicity are

- frenzied work atmosphere
- frustration caused by the personal, the business or the technological factors
- poor procedures and processes
- unclear roles – lack of accountability and responsibility
- repeated exposure to failure (Jackman, 1998)

14.2.6.3 Stages of a team

Project teams are adhoc organizational units. They are created for the completion of a project and disbanded at its completion.

Psychologist Bruce Tuckman first came up with a model for the stages of a team. The five stages he identified are forming, storming, norming, performing and adjourning (Tuckman, 1965)[57].

Earlier we debated on the suitability of Type X vs. Y managers. In the initial stages of a team, the manager should adopt the command and control style and progressively move to the democratic style.

The desirable leadership style and the role of a manager at different stages are discussed below:

14.2.6.3.1 Forming stage

At this stage, the members are pooled together and the team is just in the process of getting formed. The members may still be new to each other and the manager will need to adopt a directive style. (S)he should tell the staff what is expected of them in no uncertain terms and clearly delineate what is acceptable and what is not in the team and should also enforce them. Initial successes motivate the members a lot. So the manager should assign simple, but not trivial tasks to the members appropriate to their skill levels.

14.2.6.3.2 Storming stage

This is the stage when the members have a better understanding of the task, but still the relationship among the individuals is fragile. Misunderstandings and prejudices persist leading to accentuated conflicts among the staff. At this stage, the energies of the team are wasted in unproductive quarrels.

The project manager should continue to be directive. The unseemly conflicts might demotivate some staff and they may start wondering whether this is the team in which they are going to work till the completion of the project. The manager should confront the problems and counsel the demotivated staff that

---

[57] The initial model of Tuckman had only the first four stages. In 1977 Tuckman added the fifth stage - Adjourning

this is a passing phase. This is a point of failure for many teams and the success of the manager lies in tiding over this stage.

14.2.6.3.3 Norming stage

This is the stage at which the understanding among the staff improves and the team becomes cohesive and task-oriented. The manager adopts a more supportive role. The manager's main task is to motivate the team to maximize its output.

14.2.6.3.4 Performing stage

The performance of the team progressively improves to reach a peak level. At this stage the team is self-motivated. The manager's role is totally supportive and (s)he should ensure that all the resources necessary are available, so that the project could go on uninterrupted. The manager should delegate a part of his / her authority to groom the successors. If properly planned, the manager might even be absent at least for a part of this period and still the team will achieve the results.

14.2.6.3.5 Adjourning

The team has completed the task. This is the time the team needs to be disbanded. The manager should thank the team and show personal appreciation of each member. (S)he should ensure that all the documentation is complete including the project diary, documenting the experiences in the project and loaded into the project repository of the organization.

The celebration of the successful completion is an important activity at this stage. The manager should also ensure that the team's success is communicated across the organization.

The on-site teams, away from the head quarters for a long time, show the pangs of anxiety at this point of time – what next? The manager should apprise them of the future possibilities for them.

The on-site teams, which have been through several adversities in a new land with different food habits and culture, develop a strong bondage among themselves that disbanding the team proves to be a traumatic experience for many. It is for this reason that this stage is also called the mourning stage. It is the manager's responsibility to play a highly supportive role at this stage and cheer up the team to look for brighter things.

Practice Questions

1. State whether true or false:

   a. The project managers are assessed only on the technical aspects and not for the behavioural traits.
   b. Brainstorming is a technique of problem solving.
   c. Intuition has a role in the managerial decision-making.
   d. Decisions should always be made only on their merits.
   e. Organizational psychologists agree that money is a great motivator.
   f. Motivational lectures motivate programmers.
   g. The technical staff prefer the internal projects to the client projects.
   h. When choosing a solution, we need not worry about its implementability.
   i. Brainstorming is very effective, because it helps generate implementable ideas only.
   j. Programmer's work is autonomous.
   k. Expertise in coding makes a good project manager.
   l. By being unpredictable, a project manager can instil fear in his staff and thus can be a good manager.
   m. An assembly line worker will feel high task identity.
   n. Programmers cannot be motivated by any external agency.
   o. Successful project managers review the code line-by-line.
   p. Just terrorize the team members for no reason periodically. That way you will have a good control over your team.
   q. Setting unachievable deadlines for the team is an effective way to make them feel deficient and a project manager should exploit this to have a tight control over them.
   r. When half the work is completed, advance the deadline by 20% to create a challenge and keep repeating this for the balance portion as well to keep the team members motivated.
   s. A leader is a good listener.
   t. Feelings do not have a place in a software organization.
   u. A team has the capability to generate more and better ideas than the individuals in the team.

v. Lax project managers are more popular among the team members than the demanding ones.

w. While fairness is a good idea, it does not work well in the team management.

x. Personal problems affect the performance of a person as a team member.

y. Praising a team should be avoided by a project manager, as it goes to their heads.

z. In a large team, it is not necessary for a project manager to attempt knowing each member individually.

aa. Successful project managers manage large teams by having a few trusted lieutenants who are given no job but to spy on the other members and report to them.

ab. At the adjourning stage, it is likely that the team members are emotionally drained.

ac. When you run from crisis to crisis, the team cohesion improves.

ad. Since problems are a passing phase, the team leader should ignore the problems in the storming stage.

ae. Partying ----- (helps / inhibits) the team morale.

af. Very bright people find it more difficult to fit into a team than the average people.

ag. When an immediate action needs to be taken, email is the best form of communication.

ah. Emotions can be better expressed in email.

ai. When the number of attendees is large, the conduct of the meeting becomes difficult.

aj. It is a good practice to rehearse a presentation.

ak. If you are adept in the subject, you need not have slides for a formal presentation.

al. Listening is different from communication.

am. It is a good practice to specify the end time of a meeting.

an. The action items are meaningful only when they are assigned to (a) specific person(s).

2. Fill in the blanks with the appropriate terms:

    a. Staff attrition is a ------ (problem / symptom).

    b. For a problem, it is better to evaluate ---- (one/many) solution(s).

    c. Vroom's model postulates that the perceived value of reward should match ---- (expectancy / instrumentality).

    d. The command style of decision-making conforms to the theory --- (X/Y) of management.

    e. The monetary incentives are considered to be ------ (hygiene factors / motivators).

    f. Whose role has a higher task significance? Programmer or Project Manager? -----

    g. The team morale will be high under the ----- (command / consensus) style of decision-making.

    h. Brainstorming emphasizes on the ------- (quality / quantity) of ideas generated.

    i. When the acceptance is more important than the quality, the style of decision-making adopted is ------.

    j. A good project manager creates the circumstances in which a team member ---- (fears / trusts) him / her.

    k. As the team becomes more and more cohesive, the project manager needs to have a (less / more) tight control over the team.

    l. The productivity of a team is the highest in the ----- stage.

    m. Challenging targets ------ (motivate / frustrate) the team members.

    n. In the ------ (norming / storming) stage, the team leader should show a higher level of directive management.

    o. In the ----- stage, it is more likely that the team leader will lead from behind.

    p. In the -----stage, the difference of opinion among the team members is accentuated.

    q. The application developed in an obsolete technology failed repeatedly. Would this affect the morale of a team? ----

    r. Ahead of the meeting, the purpose of the meeting should be expressed in the meeting ------ (agenda / minutes).

    s. The team is stuck in converting the business logic to code. This is addressed in the ------ meeting.

t.   Summarizing discussions in your own words periodically is ------.

u.   The ----- (negative / positive) criticism is ok, provided it helps in the ----- (demolition / improvement) of the employee.

3.   Choose the most appropriate answer:

a.   Which of the following may be said to include the other three traits?
   i.   Decision-making
   ii.   Leadership
   iii. Motivation
   iv.   Problem solving

b.   Which is not an explicit criterion for the evaluation of the solutions?
   i.   Cost of implementation
   ii.   Ease of implementation
   iii. Feasibility of the solution
   iv.   Quality of the solution

c.   The mathematical solutions may be classified under ------
   i.   fuzzy solutions
   ii.   heuristics
   iii. intuition
   iv.   rational decisions

d.   Fishbone diagram is used to
   i.   evaluate solutions.
   ii.   generate ideas.
   iii. conduct root cause analysis.
   iv.   arrive at an unique solution.

e.   Which of the following is not a group decision-making?
   i.   Brainstorming
   ii.   Consensus
   iii. Consultation
   iv.   Optimization

f. A project manager can empower his team members by

   i.   delegation of authority

   ii. provision of adequate resources

   iii. reward and punishment

   iv. setting ambitious targets

g. Which of the following can affect a team adversely?

   i.   Challenging assignment

   ii. Prolonged client exposure

   iii. Inconsistent travel policies

   iv. Working on multiple technologies.

h. At which stage are the team expectations set?

   i.   Forming

   ii. Norming

   iii. Performing

   iv. Storming

i. What is likely to affect the performance of a team at the performing stage?

   i.   Lack of team cohesion

   ii. Interpersonal problems

   iii. Lack of resources

   iv. Poor understanding of what is expected of the team

j. Which of the following is the best medium for feedbacks?

   i.   Email

   ii. Face-to-face

   iii. SMS

   iv. Telephone

k. In which of these situations is the video conferencing preferred?

   i.   When the body language of the participants is important for the communication

   ii. When the participants are in diverse geographies

   iii. When the cost of travel is high

   iv. All of these

l. What could be the reason for the lack of communication between the technical staff and the users?

   i.   Individual bias
   ii.   Lack of English language proficiency
   iii. Technical jargons
   iv.   Difference in the academic qualifications

m. Which is the advantage of the written communication over the oral communication?

   i.   Clarity
   ii.   Faster creation of messages
   iii. Ability to express emotions
   iv.   Ability to handle the audience questions

n. When is the telephonic message preferred over email?

   i.   When big reports need to be attached as a part of the message
   ii.   When many persons need to be communicated simultaneously
   iii. When a record of the message is necessary
   iv.   When an urgent action is needed

o. Which of the following may not be a part of the meeting minutes?

   i.   Action points
   ii.   To whom the actions are assigned
   iii. Discussion points
   iv.   Ground rules for the discussion

p. Punctual beginnings and timely endings of meetings

   i.   show the team members that the project manager means business.
   ii.   show the control the project manager has over his team.
   iii. are difficult to enforce in the software organizations.
   iv.   help organize several meetings in a day.

q. Gantt chart is presented as a part of the

   i.   problem resolution meeting
   ii.   project review meeting
   iii. stand-up meeting
   iv.   daily status meeting

r. Paraphrasing is a method of

    i.   understanding the background

    ii. checking back

    iii. clarity of expression

    iv. increasing credibility

s. A lab session is the ------ phase of training

    i.   do

    ii. review

    iii. show

    iv. tell

t. Which is an advantage of email?

    i.   Ease of use

    ii. Ability to capture emotions

    iii. Suitable for immediate action

    iv. Suited for personal interaction

u. Which of the following may not be decided before a meeting?

    i.   Action plan

    ii. Attendees

    iii. Duration

    iv. Purpose

v. What should a project manager do to keep the meeting moving?

    i.   Conduct the meeting in the brainstorming mode.

    ii. Keep the end time of the meeting open to facilitate the closure of all the pending issues.

    iii. Whenever the team is stuck in a point going round and round, insist that the issue is resolved before moving to the next point.

    iv. Periodic summary of discussions thus far.

w. The daily status meetings are better conducted in

    i.   a conference room

    ii. the development area

    iii. the project manager's cabin

    iv. the sponsor's cabin

x. Stand-up meetings are preferred

    i.   for the client meetings.
    ii. for the formal presentations.
    iii. when a solution to a technical problem is sought.
    iv. for quick regular updates.

y. Which of the following causes message distortion?

    i.   Converting from analogue to digital
    ii. Usage of email
    iii. Choice of an inappropriate expression
    iv. Use of the local language

z. What could be a possible issue in observing an employee whether (s)he abides by your instruction?

    i.   Once the job is given to the employee, better leave him / her alone.
    ii. Observations tend to be impersonal.
    iii. Observations tend to become intrusive.
    iv. It takes a lot of time of the supervisor.

aa. Fairness of observation is ensured by

    i.   checking your conclusions with the employee.
    ii. being comforting.
    iii. concentrating on the important aspects of the job.
    iv. being fast.

ab. Which phase of training gives feedback?

    i.   Doing
    ii. Reviewing
    iii. Showing
    iv. Telling

ac. Which of the following is a good personal feedback?

    i.   You are stammering and hence unfit for presentations.

    ii. Initial test reports showed that your error rate was nearly 3 per 1000 lines. In the last quarter, it has improved to 2 /1000.

    iii. You are a dull person.

    iv. The Java programmers generally tend to be less productive than the VB programmers.

4. CEOs switch companies for higher economic returns. Does it mean that their basic needs have not been fulfilled? How can this be explained in terms of Maslow's hierarchy of needs?

5. What would be the criteria you would apply in deciding to follow the X or the Y style of management?

6. Describe the typical traits of a laissez-faire manager.

7. The people management skills are more important than the technical skills for a project manager - Discuss.

8. Software personnel find it challenging to work in teams. As a project manager, how would you address this issue?

9. In every project, the work output of some teams is more critical to the success of the project than the others. Sometimes, these team leaders and members expect a preferential treatment. As a project manager how would you handle this situation so that all the team members remain motivated?

15

MONITORING AND CONTROLLING A PROJECT

The ruler attains wholeness in the correct governance of the people. - Lao Tzu

15.1 Learning objectives

The control mechanisms during the execution of a project are discussed here. Under this head we will learn about

- the reports that are needed to be obtained by a project manager from his / her team and the reports submitted by the project manager.
- a cost control technique called the Earned Value Management.

15.2 Activities during this phase

Monitoring the schedule, the cost and the scope are the important activities in this phase. Towards this, a project manager needs to establish

- a reporting mechanism which includes the report format, the audience, the medium and the frequency
- an effective cost control mechanism.

- a method to manage the scope changes.
- an approach to the problem escalation.

With a lot of day-to-day activities and continuous interaction with the users, the execution phase is subject to a high level of external influences and that is why control is included as a concurrent activity with this phase.

15.3 Project status reporting

The project manager should elicit reports from his / her team leaders on a periodic basis and (s)he in turn should send reports to the higher level management and the client management. The reports could be

- for the current period only – covering changes since the last report.
- cumulative – total of what happened from the beginning.
- exception report – highlighting only the deviant areas requiring the management attention

Typical reports in a project:

15.3.1 Team's status report to project manager

The first level status reports submitted by the team leads to the project manager are normally submitted every week and these should contain the following:

- Which are the activities that were scheduled to start last week?
- Were they all started as per the schedule?
- Which are the activities that were scheduled to complete last week?
- Were they all completed as per the schedule?
- In case of delay, reasons:
  - o   Delayed start / completion of previous activit(y/ies)
  - o   Non-availability of resources – human, hardware, software
  - o   Pending from the client side
- Action required from the team / project manager / management / client management

- Action planned from the team side
- Will the delay impact the project schedule?
- Should this be communicated to the management?
- Should this be communicated to the client management?

(The last two questions are necessary such that the delays that are controllable within the team are not propagated and unnecessary panic avoided).

- Any other unscheduled activity that was undertaken last week.

15.3.2 Project manager's status report to the management / client

Normally this is done on a monthly basis and is consolidated from the teams' reports and is at a higher level of detail.

The project manager may also be required to make a presentation on the status, when (s)he may use more graphical tools such as the Work Breakdown structure, the Gantt chart or the network diagrams to show the planned vs. actual activities.

15.3.3 Exception reports

The status report may also be prepared as an exception report showing only the deviations from the schedule. When there are a large number of activities, these reports are useful.

The stoplight report is a form of an exception report; it is an effective presentation method, which shows the status of activities with a colour indicator:

Green	Amber	Red
Under Control	Deviation, but can be controlled	Deviation, needs intervention from the higher levels

Fig. 15.1. Exception Reports

15.3.4 Variance reports

These reports talk about the cost management of a project. The head wise cumulative allocations of the budget are compared with the cumulative expenses till that period and the variances are highlighted. The reasons for the adverse variances need to be explained by the project manager.

15.4 Cost control

We already discussed that this is the weakest area of many project managers because of their technical background.

Let us take this example of Elate Enterprises to understand the issues in cost control and progress reporting:

Elate Enterprises

Elate Enterprises is a small software company promoted by the two sisters, Ms. Articulate and Ms. Emulate.

The company is currently developing a software solution and has budgeted an amount of INR 15 million for it.

Following is the latest project progress report on the table of Ms.Articulate:

Task	Budgeted person days	Actual person days
Feasibility Study	2	5
System Study	15	22
Design	25	45
Code & Test	30	
System integration	3	

Ms. Palate, the Financial Controller is happy that only 80% of the money allocated for the project has been spent and she congratulates Mr. Simulate, the Project lead for an effective cost control. Can you unveil the true picture?

The technology-specific terms used by a project manager may not convey much to the senior management. There is also a problem in comparing different projects and their progress. A good method would be to bring all the reporting to a single measure, meaningful to the managements – money.

15.4.1 Earned value management

15.4.1.1 Terms

- The **planned value (PV),** formerly called the budgeted cost of work scheduled (BCWS), is that portion of the approved total cost estimate planned to be spent on an activity during a given period.
- **Actual cost (AC),** formerly called the actual cost of work performed (ACWP), is the total of direct and indirect costs incurred in accomplishing an activity during a given period.
- The **earned value (EV),** formerly called the budgeted cost of work performed (BCWP), is an estimate of the value of the physical work actually completed.

15.4.1.2 Formulas

- Schedule variance   SV = EV – PV
- Cost variance   CV = EV – AC

The same may be expressed as ratios:

- Schedule performance index   SPI = EV / PV
- Cost performance index   CPI = EV / AC
- Control ratio   CR = SPI * CPI

The control ratio could be a comparative measure across projects. Based on the indexes, we can recompute the target date of completion and the budget.

- Estimated time to complete = Original estimate / SPI
- Cost at completion = original budget / CPI

Using these formulas analyze the performance of Elate Enterprises.

Practice Questions

1. State whether true or false:

    a. Cumulative report includes the current period data.
    b. Gantt Chart can show the progress of a project on a particular date.
    c. EV can never be > PV.
    d. On the basis of the EV calculations, we may conclude that the Elate Enterprises project is under control.
    e. Control ratio could be a good performance indicator of a project to compare with other projects.

2. Fill in the blanks with the appropriate terms:

    a. The difference between the actual and the planned costs is called ------.
    b. The higher levels of management prefer a ----- (detailed / summary) report.
    c. When a report highlights only the delayed activities, it is a(n) ------ (exception / stoplight) report.
    d. In a stoplight report, the activities which are under control will be shown with a ----- colour indicator.
    e. Graphs ----- (improve / reduce) the expressiveness of a report.
    f. PV is also referred to as -----.
    g. Against a PV of 15 million, EV is 12 million; Project completion is ----%.

3. Choose the most appropriate answer:

    a. The formatting of a report is required to improve the
        i.   utility for decision-making
        ii. readability
        iii. understandability
        iv. all of these

b. Why does the senior management prefer the summary reports?

   i. Details are not helpful in the managerial decision making.

   ii. Details may camouflage a holistic perspective.

   iii. The graphical outputs cannot be prepared from the details.

   iv. The senior management may find it difficult to understand the details.

c. Which activities in a stoplight report do not require intervention from outside the team?

   i. Green and Red

   ii. Red and Amber

   iii. Only Red

   iv. Amber and Green

d. On which of the activities should a project manages focus more?

   i. Amber

   ii. Green

   iii. Red

   iv. All of these

e. Which of these data will be available from the Accounts department?

   i. AC

   ii. BCWS

   iii. EV

   iv. PV

f. Which is an indicator of the project progress?

   i. AC

   ii. ACWP

   iii. EV

   iv. PV

g. No more budgetary allocation is required when

   i. $CPI < 1$

   ii. $CPI = 1$

   iii. $SPI < 1$

   iv. $SPI = 1$

h. A change in SV will directly impact

    i.   CV

    ii. CPI

    iii. EV

    iv. SPI

i. The activity completion report is the best, when presented

    i.   as a listing of the balance activities.

    ii. in a chronological order of planned vs. actual dates of completion.

    iii. as separate reports of critical and non-critical activities.

    iv. in the order of the importance of the activities.

j. Gantt Chart is a(n) ------ report

    i.   exception

    ii. project status

    iii. stoplight

    iv. variance

k. PV is not included in the calculation of the

    i.   cost variance

    ii. estimated time to complete

    iii. schedule performance index

    iv. schedule variance

4. "War too is a project" declared Caesar. He could see that this war, of all his wars is slipping out of hands. "In 10 days flat, the Gauls should have been out. But it is 11 days since we started the war and still we have progressed only 10%. On manpower we have replenished all the attritions and so that cannot be an excuse. My treasury is becoming bankrupt with this war. I did not estimate that we would have to spend more than 2 m liras for the whole war and we are already down by 3.5 m liras". Could you decipher when the war would come to an end and how much would it cost at this rate?

16

CHANGE CONTROL AND CONFIGURATION MANAGEMENT

Life is a series of spontaneous and natural changes. Don't resist them
- that only creates sorrow. Let reality be reality – Lao Tzu

16.1 Learning objectives

This chapter describes in detail:

*   What is configuration management?
*   How challenging is the configuration management?
*   Tasks involved in the configuration management.

As part of the configuration management, the steps in change control are discussed in detail.

16.2 What is configuration management?

Identifying, organizing, controlling and communicating the modifications to software is called the configuration management.

16.3 **What is software configuration?**

What constitutes software? At the beginning of the book we asked this question to be answered later. Now is the time.

Often the words programs and software are used synonymously. But the very suffix 'ware' indicates that software consists of more than one component.

Software consists of

- Programs (both at the source and the executable levels)
- Documents, which are the records of the processes underlying the programs
- Data required to test the program

All these components need to be stored together. The complication arises because programs are changed frequently and any change in a program will certainly impact the executable and the associated documentation and may also have an impact on the test data.

Each component of the software configuration is referred to as a configuration object or item.

16.4 **Challenges in software configuration management**

As the software project progresses, a large number of changes will be initiated. Imagine when hundreds of programs and documents undergo changes by different people - what could be their impact? With so many versions of each program available, there is a possibility that somebody may not use the current corrected version of the program; also there may be an inconsistency between what the program does and what the program document portrays it to be doing. The problem could become more acute, when the program is handed over for maintenance without the correct documentation.

That is why the configuration management is considered to be a very important process in a software organization and the capability maturity model specifies this as a key process area in the level 2 itself.

16.5 Baseline

Since each of the configuration items – programs, documents and data files - will undergo several changes, there should be an approved version of each of these at any point of time: we define a baseline for each of these items in this context.

Baseline is defined as a *specification / product that has been formally reviewed and agreed upon that thereafter serves as the basis for further development and that can be changed only through the formal change control procedures.*

Defining a baseline is important because the baseline is the current version of the configuration object and thus any change requested has to be made only on this. A role identified as the configuration controller will maintain all the configuration items of a project along with the history of the versions of the item. This is important to understand how an item has evolved over different versions. In case any change in a configuration item does not produce the desired result, then the changes need to be rolled back to the baselined version.

16.6 Functions of configuration management

Organizations maintain separate directories / servers for development, testing and production. In a development organization, the production server, which has the image of the product components available in the client environments, will be under the custody of the configuration controller, whose responsibilities include

- Maintaining a directory of the different components required to build a product with a brief description of each component;
- providing version numbers for all the configuration items facilitating unique identification;
- controlling the access to and the change of the components;
- providing the information on the impact of the possible changes;
- maintaining a matrix of which component is linked to which other;
- providing information on the status of the configuration items.

16.7 Software Configuration Management (SCM) tasks

16.7.1 Identification of configuration items

There are a large number of configuration items in each project – programs, documents such as the SRS, the design document, the project plan, the test plan etc. and the data files. Each of them need to be tracked through several changes. So each of these items needs to be uniquely identified. A good identifier would be

Client name / project name/ type of item (such as prog. doc) / sub classification (SRS, executable) / identifier (prog. no., doc no.)

The level of granularity of an item that needs an unique identification needs to be determined. For example, an SRS could be identified as an object (aggregate object), with each of its chapters as a basic object. An aggregate object is thus a collection of the basic objects. The question arises whether a chapter should be a basic object or a paragraph in a chapter.

The granularity is an important decision. If a whole document is identified as an object, for every few changes the entire document and its version number need to be changed. On the other hand, defining the identifiers at a detailed level will increase the number of items to be monitored.

A directory is created with the items thus identified. This list will also contain the set of items that are associated with each of these items. For example, a program will be linked to the data referenced by it, the program specification, the user documentation etc.

A typical configuration directory will have the following information:

- Project identifier
- Item identifier
- Baselined version
- Item description
- Date on which the baseline was created

- Item attributes
- Owner
- Users
- Producer

(For example, the owner of an inventory program is inventory / stores manager, the users are the stores clerks and the producer is the concerned programmer)

- Linked items
- Location of the item (directory and path)
- Status (such as the item released for change, under test, under review, approved, installed at client site)
- Copies available at (if a copy of an item is stored in some other location(s) (the location could be a physical location or another directory / server) – for example, the project plan may be available on the organizational intranet and on-site in a physical form. This information is recorded so that any change in the item needs to be reflected in all the locations to ensure consistency).
- Date released for change (in case an item has been released for change)
- Reference: issue ticket no(s) against which this version has been created

The configuration directory will also maintain the relationship of objects with version numbers such as

Design document 4.5 = Chapter 1 4.3+Chapter 2 5.6+........+ chapter n 5.7

16.7.2 Version control

Version control is the core of the configuration management. The complexity of the version control increases with a need to maintain multiple baselined versions of a program and hence the associated objects simultaneously.

For example, a gaming app may be released for Android and IOS. This would mean that there will be a common base component and a part of the application will be specific to each operating system and each of the components in this part will have two baselined versions.

Maintaining the version history assumes an additional importance in the product companies, which need to track the version number of the product at the client sites. Whenever there is a change / upgrade request from a client, the information on the current version number, from which the upgrade is requested, is important.

16.7.3 Change control

Right from the beginning, we have been arguing that change is a reality right through the development life cycle and beyond and hence a challenge in a software project. While the outright rejection of the change requests is a privilege not available to the software project managers (unlike in several other disciplines), accepting all the change requests would land the project in trouble. How best a project manager is able to control change determines his / her success. Change control is a multi-step elaborate procedure and a project manager should ensure the discipline of change control.

Steps in change control:

- Change request: The request for change normally comes from the user. It could be due to an enhanced scope or because of a bug in a program. At times the developer himself/herself might propose to make a change / improvement in the program. A sample change request form is shown in Fig. 16.1. Each change request is given a serial number. The date is important because the resolution cycle time is an important metric for the change control. In case the resolution does not happen within the pre-agreed time, the issue needs to be escalated and the escalation matrix as to whom and after the lapse of how much time an issue should be escalated should be shared with the client.

Change request no.	Date

Project name

Change requested by

Description of the change requested

Impact of the change (to be filled by a technical member of the project team)

Business justification

Action (to be filled by the change control authority)

Approved by	Date

Fig 16.1. Change request form

- Evaluation by the developer: When a user requests a functionality change / scope extension / user interface modification, (s)he may not understand the effort involved in implementing the change. A change in one part of the program could undo some other feature. In extreme cases, it may also require architectural changes. The developers, who have an understanding of the program, need to make an evaluation of the impact of the change request, particularly in terms of the schedule and the cost. In some cases, the impact may be on the quality aspect of the application such as reliability and may also be on the risk exposure. Incorporating these, the developer(s) prepare(s) an impact report.

- Decision by the change control authority: Every user organization should have an identified role of a change control authority; some prefer a group called the change control board. It is a (group of) business manager(s), capable of assessing a change from the business perspective, who should don this role. Users at the operating level often request for changes without understanding the cost involved. A business manager could assess the business justification of the change request and weigh it against the costs involved and make a decision of accepting wholly or partly / rejecting the change request.
- Generation of change order: For the accepted change requests, the project manager raises a change order, which is essentially a request / authorization for the configuration controller to release the relevant programs and also assigns the programmer(s) who would implement the change.
- Release of the configuration objects: The configuration controller moves a copy of the relevant configuration objects with a password assigned to them to the development directory. This process is called the check-out. The password is then released to the assigned programmer(s). This is to ensure the accountability for the changes made. Any unintended change introduced in the program inadvertently or otherwise, if detected later, can be traced back to the perpetrator.
- Change in the configuration objects: Not only are the programs changed in this step, but the associated configuration items such as the documents too. In fact, a good programming discipline warrants that the change is made in the document first and then in the program. "Write, do what is written and then check what you have done is what you have written" is the sequence of steps recommended for the effective change management.
- Quality control tasks: The changed programs are tested and the document changes reviewed. The data changes, if any, are also checked.
- Baseline for the changed configuration items: The configuration controller updates the configuration directory with the changes made and increments the version number of the changed configuration items
- Rebuilding the software: The configuration controller moves the changed objects to the configuration directory / server – this is called the check-in. Then (s)he builds the new version of the software and on

a date, agreed with the users, releases it to the production environment. Normally, the configuration controller will consolidate a few change requests to build a new version. The users are intimated on the changes made and the reasons thereof beforehand.

16.7.3.1 Change control issues

We have already discussed the access control issue, which is resolved through a password. Another issue that is needed to be addressed is when simultaneously the same program is assigned to two programmers for changes. In such a situation, the program that is checked in later will overwrite the changes made earlier. This is addressed by the synchronization control, which locks any object released for change, so that it is again not released for another change. Only when the changed object is checked in, the object is released for any further change. There are tools available in the market which can manage concurrent changes as well without losing any change.

16.7.4 Configuration audit

Elaborate change control procedures have to be adopted to ensure the configuration integrity. A single omission by one individual can lead to the application failure. The configuration audit is a control measure to prevent this. On a periodic basis, this audit is performed. A few change requests are selected at random and their entire sequence of actions till the version release is checked to ascertain that the change control procedures have been religiously followed. And the compliance or otherwise is reported to the management.

The configuration management, being elaborate and rule bound, is better managed by tools. Microsoft Visual SourceSafe (VSS), Concurrent Version System (CVS) and Rational Clearcase are some of the most popular configuration management tools.

Practice Questions

1. State whether true or false:

   a. Once a project has started, no change in the scope should be entertained.
   b. The rules imposed by an external agency other than the client will not have any impact on the software.
   c. During the course of the development, the user should not suggest any improvement to the software.
   d. All components will have the same version number as the product.
   e. A justification is mandatory for a change request.
   f. Every change request will result in a new version of the product.
   g. Every change may not require a review by the QA.
   h. The configuration objects are those which undergo changes.
   i. Only the customer can initiate a change and not the software supplier.
   j. Only the functional requirements and not the non-functional requirements will impact a change in the scope.
   k. The current version of the software in use by the users is the baselined version.
   l. Any change requested by a user, by default, will be implemented in the baselined version.
   m. Basic objects do not have a version number.
   n. More than one version of a component cannot be active simultaneously.
   o. With the change of a few components, an Android app may be able to work under IOS.
   p. A change request can be initiated only by the change control authority.
   q. A baseline is maintained only for the product and not for each component.
   r. After a change in the components, the product may be released with the same version number as the previous one.
   s. When the delivery date is nearing, a project manager may say no to a change request.
   t. All changes will affect the schedule of a project.

2. Fill in the blanks with the appropriate terms:

  a. Configuration management is a key process area in CMM level ----.
  b. Programs may be available in two states: ------ and -----.
  c. Identifying the objects at a higher granular level will result in ----
      (more / less) frequent version changes of the final product.
  d. The ------ management is a process required as a consequence of the ---
      -- management (change, configuration)
  e. The change management addresses the changes in ----- (schedule /
      scope / cost) of a project.
  f. System manual is a(n) ------- (aggregate / basic) object.
  g. A(n) ----- object consists of ----- objects (aggregate, basic).
  h. When a program is changed, there will necessarily be a change in -----.
  i. When the copy of the programs are moved from the production
      directory to the development directory, it is called -----.

3. Choose the most appropriate answer:

  a. Software configuration denotes
      i.   data
      ii.   documentation
      iii. programs
      iv.   all of the above

  b. Which is a good configuration identifier?
      i.   Data 5.2
      ii.   .exe
      iii. FinAccts program
      iv.   SPM / doc / Usermanual 5.3

  c. The access control for changes will
      i.   ensure accountability.
      ii.   improve the confidentiality of the product.
      iii. allow simultaneous changes in the same program.
      iv.   improve security.

d. Which is the responsibility covered under the software configuration management?

    i. Studying the impact of the change requested

    ii. Maintaining the information of the components used and their versions

    iii. Resolving the customer issues

    iv. Maintaining information on the server configuration

e. Which of the following is a configuration object?

    i. Change request

    ii. CPU

    iii. SRS

    iv. Variables

f. The impact of a change is studied by the

    i. change control authority

    ii. developer

    iii. project manager

    iv. user

g. A change may have an impact on

    i. cost of the project

    ii. quality of deliverables

    iii. schedule of the project

    iv. all of the above

h. When there are too many change requests, most of them genuine, which is the best option for a Project Manager?

    i. Accept the requests and delay the delivery.

    ii. Decline the requests.

    iii. Implement the more important changes, make a delivery, move the remaining changes to the next release.

    iv. Implement the changes, but save time by reducing the QA tasks.

i. Synchronization control will

    i.   allow only the authorized access.

    ii. limit the number of changes.

    iii. prevent parallel access to the same program.

    iv. synchronize the production directory with the development directory.

j. Releasing the programs for change is the responsibility of the

    i.   change control authority

    ii. configuration controller

    iii. developer

    iv. project manager

k. The checked out object remains locked by synchronization control until

    i.   the engineer modifies the object.

    ii. the QA review of the changes.

    iii. the object is checked in.

    iv. a new version is released.

l. The configuration audit ensures that

    i.   the unauthorized changes have not taken place.

    ii. the change control process is in place.

    iii. all the identified configuration objects are available.

    iv. all of the above

17

RELEASE MANAGEMENT

There are really three parts to the creative process. First there is inspiration, then there is execution and finally there is the release. – Eddie Van Halen

17.1 Learning objectives

This chapter details the function of the release management:

- Importance of the release management
- Responsibilities of the function
- Challenges involved in discharging the function

17.2 What is release management?

An elaborate release management function is unique to the product companies and normally falls under the ambit of the product support. A product working in several client installations needs to be provided with the bug fixes – also known as patches – and the product enhancements.

17.2.1 Functions of release management

A software product is composed of several components. These components need to be integrated as a package. Release management should ensure that

- the right components are included.
- all the components included have reached the approved status - we addressed both these issues as a part of the configuration management.
- all the associated information (details of which are listed in a later paragraph) with each release is included in the release package.
- the customer is informed of the changes from the previous release.
- the release is distributed to the different sites.
- the customer installation is rolled back to the previous release, in case the new release encounters some problems at the site.
- a directory is maintained with location wise version details with the operating environment information.

17.3 Why is release management challenging?

- When multiple components are included, how do we ensure that all the components are the right ones and have reached the 'approved' status?
- Many products are released for multiple operating environments. Release management needs to ensure that the right components appropriate to the environment, be sent to each site.
- An operational product is changed to a new version. How do we ensure that the changes do not result in a malfunctioning product?
- The situation becomes more complicated when different sites use different versions of the product. The release manager has to maintain this information and send the appropriate upgrades / patches.
- When a large number of the sites requires an upgrade, it is difficult to send the engineers for installation at each of the sites. The product development organizations send the upgrade, requiring the customers to install by themselves. This puts an added responsibility on the release management. The instructions for the installation and any batch file required for the installation should accompany the release package.

- Another issue that needs to be addressed is whether the entire changed product be released every time or only the changed components.
- Similarly, should a new set of documentation be sent for the entire product or only the changes need to be communicated?

17.4 Release identifier

Software releases are normally numbered as $n_1.n_2$ for example Windows 8.1.

Whenever the product has a substantially changed functionality, the version is incremented. For example, Oracle database 12 will have many features and functionalities distinctly different from version 11.

The second number is incremented when there are bug fixes or minor changes. For example ver12.1 will have minor changes over ver12.

17.5 Release package

The release manager creates a set of items to be included along with the software package. These include

- release name and identifier such as Oracle 12.1
- date of the release
- contact mail id and phone no of the concerned role in the release management function: these details are required for the client to contact in case of any issue
- a brief description of the release
  - o   Reason for the release
  - o   Benefits due to the release
- requisites for the installation
- steps in the installation
- date till which the previous version will be supported
- acknowledgement: this is a turn-around document which will be signed by the customer on receipt of the package and returned to the vendor.

Practice Questions

1. State whether true or false:

   a. Every new release will be an enhanced product over the previous one.
   b. The choice of the components for a package will be dependent on the operating environment in which the package will be used.
   c. Infrequent release of versions is an indication of a stable product.
   d. Software product organizations are obligated to service all the versions of the product perpetually.

2. Fill in the blanks with the appropriate terms:

   a. ------- is the function that ensures all the components ready for release have reached the 'approved' status.
   b. Release management is critical for a software ------ (product / project) company.
   c. Bug fixes are also known as -----.
   d. A batch file for installation is more useful when the ------ (customer / support engineer) installs the product.

3. Choose the most appropriate answer:

   a. The components for release will be picked from the
      i. configuration directory
      ii. customer installation
      iii. development directory
      iv. test directory

b. The customer complained that they have received the package for Linux, when they were operating in Windows. Which function could be responsible for this?

   i.   Configuration management
   ii. Development team
   iii. Quality assurance
   iv. Release management

c. When a new release malfunctions, which could be the best option for the client?

   i.   Debug the program.
   ii. Move the operating environment to the previous version.
   iii. Wait for the new release.
   iv. Roll back to the previous version.

d. The baselined version of the product is 6.1. Which of the following versions is likely to have a distinctly enhanced functionality?

   i.   6
   ii. 6.2
   iii. 7
   iv. Cannot say

e. Which of the following is a turn-around document?

   i.   Product acknowledgement
   ii. Change request
   iii. Configuration directory
   iv. Release note

18

EXPECTATION MANAGEMENT

Oft expectation fails, and most oft there
Where most it promises, and oft it hits
Where hope is coldest, and despair most fits
            -William Shakespeare in 'All's well that ends well'

18.1 Lesson objectives

This chapter discusses the following

- What is expectation management?
- What could be the possible ways in which a project manager may manage the customer expectations?

18.2 What is expectation management?

In the scope document, we defined the success criteria and at that time we said that these criteria should be defined from the user perspective. The purpose of the software projects is to meet the customer expectations. To emphasize the importance of expectations, the project triangle is redefined as the project diamond with expectations in the middle.

Fig. 18.1. Project triangle

Fig. 18.2. Project Diamond
(Adapted from Hamil (2005))

The following two extreme instances are often encountered in the software projects, when the CEO of the software development organization meets the senior management / CEO of the client organization:

Scenario 1:

The client gives a feedback on a project completed: "True, your team completed the project within time and the cost budget, but their client interactions could have been smoother" and several other faults of the team are narrated after the 'but'. Which means that somewhere the project team has fallen short of meeting the client expectations.

Scenario 2:

The client says "Yes. The project is delayed; but we believe that your team can make up for the delay. We appreciate their sincere efforts". Several such positive expressions follow for a project that has not met the deadline.

So the objective of a project is not just to meet the scope and the deadline requirements of the client, which are important by themselves, but there is something more that needs to be achieved to meet the client expectations.

Look at the following example:

- The customer wants an elephant to be arranged for a wedding at home.
  - Situation 1: You deliver a sick elephant on the wedding day.
  - Situation 2: You told the customer one week before the wedding that you can only arrange for a horse and arranged for a horse on the wedding day.

In which of the cases have you managed the customer expectation better? How is that in the second instance even though the delivery falls short of the original specification, the customer is found more satisfied than in situation 1? Is it just because you alerted the client one week before?

To an extent we discussed this as a part of the scope management process (Recall Fig. 3.1). The customer expectations are not only affected by what you deliver, but also how you deliver.

Look at this example for the process differentiation:

In a restaurant

Waiter 1 served whatever you ordered, but with no smile on his face and he also placed the plates with a thud.

Waiter 2 spilled water on your pant, but was profusely apologetic and wiped your trousers with tissues.

What makes you more inclined to appreciate the services(?) of the second waiter, even though there was a clear service deficiency?

In the hospitality industry, the process differentiators in the service offerings may easily be visible. What could be the differentiators in the software industry?

Expectation management is about managing the perceptions of a client. A project manager's success would depend upon how well (s)he is able to influence the stakeholders.

18.3 When is expectation management important?

In the SDLC, when do we start worrying about the expectation management? In fact, this precedes the SDLC. The customer expectations are built at the pre-sales stage itself. In fact, during the sales stage, a hype is created about the deliveries that when the project is initiated, the customer starts with exaggerated expectations – some of them unrealistic. The project manager's job is rendered more challenging because of this. (S)he has to start moderating the expectations without creating any disillusionment in the minds of the customer.

Modelled after Gartner's hype cycle[58], we may look at the expectation cycle in the following way[59]:

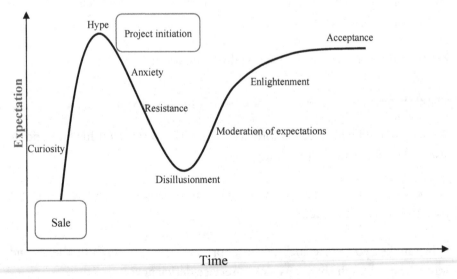

Fig 18.3. Expectation Cycle

---

[58]   Gartner Hype Cycle is a graphical representation of the maturity and adoption of technologies and applications.
[59]   A similar curve – emotional journey – is described by Ian Gambles (Gambles, 2009)

The reality starts dawning on the customer when the application development starts; but the expectation continues to be rising even as the development progresses. So the responsibility of the expectation management continues through the entire development life cycle. It needs to be recognized that the customer satisfaction is not just influenced by what is delivered but what is perceived to have been delivered.

A cautionary note here: there will be a large number of users in any client organization. Trying to match everybody's expectation is a losing game. The project manager should recognize who the decision-makers and who the passengers are.

18.4 A technique for expectation management

Hamil (2005) suggests a technique called the Expectation Management Matrix (EMM), which may be useful. Hamil argues that among the parameters of the scope triangle, there is a priority, which could be different for different projects. But when you ask the users they will always say that all are of equal importance. It is for the business analyst / project manager to unearth the priorities.

Priority Parameter	1	2	3
Cost			
Time			
Scope and Quality			

Fig 18.4. Expectation Management Matrix

Hamil goes on to explain how the priorities could be identified by taking a famous example – perhaps the most famous project of the last century – man's moon landing mission.

President Kennedy committed the nation to the grand project by the visionary statement "....before this decade is out, of landing a man on the moon and returning him safely to the Earth"[60]. As for the budget, "I am asking the

---

[60] This speech was delivered before a joint session of Congress on May 25, 1961.

Congress and the country to accept a firm commitment to a new course of action, a course which will last for many years and carry very heavy costs: 531 million dollars in fiscal '62--an estimated 7 to 9 billion dollars additional over the next five years"[61].

Now let us apply EMM to this historic project: From our understanding of the project, it is not difficult to identify that for this project, the scope is of the highest priority. The time will assume precedence over the cost, being more visible to the public.

Parameter \ Priority	1	2	3
Cost $ 9.5 billion till 67			✓
Time Till the end of 1969		✓	
Scope and Quality 1. landing a man on the moon 2. returning him safely to the earth	✓		

That NASA'a Apollo 11 mission landed two men on the moon on July 26. 1969 just before the end of the decade and Kennedy and his mission are remembered by the USA with pride and gratitude.

Does anybody know / care to know / remember that this project had a heavy cost overrun? Even if it was known, does it reduce the magnitude of the achievement? In fact Kennedy himself highlighted the need to commit unconstrained resources, when he said "If we are to go only half way, or reduce

61   http://www.space.com/11772-president-kennedy-historic-speech-moon-space.html accessed at 10.40 pm on 30/08/15.

our sights in the face of difficulty, in my judgment it would be better not to go at all."

This powerful example would have convinced you that it is possible to prioritize the parameters in every project. One thing that should be remembered is that the priority is not set from the perspective of the project team, but of the users. So a project manager should educate the users on the concept of the EMM and facilitate them to agree to the fact that there are priorities among the parameters and to identify the priorities. The expectation mismatch arises because of poor understanding of the priorities or trying to optimize all the parameters. Imagine NASA had made some compromises in their rockets with a view on the cost control!

Now have a relook at the project Annalakshmi (Chapter 14). Debate on what could be the priorities in this project,

- Should the project manager put the scope as the top priority and deliver all the functional requirements? Or should the portion related to the customer complaints be delivered first?
- Is the user-friendliness of the interface important? Or can the user-friendliness be sacrificed for some other feature / functionality?
- Should the functionalities be delivered before the election time to satisfy the ruling party?
- Should the project manager worry about the delays and the heavy costs of the changed functionalities suggested by the consultants and say no to them?
  And so on.

Based on the questions identify the priorities.

18.5 Prerequisites for managing expectations

Identification of the priorities helps a project manager choose the trade-offs in case of a conflict among the parameters of the scope triangle. In spite of the overt or covert identification of the priorities, the project manager cannot expect the client to stand by him / her in case of such trade-offs.

Towards managing expectation, the Project manager should additionally strive to cultivate trust among the users (Martin, 2011). If an atmosphere of trust is established, the users will stand by the project team at times of gaps in expectations.

Regular communication is an important step in establishing trust with the users. Higher user involvement results in greater user ownership of the project. By making them the owners of the project, the project manager makes them the stakeholders in managing the expectations. Once the dichotomous 'we-they' relationship is changed to 'we', the project manager has succeeded in influencing and managing the expectations.

With several users, it is always possible that everybody may not respond to the project manager's efforts uniformly. There will always be some converts and some sceptics and the majority neutral with neither affiliation nor animosity towards the project and / or the project team. The project manager should use the champions to convince the sceptics and convert the neutral majority. Meeting the adversaries in private individually rather than confronting them collectively could also be another strategy. (Recall consultation-based decision-making discussed in Chapter 14).

A consultant team has an accelerated exposure to several organizations, while the users have an in-depth exposure to one organization. Citing relevant examples from experience without hurting the organizational pride is a way to gain the respect and the trust of the users. Demonstration of knowledge, experience and expertise helps a project manager establish credibility with the client.

18.6 Technology – a tool in managing expectation

Right in the beginning, we identified the intangibility of software as a challenge in the project management. This is one of the main reasons why perceptions reign over reality in the software projects much more than in any other. It is not unusual in the case of software that on delivery the customer declares that this is not what (s)he wanted!

Technology today provides the tools and the techniques to overcome this:

- Prototypes: These could be used to show the customer and make him / her experience the look and feel of the final product. The mid-course corrections are easy and less costly.
- Proof-of-concept: A methodology / an application may be demonstrated on a pilot scale to convince the user of its efficacy.
- Agile methodology: Creating the working products in short sprints and evolving them over several such sprints is a preferred methodology for the applications with fuzzy requirements.

Practice Questions

1. State whether true or false:

    a. The customer expectations are influenced by how you deliver irrespective of what you deliver.
    b. When you manage reality, perceptions are automatically managed.
    c. As the project progresses, the customer expectations are hyped up.
    d. When a customer feels disillusioned, it is an indication of the project failure.
    e. When all the three parameters of the scope triangle are of equal importance, the EMM is not applicable.
    f. If the cost is of the lowest priority in a project, it means that the customer will not be worried about cost overruns.
    g. India's Mars Orbiter Mangalyan mission is admired for its remarkable economy in the investment. If we construct an EMM for this project, the cost will be of the highest priority.
    h. Scope will be of the highest priority in all projects.
    i. Higher user involvement in the project leads to inflated expectations.
    j. Trying to influence all the users together is an effective way of managing the expectations.
    k. A project will be deemed a failure even if one user's expectation is not met.
    l. Once a prototype is constructed, any change in the application is not possible.

2. Fill in the blank with an appropriate term:

    a. A project manager should attempt to satisfy the customer ------- (needs / wants).

3. Choose the most appropriate answer:

   a. Which is the parameter that is in the project triangle but not in the project diamond?
      i.   Cost
      ii. Scope
      iii. Time
      iv. None of these

   b. When does the expectation management start?
      i.   Pre-sales
      ii. Project initiation stage
      iii. Prototyping stage
      iv. Requirements elicitation stage

   c. What could be the implication of the cost being of the highest priority in the moon landing project?
      i.   If the available budget is not considered adequate for the project, the project will be aborted.
      ii. The mission will be achieved irrespective of the cost.
      iii. NASA will complete the project to the extent the budget permits.
      iv. The cost overruns will be compensated by the schedule overruns.

   d. A consultant wields influence over the client through
      i.   charisma
      ii. knowledge and experience
      iii. organizational position
      iv. explicitly stated rules

   e. The advantage of a prototype is that it
      i.   obviates the need for the system documentation.
      ii. exposes the user to the look and feel of the product early in the development cycle.
      iii. optimizes the processing part in the application.
      iv. reduces the time of development.

f. For which of the following applications is the agile methodology the most suitable?

    i.   Core banking application

    ii. Gaming

    iii. Rocket launch

    iv. Waterfall model applications

19

CLOSING A PROJECT

Again and again one is born, again and again one dies.
— Adi Sankaracharya

19.1 Lesson objectives

The project comes to a closure in this phase. This chapter details the activities done during this phase.

19.2 Steps in project closure

- Completing all the documentation
- Handing over the project deliverables to the client
- Obtaining the client acceptance
- Conducting the post-implementation audit
- Celebrating success

19.2.1 Project documentation

At this point of time, the current version of all the software documentation, incorporating all the changes to date, should be ready.

A representative list of documents:

- Scope document / Business case
- Proposal
- Business requirement document (BRD) / Product requirement document (PRD)
- Functional specification document (FSD) / System requirement specifications (SRS)
- Contract
- Work breakdown structure (WBS)
- WBS Dictionary
- Estimate with the basis of assumptions
- Schedule – Gantt chart / network diagrams
- Quality plan
- Project plan
- Design document
- Review reports
- Test reports
- Minutes of all the meetings
- Status reports
- Change notices, impact assessments, decisions by the change control authority
- Sample deliverables
- UAT reports
- System manual
- User manual
- Client acceptance certificate
- Post implementation audit report

Not all of these documents will be there in all the projects. While all the documents of a project will be uploaded in the project repository of the development organization, the selected ones, based on need and the contract specifications, will be handed over to the client.

- It is recommended that the project manager maintain a project diary right from the beginning of the project. This is a free format document in which the project manager will note down the important happenings in the project – particularly the problems and how they were overcome. This is a valuable learning for any organization and should be preserved in the repository for the future reference.

19.2.2 Deliverables

The fully tested software, after the user acceptance tests, is installed in the target server with the associated utilities. Apart from the software, there are several deliverables that need to be handed over to the client:

- Source code, if the contract demands it
- Documentation – selected from the list shown above as per the contract
- Training – Different sessions need to be planned for the Senior management, the IT department and the users
- Any other, as specified in the contract – for example, some organizations may request on-site support for a fixed period after installation.

19.2.3 Client acceptance

This is a critical and the final milestone in a project. On the basis of the satisfactory completion of the UAT and the full / substantial resolution of the issues that the users had raised, the client management, normally the project sponsor, signs an acceptance certificate. The final instalment of the project payment is normally tied to this and this is the documentary evidence for the project manager to communicate the successful completion of the project back home!

19.2.4 Post-implementation audit

Every software project has a purpose; it has an identified problem to address. This was what was specified at the initiation stage, when the scope document / business case was created. Now that the software has been implemented, it is the time to review whether the stated objectives have been fulfilled. This is also the time to review not only what was achieved but also how it was achieved. The review may be conducted by one level higher than the project manager along with the senior persons picked from the departments such as quality and the information security. Depending on the criticality of the project to the organization and to the client organization, even more senior people might be involved.

A sample set of questions that need to be addressed are

- Were the business objectives of the project fulfilled? Some objectives may be realized only after a few months of the run of the software. For example, for the inventory management software, we may have identified increase in the inventory ratio as an objective. Achieving the target inventory ratio may take a few months, but what may be checked is whether the ratio shows a non-trivial increasing trend.
- Was the project completed within the originally specified time and cost?
- Was the quality level achieved acceptable?
- Were the processes followed as per the standards specified by the organization / client?
- What were the lessons learned from the project? If we have to redo the same project, which are the activities we will do differently? Why?

Opinions of the actual users of the software and the senior management of the client organization are also elicited at this point of time to check if their expectations have been met.

19.2.5 Recognize the team's achievement

Recognition of the team's accomplishment is an important motivator. A project manager should not fail to recognize every individual's contribution in public.

The project manager should also ensure the celebration of the success in a get-together..

The success should also be communicated across the organization through the formal channels.

All's well that ends well – William Shakespeare

_____*****_____

Practice Questions

1. State whether true or false:

    a. At the time of the software hand-over, all the issues would invariably have been resolved.

2. Fill in the blanks with the appropriate terms:

    a. Documents are a part of the ------- (deliverables / process areas) in a software project.
    b. The project success criteria are defined in the ----- (business / technical) terms.
    c. Which document will contain the lessons learned in a project? -----
    d. Status reports need to be submitted to the ----- (client / team).

3. Choose the most appropriate answer:

    a. Which of the following document should be handed over to the client at the end of a project?
        i.   Non-disclosure agreement
        ii. Proposal
        iii. RFP
        iv. User manual

    b. In a scope document, under which head are the business value expectations of the project mentioned?
        i.   Functional requirements
        ii. Objectives
        iii. Impact on the organization
        iv. Success criteria

c. The report formats are likely to be included in the

    i.   project diary

    ii. SRS

    iii. system manual

    iv. user manual

d. In which document are the acceptance criteria detailed?

    i.   Design document

    ii. Scope document

    iii. SRS

    iv. UAT

e. A system manual contains the same details as the

    i.   business requirement document

    ii. design document

    iii. SRS

    iv. user manual

f. Chronologically, which is the document that is created first in a project life cycle?

    i.   Business case

    ii. Gantt chart

    iii. Project plan

    iv. WBS dictionary

g. Client acceptance procedures are derived from the

    i.   acceptance certificate

    ii. acceptance criteria

    iii. post implementation audit

    iv. user acceptance tests

h. Identify a project deliverable.

    i.   Business case

    ii. Maintenance contract

    iii. Server license

    iv. User training

i. Which of the following is critical for considering the project to be complete?

   i.   Software installation
   ii. Post-implementation audit
   iii. Sign-off by the customer
   iv. Completion of user acceptance tests

j. Which process checks the fulfilment of the success criteria?

   i.   Documentation
   ii. Post-implementation audit
   iii. Sign-off by the customer
   iv. User acceptance tests

k. In which phase should the acceptance criteria be defined?

   i.   Controlling
   ii. Execution
   iii. Initiation
   iv. Planning

l. In case the customer disputes the completion of the project, the arbitrator will check (the fulfilment of) the

   i.   acceptance criteria
   ii. contract clauses
   iii. proposal commitments
   iv. user acceptance test results

m. Which of these activities is performed at the project closure stage?

   i.   Budgeting
   ii. Celebrating success
   iii. Controlling
   iv. Project definition

4. What is the importance of data migration in a software project?

5. Establish the criticality of documentation in a software project.

6. Some team members deliberately avoid concurrent documentation to create indispensability. How would you ensure that this does not happen?

Annexure I

TECHNIQUES OF COST-BENEFIT ANALYSIS

<u>Return on Investment (RoI) method:</u> RoI is the ratio of the net gain to the investment in the project. This method is particularly useful when multiple projects need to be compared.

Net gain =benefits from the project in the monetary terms – cost of the project

RoI = Net gain / Cost of the project

<u>Risk adjusted RoI:</u> The Net Present Values (NPV) of the costs and the benefits are calculated for the RoI calculation. The NPV method takes into account the time value of money and is discussed in the next paragraph.

<u>Net Present value method:</u> This method is also called the Discounted Cash Flow Method. Since a project may span across a long duration and its benefits will flow over a period for several years, it is necessary to take into account the time value of money in calculating the returns. The NPV method does this by bringing all the costs and the benefits to the current period applying a rate suggested by the management as the desired return rate.

NPV = Total benefits discounted to the current period – total cash outflows discounted to the current period.

The project is undertaken only if NPV $\geq$ 0. In case the NPV is negative, the project is dropped.

Internal Rate of Return (IRR) method: IRR is the discount rate at which NPV = 0

NPV = PV of the future cash flows – initial investment

$$PV = \frac{CF_1}{(1+r)} + \frac{CF_2}{(1+r)^2} + \frac{CF_3}{(1+r)^3} + \dots\dots$$

,

r is the internal rate of return;

CF_1 is the period one net cash inflow;

CF_2 is the period two net cash inflow,

CF_3 is the period three net cash inflow and so on ...

Through iterations the value of r is calculated. This should be equal to or more than the rate suggested by the management. Normally this rate is the cost of the capital. If IRR is lower, then the project is dropped.

Payback period method: This is the simplest of the methods and a crude way of evaluating the acceptance or rejection of a project. The payback period is the time in which the investment in a project is recovered. This is the time in which the project is said to have achieved the break even. The time value of money is not taken into account in this method.

Bibliography

1. Amabile, Teresa, Motivational Synergy: Toward New Conceptualization of Intrinsic and Extrinsic Motivation in the Workplace, Human Resource Management Review, Elsevier, 1993

2. Bloch, Michael, Sven Blumberg and Jürgen Laartz, Delivering Large-scale IT Projects on Time, on Budget, and on Value, McKinsey on Business Technology, October 2012.

3. Boehm, Barry W., Software Engineering Economics, Prentice-Hall, 1981 ISBN 0-13-822122-7

4. Bollinger, Terry, The interplay of art and science in software, IEEE Computer, Oct 1997, pp128,125-126

5. Boukouchi, Youness, Abdelaziz Marzak, Habib Benlahmer and HichamMoutachaoui, "Comparative Study of Software Quality Models", IJCSI International Journal of Computer Science Issues, Vol. 10, Issue 6, No 1, November 2013

6. Brooke, J. (1996). "SUS: A "Quick and Dirty" Usability Scale. in P. W. Jordan, B. Thomas, B. A. Weerdmeester, & A. L. McClelland (Eds.), Usability Evaluation in Industry. London: Taylor and Francis.

7. Brooks, Frederick P., The Mythical Manmonth, Addison Wesley Pub. Co., 1975

8. Brykczynski, Bill and Richard D Stutz, Software Engineering Project Management, John Wiley & Sons, 2006

9. Charlette, Robert N., Why Software Fails, IEEE Spectrum, http://spectrum.ieee.org/computing/software/why-software-fails, 2nd Sep 2005 accessed at 5.10 pm on 01/06/15

10. DeMarco, Tom, Controlling Software Projects, Prentice-Hall, 1982

11. Flyvbjerg, Bent and Alexander Budzier, Why Your IT Project Might be Riskier Than You Think, Harvard Business Review, September 2011

12. Gambles, Ian, Making the Business Case: Proposals that Succeed for Projects that Work, Gower Publishing Ltd, ISBN 9780566087455, 2009

13. Gilb, T., Principles of Software Engineering Management, Addison-Wesley, 1988.

14. Glen, Paul, Leading Geeks: How to Manage People Who Deliver Technology, Jossey – Bass, 2003, Ch. 6

15. Hamil, David L., Expectation Management: A Gateway to Project Success – Client Satisfaction, A professional development symposium whitepaper, symposium sponsored by North Alabama Chapter of Project Management Institute (PMI) and Defense Acquisition University (DAU), 15th Sep 2005

16. Humphrey, Watts S., Characterizing the Software Process A Maturity Framework, Software Engineering Institute, Carnegie Mellon University, June 1987

17. Humphrey, Watts S., Characterizing the Software Process A Maturity Framework, IEEE Software 5 (2), 73 – 79, March 1988

18. Humphrey, Watts S, Managing the Software Process. SEI series in software engineering. Reading, Mass.: Addison-Wesley. ISBN 0-201-18095-2, 1990

19. ISO 9001: Quality systems – Model for Quality Assurance in Design, Development, Production, Installation and Servicing 2nd edition, Geneva: International Organization for Standardization (ISO), 1994

20. Jackman M. Homeopathic Remedies for Team Toxicity, IEEE Software, Jul 1998, pp 43-45

21. Jones, Capers, Patterns of Software System Failure and Success, Dec. 1995

22. Jones, Capers, A Short History of Lines of Code (LOC) Metric Ver 7.0, Jun 27, 2013

23. Kepner, Charles H. and Benjamin B. Tregoe, The New Rational Manager, Princeton, NJ, 1981

24. Martin, Nita A., Project Politics: A Systematic Approach to Managing Complex Relationships, Gower publishing Ltd., 2011

25. McCall, Jim A., Paul K. Richards and Gene F. Walters, Factors in Software Quality, Concepts and Definitions of Software Quality, Volume 1, Final technical report, General Electric company, November 1977

26. McConnel, Steve, Software Project Survival Guide, Microsoft press, 1998

27. Myers, David G., Intuition: Its Powers and Perils, Yale University Press, 2004

28. Myers, I.B. and P.B. Myers, Gifts Differing: Understanding Personality Type (Davies-Black Publishing), 1995

29. Pressman, Roger S., Software Engineering – A Practitioner's Approach, Fifth Edition, McGraw Hill, 2001

30. Park, Robert E., Software Size Measurement: A Framework for Counting Source Statements, Software Engineering Institute, Carnegie Mellon University Pittsburgh, Pennsylvania 15213, Sep 1992

31. Sackman, H., W.J. Erikson, and E. E. Grant, Exploratory Experimental Studies Comparing Online and Offline Programming Performance, Communications of the ACM 11, no. 1 January 1968, 3-11.

32. Schwarz, Roger, How Criticizing in Private Undermines Your Team, Harvard Business Review, Mar 25, 2013

33. Tuckman, Bruce W., Psychological Bulletin, Vol 63(6), Jun 1965, 384-399.

34. Verma, Vijay K. Managing the Project Team: The Human Aspects of Project Management, Volume 3, Project Management Institute, 1997

35. Waligora, Sharon and Richard Coon, Improving the Software Testing Process in NASA's Software Engineering Laboratory, Computer Sciences Corporation

36. Wyzocki, Robert K. and Rudd McGary, Effective Project Management: Traditional, Agile, Extreme Managing Complexity in the Face of Uncertainty, Third edition, Wiley, 2010

Index

Agile methodology, 331

Albrecht, Allan, 98, 99, 100

Amabile, Teresa, 264

Assumptions, 46, 50, 52, 53, 66, 67, 76, 78, 212

Atos, 36, 55, 57, 58, 59, 60, 61, 62, 63

Baseline, 307

Benefits, 53, 75, 198

Boehm model, 161

Boehm, Barry W, 126, 345

Business analyst, 230

Business case, 52

   Executive Summary, 52

Capability maturity model

   Optimizing level, 169

Capability Maturity Model, 124, 167

   Defined level, 166, 168

   Initial level, 167

   Managed level, 168

   Optimizing level, 169

   Repeatable level, 168

Change control, 310

   Access control, 313

   Change order, 312

   Check-in, 312

   Check-out, 312

   Synchronization control, 313

Change control authority, 312

Change control board, 312, *See* Change control authority

Change request, 310

CMMI, 169

COCOMO, 205, 206, 207, 208, 214, 215, 217

   Cost Drivers, 207

   Detailed COCOMO, 208

   Effort Adjustment Factor, 206, 207

   Scale factors, 206

COCOMO II, 205

Coding standards, 164, 176, 226

Communication management, 265

   Email, 266

   Providing feedback, 281

   Video-conferencing, 266

Concurrent Version System (CVS), 313

Cone of uncertainty, 126

Configuration audit, 313

Configuration controller, 312

Configuration directory, 308

Configuration items, 308

   Aggregate object, 308

   Basic object, 308

Configuration management, 163, 179, 305, 306, 307, 309, 313, 316, 319

Configuration objects:, 312

Conflict management, 258

Conflict resolution, 259

   Compromising, 260

   Forcing, 260

   Problem solving, 259

   Smoothing, 260

   Withdrawal, 260

Constraints, 46, 51, 53, 65, 183

Contract, 61, 240, 336

   Force majeure clause, 240

   Indemnification, 241

   Intellectual property rights, 240

   Jurisdiction, 241

   Non- disclosure clause, 240

   Non-compete clause, 240

   Non-poaching clause, 241

   Warranties, 241

Cost control, 188, 203, 212, 214, 299

Cost-benefit analysis, 47, 51, 53, 66, 67, 193

Critical chain method, 147

Data migration, 29

Database administrator, 230, 235

De Beers, 36, 55, 57, 61, 62, 63, 183, 258

Decision making, 252, 254

   Command, 257

   Consensus, 257

Consultation, 257

Convenience, 257

   Heuristics, 253

   Satisficing, 252

   Tolerance for ambiguity, 253

DeMarco, 124, 345

Disbenefits, 53

Discounted Cash Flow, 343, *See* Net Present Value

Documentation, 19, 24, 43, 80, 81, 141, 172, 173, 337, 341

Domain expert, 230, 235

Earned value management, 300

   Actual cost (AC), 300

   Actual cost of work performed (ACWP), 300, *See* Actual cost (AC)

   Budgeted cost of work performed (BCWP), 300, *See* Earned value (EV)

   Budgeted cost of work scheduled (BCWS). *See* Planned value (PV)

   Control ratio, 301

   Cost performance index, 301

   Cost variance, 301

   Earned value (EV), 300

   Planned value (PV), 300

   Schedule performance index, 301

   Schedule variance, 301

Estimation, 26, 80, 94, 121, 122, 132, 133

   Analogy method, 127

   Automation, 129

Expectation Cycle, 326

Expectation Management, 323, 327, 328

Expectation Management Matrix
   (EMM), 327
Fishbone diagram, 251, 252, 290
Formal Technical Reviews, 164
FORTRAN, 182
Function point, 98, 100, 101, 119, 129
   Complexity adjustment, 100, 119
   Data Element Type, 108
   External Input, 99
   External interface file, 99
   External Output, 99
   External query, 99
   File type referenced, 110
   Information domain, 99, 119
   Internal logical file, 99
   Internal logical file, 120
   Record Element Type, 108
   Unadjusted function point, 100
Functional requirements, 43
FURPS, 161
Gantt Chart, 138
Herzberg, Frederick, 262
Humphery, Watts, 124
Hype cycle, 326
IEEE, 17, 345
Internal Rate of Return, 344
International Function Point User
   Group, 99
IPMA, 17, 18
ISBSG, *127*
Ishikawa diagram. *See* Fishbone diagram
ISO, 159
ISO 25010, 162
ISO 9001, 165, 166, 345
   QMS, 165, 166

ISO 9126, 161, 162
Knowledge Areas, 29, 31
LOC, 97, 98, 118, 128, 173, 205
   SLOC, 98, 115, 128, 131, 206, 215
Maslow, Abraham, 261
McCall, 157, 161
McCall's quality model, 157
McConnel, Steve, 123
Meetings
   Daily status meetings, 269
   General problem resolution, 270
   Minutes, 266, 267, 268, 269, 289,
      292
   Progress review meetings, 269
   Project status review with
      management, 270
   Quality review, 269
   Stand-up meeting, 269
   Technical problem resolution, 270
Metrics, 95, 102, 128, 168, 176
   Function-oriented metrics, 98
   Productivity metric, 95
   Quality metric, 95, 159
   Size-oriented metrics, 97
Microsoft Visual SourceSafe (VSS), 313
Milestones, 74, 212
Module lead, 230
Motivation, 261
   Autonomy, 263
   Expectancy theory, 262
   Extrinsic motivation, 264
   Feedback, 263
   Hygiene vs motivators, 262
   Intrinsic motivation, 264
   Maslow's hierarchy of needs, 261

Oldham – Hackman model, 262
Task identity, 263
Task significance, 263
Taylorist model, 261
Theory X vs Theory Y, 261
Net Present value, 343
Network diagram, 139, 141, 142, 145
Outsourcing, 192, 228, 237
Pareto analysis, 169, 175, 179
Parkinson's law, 208
Payback period, 344
PERT / CPM, 19, 139, 143, 149, 151
Activity, 139, 140, 141, 143, 144,
145, 146, 147, 149, 150, 151
Backward pass, 144
Critical event, 145
Critical path, 145
Dangle, 141
Dummy activity, 142, 143
Forward pass, 144
Loop, 141
Node, 140
Predecessor activity, 140
Slack, 144, 145, 146, 149, 152
Successor activity, 140
Planning, 26, 33, 69, 102, 168, 212,
267, 341
PMBOK, 16, 17, 21, 31, 34, 182, 204
Post implementation audit, 29, 336
PRINCE 2, 17
Problem solving, 248, 259, 290
Five whys, 252
Process methodology, 30
Program Management, 15, 16, 61
Programmers, 230, 263

project, 56
Project, 3
Champion, 220
Initiation, 22, 33, 35, 57, 341
Planning, 21
Sponsor, 220, 294, 337
Stakeholders, 220
Project cost management, 203
Bottom-up approach, 205
Budget, 32, 211, 238, 244
Budgetary estimate, 204
Budgeting, 31, 203, 210, 214, 341
Cost estimation, 203
Definitive estimate, 204
Parametric approach, 205
ROM (Rough Order Magnitude)
estimate, 204
Top-down approach, 205
Project diary, 285, 336, 340
Project management, 1, 12, 13, 15, 16,
17, 21, 29, 31
Project Management Office (PMO), 231
Project manager, 230
Skills required of a project manager,
247
Project organization structure, 229
Matrix organization, 229
Projectized organization, 229
Project Plan, 27, 212, 278
Project pricing, 208
Project Pricing
Time and materials, 210
Project Scheduling, 135
Project staffing, 224
Eligibility, 225

Suitability, 44, 182, 225

Project status reporting, 297

Cumulative report, 297

Exception report, 297

Project manager's status report to management / client, 298

Stoplight report, 298

Team's status report to project manager, 297

Variance reports, 299

Proof-of-concept, 331

Pygmalion effect, 282

Quality, 7, 11, 16, 18, 20, 27, 28, 30, 56, 60, 61, 69, 94, 96, 98, 115, 116, 124, 154, 155, 156, 157, 159, 161, 162, 163, 164, 165, 166, 167, 169, 171, 172, 173, 174, 175, 177, 179, 180, 197, 203, 213, 221, 228, 229, 230, 233, 241, 254, 269, 311, 338

Quality factors, 157

Correctness, 157, 158, 159, 174, 175

Efficiency, 116, 158, 159, 162, 174

Flexibility, 9, 158, 159, 227

Integrity, 158, 159, 177

Interoperability, 158, 159, 161

Maintainability, 117, 158, 162

Portability, 158, 159, 162

Reliability, 46, 50, 117, 157, 158, 159, 161, 174, 177

Reusability, 113, 158, 159

Testability, 158, 162

Usability, 122, 158, 160, 162, 174

Quality management, 155, 162, 213

Quality assurance, 103, 155, 157, 322

Quality control, 94, 156, 157, 166, 169, 312

Quality planning, 155, 156

Quality standards, 163, 164, 257

RACI matrix, 231, 234, 267

Rational Clearcase, 313

Release management, 318

Release identifier, 320

Release package, 320

Request for proposal

Bidder qualification, 239, 244

Request for Proposal, 98, 238

Requirements

MOSCOW, 70

specification, 50

Resource levelling, 147

Return on Investment (RoI), 343

Risk, 181

Risk adjusted RoI, 343

Risk exposure, 186, 193, 196

Risk management, 182

Contingency plan, 194, 251

External risks, 184

Organizational risks, 184

Project management risks, 183

Risk assessment, 182, 185, 187

Risk assessment matrix, 187

Risk avoidance, 192

Risk identification, 182, 199

Risk log, 194

Risk mitigation, 182, 191

Risk monitoring and control, 182, 194

Risk reduction leverage, 194

Risk referent level, 195

Risk refinement, 190

Risk tolerance, 190
Technical risks, 182
Risk management plan, 26
Scope, 16, 19, 26, 28, 29, 30, 35, 36, 39, 42, 46, 58, 59, 61, 68, 99, 107, 129, 137, 220, 230, 238, 245, 296, 310, 311, 314, 325, 327, 328, 329
Scope document, 25, 35, 43, 46, 47, 52, 54, 64, 68, 231, 323, 337, 339
Control requirements, 45, 49
Exclusions, 43, 48
Reliability requirements, 46, 50
Success criteria, 47, 51
Scope triangle, 5, 16, 26, 203, 327, 329, 332
Seven run rule, 169, 171
Six sigma, 171, 172, 173, 180
Software configuration, 306, 316
Documents, 306
Software Engineering Institute, 98, 124, 345
Software Engineering Process Group, 162
Software Estimation, 110
Software Measurement, 93
Software project management, 1, 5, 14
Software Quality Assurance, 162, 168
Stakeholders, 220
Statement of Work, 240

Statistical process control, 170
Systems Usability Scale, 160
Taylor, Frederick, 261
Team building, 282
Adjourning, 285
Forming stage, 284
Norming stage, 285
Performing stage, 285
Storming stage, 284
Team lead, 230
Technical writer, 230
Technology environment, 44, 49
Tester, 235
Tuckman, Bruce, 284
User Acceptance Testing, 242
Vendor management, 241, 244
Transition, 242
Version control, 309
Wideband Delphi approach, 129
Work Breakdown Structure, 71, 73, 134, 138
100% rule, 71
Acceptance criteria, 77
Bottom up approach, 72
Progressive elaboration, 72
Risk events, 74
Rule of 7±2, 74
Top down approach, 71, 78
Work Breakdown Dictionary, 76

Ludwig Steiger

Construire
en bois

Ludwig Steiger

Construire
en bois

3e édition

BIRKHÄUSER
BÂLE

Table des matières

AVANT-PROPOS _7

INTRODUCTION _8

LE MATÉRIAU _9

    Le bois _9

        Croissance _9

        Humidité du bois _11

        Types de débits _13

        Propriétés _14

        Comportement statique _16

    Produits de construction en bois _18

        Bois massif _18

        Matériaux dérivés du bois _21

        Panneaux à liants minéraux _24

    Préservation du bois _25

        Sélection du bois _25

        Protection constructive _26

        Protection chimique _26

CONSTRUCTION _29

    Stabilité _29

        Système porteur _29

        Contreventement _29

    Systèmes de construction en bois _31

        Construction en bois empilés _32

        Construction à pans de bois _36

        Construction à ossature bois _38

        Construction poteaux-poutres _44

        Construction en panneaux porteurs _47

        Construction en panneaux massifs _49

ÉLÉMENTS DE CONSTRUCTION _56

    Fondations _56

        Fondations par dalle _56

        Fondations filantes _57

        Fondations individuelles _58

        Soubassement _58

    Parois extérieures _61

        Couches de construction _61

        Physique de la construction _61

        Bardage extérieur _64

        Finitions _74

        Revêtement intérieur et installations techniques _74

        Baies _77

Parois intérieures _77

    Couches de construction _77

    Raccordements _78

Planchers _80

    Planchers à solivage _81

    Couches de construction _82

    Solivage _82

    Appuis _84

    Planchers massifs _87

Toiture _89

    Toitures inclinées _90

    Toitures plates _96

CONCLUSION _99

ANNEXES _100

Normes _100

Références bibliographiques _101

Crédits iconographiques _101

L'auteur _101

Avant-propos

S'il est un des matériaux de construction les plus élémentaires et les plus anciens de l'humanité, le bois n'a rien perdu de son attrait et de son actualité. Nombreuses sont les cultures et les zones climatiques où les habitations en bois comptent, avec les édifices en maçonnerie, parmi les formes bâties dominantes. De nos jours, la construction en bois est stimulée par le fait que le bois est en principe neutre en CO_2 et qu'il consomme beaucoup moins d'énergie, sur l'ensemble de son cycle de vie, que des éléments massifs comme ceux réalisés, par exemple, en béton.

Le bois se révèle d'ailleurs d'autant plus durable qu'il représente une ressource renouvelable. Matériau vivant, léger et facile à façonner, il confère aux bâtiments qui en sont faits un caractère tout à fait unique.

Les premiers projets que les étudiants en architecture ont à concevoir sont souvent des bâtiments en bois, car ce matériau leur permet de se familiariser de façon concrète et immédiate avec les modes et principes de construction fondamentaux. Pour les y aider, l'auteur présente dans un premier temps les propriétés du matériau naturel qu'est le bois, décrit ensuite les systèmes usuels de construction en bois et leurs règles spécifiques, et montre enfin, en s'appuyant sur des exemples, comment ces règles s'appliquent aux divers éléments de construction et à leurs raccords.

Cette troisième édition traite désormais aussi de la construction en panneaux de bois massifs, qui gagne depuis quelques années du terrain par rapport à la construction en maçonnerie ou en béton. Par ailleurs, certains règlements sur les constructions admettent aujourd'hui la réalisation de bâtiments en bois de plusieurs étages, qu'une combinaison ciblée avec des éléments en béton armé permet de rendre tout à fait conformes aux exigences en matière de protection incendie.

En permettant aux étudiants de reconnaître les différents systèmes de construction en bois et d'en comprendre les principes, le présent volume les rend à même de choisir le plus approprié à leur projet, et de le développer jusque dans les détails.

Bert Bielefeld
Directeur de collection

Introduction

Dans un essai consacré à la formation d'architecte, Mies van der Rohe écrivait en 1937 : « Où la structure d'une maison ou d'un bâtiment, l'unité entre matériau, construction et forme ressort-elle avec autant de clarté que dans les constructions en bois des Anciens ? Celles-ci recèlent la sagesse de générations entières. Quel sens du matériau et quelle puissance d'expression émanent de ces bâtiments ! Quelle chaleur ils dégagent, et comme ils sont beaux ! Ils sonnent comme d'anciens chants. » Cette citation de l'un des plus grands architectes du XXe siècle illustre à la fois la fascination qu'exerce la construction en bois et le défi qu'elle lance.

Pour pouvoir utiliser judicieusement ce matériau vivant dans un projet, l'étudiant doit disposer de vastes connaissances relatives aux essences de bois, aux nombreux systèmes constructifs existants, ainsi qu'à la composition et aux modes d'assemblage des éléments de construction en bois.

À la différence de la construction massive monolithique, en général plus familière aux étudiants, construire en bois consiste à assembler des éléments linéaires selon un ordre déterminé, basé sur une trame prédéfinie. Cela exige de la part du concepteur davantage de méthode, mais aussi un plus grand travail d'élaboration des détails et de dessin.

Cet ouvrage vise à transmettre aux étudiants, en trois temps, les bases de la construction en bois. Ainsi la première partie sera-t-elle consacrée au matériau et à ses propriétés, la deuxième aux principaux systèmes constructifs et à leurs assemblages caractéristiques, et la troisième à la composition des différents éléments de construction et à leur liaison. L'accent sera mis sur des solutions constructives simples, permettant d'illustrer les principaux problèmes que pose la conception d'un bâtiment en bois. Aussi, et bien que ce matériau s'y prête parfaitement, les structures de grande portée, comme les ponts ou les halles, ne seront-elles pas traitées dans le cadre de ce livre, le lecteur étant ici renvoyé à la littérature spécialisée.

On mentionnera toutefois une difficulté particulière survenant lorsque l'on entend présenter la construction en bois, difficulté qui est cependant aussi sa grande chance : à savoir que la technologie du bois se trouve en pleine évolution, l'industrie ne cessant de proposer, en plus des systèmes traditionnels, de nouveaux matériaux et de nouvelles techniques.

Le but de cet ouvrage est de structurer ce vaste domaine et d'en fournir un aperçu. La priorité sera donnée aux connaissances consolidées et aux constructions éprouvées, ce qui n'empêchera pas de faire à tout le moins mention des derniers produits et développements techniques en date.

LE BOIS

Dans le monde, on utilise en quantités importantes une bonne centaine d'essences de bois, ayant chacune un aspect et des propriétés spécifiques. Beaucoup sont employées dans le second œuvre et la fabrication de meubles. Dans la construction en bois, on utilise relativement peu de bois résineux. Aussi le novice n'a-t-il pas besoin d'être un expert en bois, l'important étant de comprendre la structure anatomique et de connaître les propriétés physiques fondamentales de ce matériau.

Croissance

On devrait toujours garder à l'esprit que toute pièce de bois, poutre ou planche, provient d'un organisme végétal, un arbre, dont la croissance et la qualité sont influencées par son environnement. Aucune pièce de bois n'est identique à aucune autre, ses propriétés dépendant bien sûr de l'essence dont elle provient, mais aussi de la situation qu'elle occupait à l'intérieur du tronc.

Le tronc se compose de cellules allongées en forme de tube, responsables, durant la croissance de l'arbre, du transport des substances nutritives. Les parois de ces cellules creuses sont constituées de cellulose et de lignine (ciment intercellulaire), la texture de ces parois et la structure cellulaire du bois déterminant la résistance mécanique du matériau. À la différence du béton non armé ou de la brique, le bois présente une structure orientée, correspondant au chemin suivi par les substances nutritives depuis les racines jusqu'aux branches, en passant par le tronc. On parle à cet égard du sens des fibres, ou fil du bois.

Cellules

○

○ **Remarque:** Le comportement statique d'une pièce de bois étant sensiblement différent selon qu'elle est sollicitée dans le sens des fibres ou perpendiculairement à celui-ci, il convient d'indiquer par des hachures, dans les plans et les coupes de construction, le sens dans quel on a débité le bois.

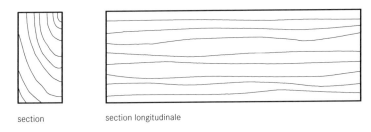

section   section longitudinale

III. 1 : Représentation du bois en section transversale et longitudinale

Les cellules se développent autour du canal médullaire central, la partie la plus ancienne du tronc. La croissance de l'arbre s'effectue selon des phases annuelles qui, dans les climats tempérés, s'étendent en général d'avril à septembre, et lors desquelles se forment les cernes annuels.

Bois initial/final   À l'intérieur de ces cernes se constituent au printemps les cellules à larges pores du bois initial, relativement tendre, et, en automne, les cellules à parois épaisses du bois final, plus dur. La proportion de bois final dont il se constitue détermine dans une large mesure la résistance mécanique du bois.

Aubier/duramen   Ce processus de croissance se « lit » aisément sur la section transversale d'un tronc. Selon l'essence en question, la zone extérieure, appelée aubier, se distingue plus ou moins clairement de la zone intérieure, plus ancienne, appelée duramen. Ce dernier n'assumant pas de fonction de conduction, il est plus sec que l'aubier, responsable du transport de la sève. Les différences entre duramen et aubier permettent de classer les différentes essences en deux catégories :

— Essences à aubier distinct
— Essences à aubier non distinct

Les essences à aubier distinct, dont font par exemple partie le chêne, le mélèze, le pin et le noyer, présentent un duramen foncé et un aubier clair et passent pour particulièrement résistantes aux intempéries.

Dans certaines essences, comme l'épicéa, le sapin, le hêtre ou l'érable, aubier et duramen présentent une différence d'humidité, mais pas de teinte. L'un est aussi clair que l'autre, le duramen étant sec et l'aubier humide.

Quant aux essences à aubier non distinct, comme le bouleau, l'aulne ou le peuplier, elles ne présentent de différence ni de coloration ni d'humidité.

III. 2 : **Différences entre duramen et aubier (troncs coupés transversalement)**

Humidité du bois

Presque toutes les propriétés physiques du bois sont influencées par sa teneur en eau. En dépendent en effet son poids, son comportement au feu, sa résistance aux parasites, son comportement statique, et surtout sa résistance à la déformation et sa stabilité dimensionnelle.

Lorsque le taux d'humidité change, le bois se rétracte ou se dilate. Lorsque le bois sèche, son volume diminue. Ce phénomène est appelé retrait, le processus inverse, qui provoque une augmentation de volume, étant appelé gonflement.

Retrait / gonflement

Ces changements de volume sont dus au fait que tant les cavités que les parois des cellules contiennent de l'eau. Le bois étant un matériau hygroscopique, il a la propriété d'absorber ou de restituer l'humidité en fonction du climat ambiant. On dit à ce propos que le bois « travaille ».

Le taux d'humidité du bois d'œuvre débité doit toujours être indiqué. On établit à cet égard la distinction suivante :

Bois saturé	plus de 30 % d'humidité
Bois mi-sec	plus de 20 % mais au maximum 30 % d'humidité
Bois sec	jusqu'à 20 % d'humidité

Le bois d'œuvre devrait toujours être posé à l'état sec, si possible à un taux d'humidité correspondant à celui qui prévaudra sur le lieu de mise en œuvre. L'humidité d'équilibre indique le taux d'humidité auquel ne se produisent plus que de légers changements de dimensions. Elle atteint les valeurs suivantes :

Locaux fermés, chauffés	9 ± 3 %
Locaux fermés, non chauffés	12 ± 3 %
Espaces couverts, non fermés	15 ± 3 %
Constructions exposées de tous côtés aux intempéries	18 ± 6 %

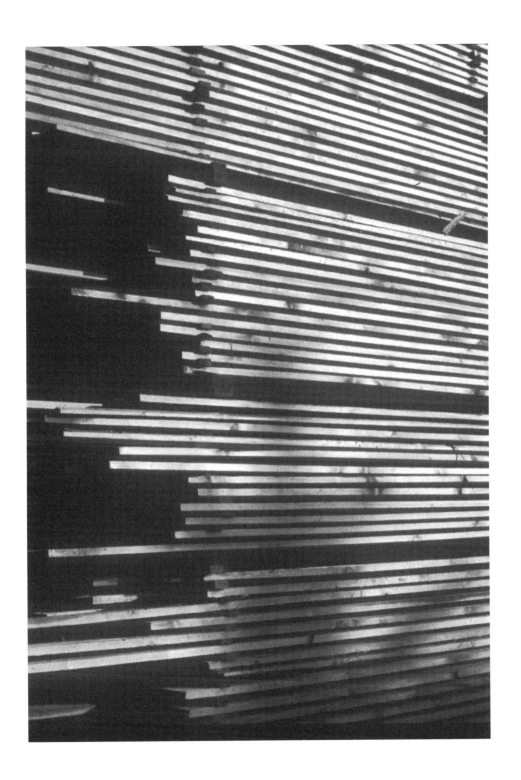

L'humidité du bois indique le pourcentage d'eau que contient le bois par rapport à son poids à l'état anhydre.

Le bois continue cependant de travailler une fois mis en œuvre ; il se gonfle et se rétracte lors des changements de saison, selon l'humidité de l'air ambiant.

○

Types de débits

En raison de la différence de teneur en eau entre aubier et duramen et, à l'intérieur des cernes annuels, entre bois initial et final, le bois débité subit des retraits différentiels, et donc des déformations. Est à cet égard déterminante la position de la pièce débitée à l'intérieur du tronc.

Le volume varie dans une mesure différente selon que la découpe est <u>tangentielle</u> ou <u>radiale</u>, c'est-à-dire perpendiculaire aux cernes annuels. Dans la plupart des essences, la rétractabilité d'une pièce débitée tangentiellement est plus de deux fois supérieure à celle d'une pièce débitée radialement. Dans le sens longitudinal, en revanche, la rétractabilité du bois est négligeable.

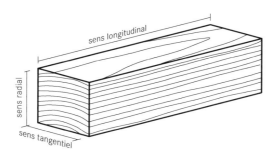

III. 3 : Bois équarri avec bout débité dans les sens radial et tangentiel

○ **Remarque:** L'une des principales règles de la construction en bois consiste à toujours mettre en œuvre le bois de manière à ne pas empêcher les mouvements dus au retrait et au gonflement, par exemple en ménageant entre les pièces de bois des joints assez larges. Pour permettre au bois de travailler perpendiculairement au sens des fibres, une lame de bardage ne devrait si possible être fixée qu'avec une seule vis, placée dans l'idéal au milieu ou, sinon, au bord de la planche.

Ces différences de comportement impliquent que des planches ou des bois équarris débités perpendiculairement les uns aux autres dans un même tronc se déforment différemment. Du fait du rétrécissement de leurs cernes, orientés dans le sens de la longueur, les planches découpées tangentiellement se cintrent vers l'extérieur, du côté opposé au duramen (tuilage). Seule la planche centrale, dite planche de cœur, reste droite, tout en s'amincissant cependant au niveau de l'aubier. L'illustration 4 montre la diminution de volume que subissent, lors du processus de retrait, les différents sciages.

Propriétés

Du fait de sa structure à pores fins, le bois est un assez bon isolant. Le coefficient de conductivité thermique de résineux comme l'épicéa, le pin et le sapin est de 0,13 W/mK, celui de feuillus comme le hêtre et le chêne de 0,23 W/mK. Sachant que la conductivité thermique de la brique de terre cuite est de 0,44 W/mK et celle du béton de 1,8 W/mK, le bois se révèle posséder de bien meilleures propriétés isolantes que beaucoup d'autres matériaux.

La dilatabilité thermique du bois est par ailleurs si faible – à la différence de celle de l'acier ou du béton, par exemple – que son incidence est négligeable dans la construction.

Masse volumique

En raison de sa faible masse volumique, le bois présente une capacité d'accumulation thermique inférieure à celle de matériaux massifs comme la maçonnerie ou le béton. Ainsi le coefficient d'accumulation thermique de l'épicéa et du sapin est-il de 350 Wh/m^{3}K, alors que celui du béton normal se monte à 660 Wh/m^{3}K. Cela se révèle particulièrement problématique lorsqu'il s'agit d'assurer une protection thermique estivale efficace. L'équilibrage des températures entre nuits fraîches et jours chauds est moins bon dans les bâtiments en bois que dans les constructions massives.

C'est aussi du fait de sa faible masse volumique que le bois présente un faible indice d'affaiblissement phonique, mais une bonne capacité d'absorption acoustique, due à ses cellules ouvertes.

○ **Remarque:** La face opposée au duramen d'une pièce débitée tangentiellement est appelée face gauche, celle tournée vers le duramen, face droite. Lors de la mise en œuvre, on tiendra compte des déformations susceptibles d'affecter une telle pièce.

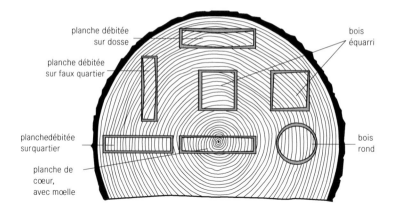

planche débitée sur dosse

bois équarri

planche débitée sur faux quartier

planchedébitée surquartier

bois rond

planche de cœur, avec moelle

III. 4 : Coupe transversale d'un tronc, types de débits

Il n'est possible d'améliorer la capacité d'accumulation thermique et la protection phonique d'une construction en bois qu'en y ajoutant des matériaux lourds, c'est-à-dire dotés d'une masse volumique plus importante, par exemple des panneaux de placoplâtre ou de fibrociment pour les murs, ou des revêtements de sol d'un certain poids.

Bien que le bois soit un matériau combustible (normalement inflammable), son comportement au feu est moins défavorable qu'il n'y paraît au premier abord. En effet, du fait de la couche carbonisée qui se forme à sa surface, une pièce de bois de grande section se consume relativement lentement et de façon régulière, si bien qu'elle ne perd sa capacité porteuse qu'après un certain temps – à la différence, par exemple, d'une poutre en acier qui, à haute température, et bien qu'incombustible, se déforme et perd sa résistance statique.

La vitesse de combustion du bois est d'autant plus faible qu'il est humide. Perpendiculairement au sens des fibres, cette vitesse atteint

Protection contre le feu

○ **Remarque:** La masse volumique indique la densité d'un matériau. Elle dépend de son poids, et s'exprime en kg/m^3. La masse volumique des bois de résineux atteint entre 450 et 600 kg/m^3, celle des bois de feuillus européens 700 kg/m^3 et celle des bois de feuillus d'outre-mer jusqu'à 1000 kg/m^3. À titre de comparaison, celle du béton normal varie entre 2000 et 2800 kg/m^3.

environ 0,6 à 0,8 mm/min pour les bois résineux et environ 0,4 mm/min
pour le chêne. Le comportement au feu d'une pièce de bois dépend en
outre de sa forme extérieure : plus sa surface est importante à volume
○ égal, plus faible est sa résistance au feu. Cela se manifeste en particulier lorsqu'une pièce en bois massif présente des gerces dues au retrait,
et c'est ce qui explique que la durée de résistance au feu du bois lamellé-
collé, dépourvu de gerces, soit supérieure et calculable avec plus de précision que celle du bois massif.

Dimensionné en conséquence, le bois est donc tout à fait en mesure
de répondre aux exigences de la protection anti-incendie.

Comportement statique

À la différence de la maçonnerie, destinée à être essentiellement
sollicitée en compression, le bois est capable de reprendre dans la même
mesure ou presque les efforts de compression et de traction. En raison
de sa structure cellulaire tubulaire, cependant, la direction dans laquelle
s'appliquent les forces est déterminante. Dans le sens du fil, le bois peut
reprendre des efforts de compression environ quatre fois plus impor-
tants que transversalement aux fibres. L'illustration 5 donne, sous forme
de contraintes admissibles exprimées en N/mm^2, les différentes valeurs
de résistance des bois résineux (S 10), telles que définies dans les
normes allemandes.

Lors de la mise en œuvre, on devra donc veiller à ce que le bois soit,
si possible, sollicité dans le sens du fil, plus performant tant en compression qu'en traction.

De manière générale, le comportement statique du bois dépend de
la proportion de ses cellules à parois épaisses, et donc de sa densité.
C'est pour cette raison que les bois de feuillus durs, comme le chêne, se
prêtent particulièrement aux sollicitations en compression (telles qu'en
subissent par exemple les lisses basses), alors que les sollicitations en
flexion seront avantageusement reprises par un bois résineux à fibres
allongées.

Classement   Le bois d'œuvre débité présentant toutes les irrégularités inhérentes
à un matériau naturel organique, le comportement statique que l'on en
attend n'est pas garanti d'avance. Aussi le bois fait-il l'objet d'un classement visuel et automatique, ainsi que d'un marquage commercial, selon

○ **Remarque:** En Suisse, les classes de résistance
au feu F30, F60 ou F90 indiquent qu'un élément
de structure reste, sous l'effet des flammes, en état
de fonctionner pendant 30, 60 ou 90 minutes.

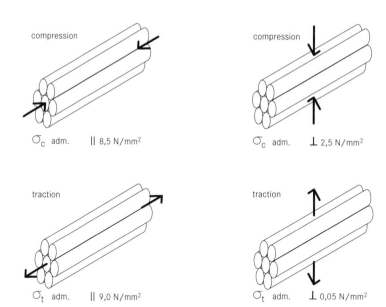

compression

σ_c adm. $\parallel$ 8,5 N/mm²

compression

σ_c adm. $\perp$ 2,5 N/mm²

traction

σ_t adm. $\parallel$ 9,0 N/mm²

traction

σ_t adm. $\perp$ 0,05 N/mm²

III. 5 : Contraintes de compression et de traction admissibles

Tab. 1: Classes de sélection et de qualité en Allemagne

Classe de sélection	Classe de qualité	Capacité porteuse
S 13	I	supérieure à la moyenne
S 10	II	ordinaire
S 7	III	faible

des critères tels que le nombre et la taille de ses nœuds, les défauts de son fil et ses gerces, mais aussi sa masse volumique et son élasticité.

En Allemagne, les bois d'œuvre débités sont répartis en trois classes de sélection et de qualité, en fonction desquelles sont indiquées les valeurs de résistance à utiliser dans les calculs statiques. > Tab. 1

Dans certains pays, la classification est encore plus fine. Aux États-Unis, par exemple, tous les bois d'œuvre sont dotés d'une estampille spécifiant la classe de qualité du bois, l'organisme chargé du contrôle de cette qualité, le numéro de scierie, l'essence du bois, son taux d'humidité, son module d'élasticité, sa résistance à la flexion et son utilisation.

De telles spécifications facilitent considérablement la distribution des bois sur le chantier, ainsi que leur contrôle par l'autorité de surveillance des travaux.

PRODUITS DE CONSTRUCTION EN BOIS

Les produits présentés ci-après vont du bois massif aux panneaux liés à d'autres matériaux, comme le ciment ou le plâtre, en passant par les matériaux dérivés du bois, dans lesquels la structure du matériau de départ est sensiblement modifiée.

Bois massif

Le terme « bois massif » désigne du bois rond ou débité écorcé, tiré de résineux ou de feuillus. Le bois d'œuvre débité est fourni par les scieries sous forme de bois de stockage équarri, disponible dans des sections et des longueurs déterminées. Selon le rapport entre l'épaisseur et la largeur des pièces, on parlera de lattes, de planches, de madriers ou de bois équarris. > Tab. 2

Dimensions Les dimensions indiquées au tableau 3 correspondent à des sections courantes. Les autres gammes de dimensions standardisées ne diffèrent que légèrement de ces valeurs

D'ordinaire, le bois d'œuvre débité est utilisé brut de scierie, c'est-à-dire non raboté. Lorsque les planches et madriers doivent cependant être rabotés des deux côtés, par exemple en vue d'une mise en œuvre apparente en intérieur, il s'agit de retrancher environ 2,5 mm aux dimensions indiquées.

La longueur des pièces va de 1,5 à 6,0 m, par augmentations graduelles de 25 ou 30 cm.

Le bois de stockage équarri est fourni dans des sections carrées ou rectangulaires en centimètres entiers. Les sections indiquées au tableau 4 représentent des dimensions préférentielles.

Les sections des bois de stockage équarris américains > Tab. 5 se basent sur l'inch (in), unité de mesure correspondant au pouce européen (1 po = 25,4 mm). À partir d'une largeur minimale de 2 in sont produites des sections minces, particulièrement adaptées aux montants rapprochés de la construction à ossature bois américaine. > Chap. Construction à ossature bois

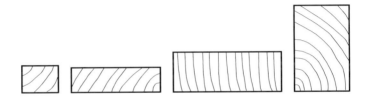

III. 6 : Section des pièces de bois massif

Tab. 2: Section des lattes, planches, madriers et bois équarris

	Épaisseur e [mm]	Largeur l [mm]
	Hauteur h [mm]	
Latte	d ≤ 40	b < 80
Planche	d ≤ 40	b ≥ 80
Madrier	d > 40	b > 3d
Bois équarri	b ≤ h ≤ 3b	b > 40

Tab. 3: Sections courantes

Sections de lattes	24/48, 30/50, 40/60
Épaisseurs de planches	16, 18, 22, 24, 28, 38
Épaisseurs de madriers	44, 48, 50, 63, 70, 75
Largeurs de planches/madriers	80, 100, 115, 120, 125, 140, 150, 160, 175

Tab. 4: Dimensions courantes pour les bois équarris

6/6, 6/8, 6/12, 6/14, 6/16, 6/18
8/8, 8/10, 8/12, 8/16, 8/18
10/10, 10/12, 10/20, 10/22, 10/24
12/12, 12/14, 12/16, 12/20, 12/22
14/14, 14/16, 14/20
16/16, 16/18, 16/20
18/22, 18/24
20/20, 20/24, 20/26

Tab. 5: Dimensions des bois américains en inches

Largeurs	2, 2½, 3, 3½, 4, 4½
Hauteurs	2, 3, 4, 5, 6, 8, 10, 12, 14, 16

En Europe centrale et en Europe du Nord, des essences de bois courantes sont, par exemple, l'épicéa, le sapin, le pin, le mélèze et le douglas, en Amérique le pin douglas, le cèdre rouge (red cedar), le pin de Caroline et le pitchpin.

En poussant plus loin la transformation et la valorisation du bois massif, on obtient les produits suivants.

En plus des critères de classement habituels pour le bois massif, le bois massif de construction (BMC) est classé et marqué en fonction de

Produits en bois massif

19

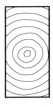
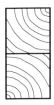
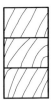

bois massif
de construction

poutre duo

poutre trio

poutre en quarts
de section

bois lamellé-
collé

III. 7 : Produits en bois massif

sa résistance et de son aspect. Il remplit donc des exigences particulières en matière de capacité porteuse, d'aspect, de stabilité dimensionnelle et de résistance à la déformation, de taux d'humidité, de largeur des gerces et de texture superficielle. Grâce à la technique de l'assemblage à entures multiples, consistant à encoller les dents usinées aux extrémités des éléments mis bout à bout, il est possible d'obtenir des pièces de n'importe quelle longueur. Les sections disponibles correspondent à celles du bois de stockage équarri.

On obtient une amélioration qualitative similaire avec les <u>poutres duo</u> ou <u>trio</u>, composées de deux ou trois madriers ou bois équarris collés à plat et à fil parallèle.

Les <u>poutres</u> composées de <u>quarts de section</u> contrecollés à fil parallèle sont faites de segments de grumes dont l'extérieur est tourné vers l'intérieur, de manière à former au cœur de la section rectangulaire obtenue une gorge centrale continue.

Le <u>bois lamellé-collé (BLC)</u> répond à de très hautes exigences en matière de résistance à la déformation et de capacité porteuse. Il se compose de planches de résineux collées sous pression sur leur face la plus large et à fil parallèle. Pour garantir un collage hydrorésistant, on utilise des résines synthétiques à base de phénol, de résorcine, de mélamine ou de polyuréthane, qui apparaissent extérieurement, au niveau des joints de collage, dans des tons allant du brun foncé au brun clair.

Avant d'être collées, les planches sont séchées et rabotées, tous les défauts du bois étant éliminés mécaniquement. Le collage par couches permet de réduire les déformations à des proportions minimes. Livrable dans des sections allant jusqu'à 200 cm de hauteur et dans des longueurs pouvant atteindre 50 m, le bois lamellé-collé est souvent mis en œuvre dans des structures de grande portée.

Matériaux dérivés du bois

Composés non seulement d'éléments tels que planches, lattes, placages ou lamelles, mais aussi de résidus issus du façonnage du bois, tels que copeaux et fibres, les produits dérivés du bois permettent une utilisation particulièrement économique du matériau.

Ces produits sont fabriqués industriellement, par assemblage sous pression à l'aide de colles à base de résine synthétique ou de liants minéraux. Les propriétés irrégulières du bois sont ainsi homogénéisées et sensiblement améliorées. Les propriétés statiques et les contraintes admissibles des dérivés du bois peuvent être déterminées avec beaucoup plus de précision que celles du bois massif, retraits et gonflements étant par ailleurs beaucoup moins marqués chez les premiers que chez le second.

Les dérivés du bois sont la plupart du temps produits sous forme de panneaux de dimensions standard.

Dans tous les pays, les dérivés du bois sont subdivisés, selon leur mode de collage, en classes indiquant dans quelle mesure ils peuvent être exposés à l'humidité. Le tableau 6 présente les désignations ayant cours en Allemagne.

■ Collage

La construction en bois américaine connaît, elle, quatre classes de collage. > Tab. 7

Tab. 6: Classes de matériaux dérivés du bois, désignations allemandes

V 20	ne tolère pas l'humidité
V 100	tolère une humidification de courte durée
V 100 G	tolère une humidification de longue durée ; propriétés antifongiques

Tab. 7: Classes de matériaux dérivés du bois, désignations américaines

Exterior	exposition durable à l'humidité
Exposure 1	haute résistance à la pluie, mais non adapté à une exposition durable aux intempéries
Exposure 2	exposition normale à l'humidité
Interior	pour les espaces intérieurs protégés, non exposés à l'humidité

■ **Astuce:** Pour garantir une utilisation économique des panneaux, il s'agit, lors de la conception, de définir la trame de construction de manière à minimiser les découpes nécessaires lors de la mise en œuvre. Si les panneaux choisis ont, par exemple, une largeur de 125 cm, on prévoira entre les montants de la structure un entraxe égal à cette largeur, ou correspondant à la moitié (62,5 cm) ou au tiers (41,6 cm) de celle-ci.

Les catégories Exterior et Exposure 1 correspondent à la classe de collage allemande V 100, la catégorie Interior étant comparable à la classe V 20.

On distingue, selon la nature de leurs composants, les catégories de panneaux en dérivés du bois suivantes :

— Panneaux contreplaqués et multiplis
— Panneaux de particules
— Panneaux de fibres

Panneaux contreplaqués et multiplis

Les panneaux contreplaqués et multiplis se composent d'au moins trois couches de bois (plis) collées les unes sur les autres à fil croisé.

Ce croisement des plis, appelé contreplacage, empêche le bois de travailler et confère au panneau la résistance et la stabilité voulues dans toutes les directions. Aussi les panneaux contreplaqués et multiplis se prêtent-ils particulièrement bien au contreventement des constructions en bois. Selon le type de colle utilisé, ils peuvent aussi être mis en œuvre en extérieur. Lorsqu'on les utilise comme éléments de façade, il convient cependant d'en couvrir ou d'en vitrifier les tranches, particulièrement sensibles à l'humidité.

Les panneaux contreplaqués, dont l'épaisseur varie entre 8 et 30 mm, se composent de trois, cinq, sept ou neuf plis superposés. Les panneaux présentant au moins cinq plis et une épaisseur de plus de 12 mm sont aussi appelés panneaux multiplex.

Les panneaux contreplaqués lattés et contreplaqués lamellés présentent au moins trois couches, l'âme se composant ici de lattes ou de

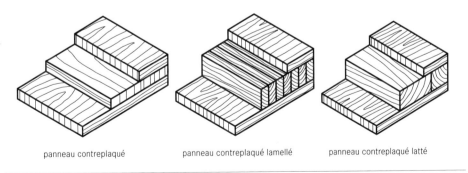

panneau contreplaqué   panneau contreplaqué lamellé   panneau contreplaqué latté

III. 8 : Panneaux contreplaqués, contreplaqués lamellés et contreplaqués lattés

22

lamelles qui, disposées perpendiculairement aux placages extérieurs, confèrent au panneau une capacité porteuse accrue.

Comptent parmi les panneaux contreplaqués et multiplis les plus utilisés les produits suivants :

— Panneaux contreplaqués de construction (BFU)
— Panneaux contreplaqués lattés et contreplaqués lamellés (ST, STAE)
— Panneaux à trois et cinq plis
— Panneaux en lamibois (LVL)
— Panneaux multiplex

Les <u>panneaux de particules</u>, composés de copeaux de sciure ou de rabotage collés sous pression, tirent parti des déchets produits par l'industrie du bois. À la différence des panneaux contreplaqués, ils ne présentent pas de plis continus, mais une structure fine non orientée. On peut les utiliser soit comme voile travaillant dans les parois, les sols, les planchers et les toitures, > Chap. Contreventement soit comme chape sèche dans les constructions de planchers. Panneaux de particules

Composés de lamelles rectangulaires relativement longues (environ 35 × 75 mm), les panneaux OSB (Oriented Strand Board), ainsi nommés en raison de leur structure orientée, sont des panneaux de particules fréquemment utilisés dans le bâtiment. L'orientation des lamelles changeant d'une couche à l'autre, les panneaux OSB présentent, comme les panneaux contreplaqués, des propriétés mécaniques dirigées. Il en résulte des valeurs de résistance deux, voire trois fois supérieures à celles des panneaux de particules standard. Panneaux OSB

Sont couramment utilisés les panneaux de particules suivants :

— Panneaux pressés à plat (FP)
— Panneaux en bois reconstitué à lamelles orientées (LSL)
— Oriented Strand Board (OSB)
— Panneaux extrudés

Les composants des <u>panneaux de fibres</u> sont encore plus petits que ceux des panneaux de particules. Le matériau de départ, du bois résineux, est broyé si fin que sa structure n'est plus reconnaissable. Que ce soit avec ou sans pression et avec ou sans colle, la fabrication par <u>procédé humide</u>, sans liant, permet d'obtenir les produits suivants : Panneaux de fibres

— Panneaux de fibres isolants (SB)
— Panneaux de fibres poreux (HFD)
— Panneaux de fibres bituminés (BPH)
— Panneaux de fibres mi-durs (MB)

Quant au procédé à sec, avec ajout de liants, il permet de produire les types de panneaux suivants :

— Panneaux de fibres de moyenne densité (MDF)
— Panneaux de fibres de haute densité (HDF)
— Panneaux de fibres durs (HB)
—

La plupart des panneaux de fibres fabriqués par procédé humide sont des panneaux tendres utilisés en intérieur, à titre d'isolation phonique et thermique ou de lambrissage de toiture. En raison de leur structure homogène, les panneaux de fibres de moyenne densité (MDF) sont très appréciés dans la fabrication de meubles et en agencement intérieur. Quant aux panneaux de fibres de haute densité (HDF) et durs (HB), on les utilise principalement comme revêtement de façade.

Panneaux à liants minéraux
À la différence des dérivés du bois contenant des liants organiques, les panneaux à liants minéraux font intervenir des liants inorganiques, et ne se composent qu'en partie de bois, ou n'en comportent même plus du tout. Il peut s'agir de
panneaux liés au ciment :

— Panneaux de particules bois-ciment
— Panneaux de fibrociment

ou de panneaux liés au plâtre :

— Panneaux de particules bois-plâtre
— Panneaux de placoplâtre
— Panneaux de fibroplâtre

Les panneaux liés au ciment se distinguent par leur grande résistance aux intempéries, au gel et aux attaques de champignons et d'insectes. Aussi sont-ils principalement utilisés comme revêtement de façade, y compris jusqu'au soubassement, en contact avec le terrain. Ils sont cependant aussi utilisables sous forme de voile travaillant.
Les panneaux liés au plâtre, en revanche, s'utilisent presque exclusivement en intérieur, les panneaux de placoplâtre principalement comme revêtement de parois et de plafonds, les panneaux de fibroplâtre, le plus souvent en multicouche, dans les constructions de chapes et de planchers. Les panneaux de placoplâtre et de fibroplâtre ne peuvent être mis en œuvre sous forme de voile travaillant extérieur que dotés d'une protection efficace et durable contre les intempéries.

PRÉSERVATION DU BOIS

Parasites du bois

À la différence de matériaux minéraux comme la maçonnerie ou le béton, le matériau organique qu'est le bois est exposé à des attaques d'origine végétale (champignons) et animale (insectes), susceptibles de provoquer non seulement une détérioration de l'aspect extérieur, mais encore une diminution de la capacité porteuse du bois, jusqu'à destruction complète du bâtiment. Aussi la protection du matériau revêt-elle, dans la construction en bois, une importance primordiale.

Pour se développer, les <u>champignons</u> ont besoin de cellulose. Ils prospèrent en particulier dans les zones humides, chaudes et sans contact avec l'air. Pour que le bois pourrisse, il faut qu'il présente une humidité d'au moins 20%.

Les <u>insectes</u>, en particulier les coléoptères, se nourrissent de l'aubier, surtout des résineux, et y déposent leurs larves. Les termites, vivant surtout dans les régions tropicales et subtropicales, mais aussi en Amérique et dans les régions méditerranéennes d'Europe, comptent parmi les insectes xylophages les plus dangereux. Pour éviter les pertes d'humidité, en effet, les termites creusent dans le bois des réseaux de galeries, si bien que leurs attaques ne sont pas visibles de l'extérieur, et que les bâtiments ou les meubles infestés peuvent s'écrouler d'un coup.

On fait la distinction entre mesures de protection <u>curatives</u>, visant à traiter un bois déjà atteint, et mesures <u>préventives</u>, destinées à empêcher les attaques biologiques.

Au stade de la conception, on s'attache avant tout aux mesures préventives, pouvant relever des trois catégories suivantes :

— Sélection du bois
— Protection constructive
— Protection chimique

Sélection du bois

On ne devrait mettre en œuvre que des bois ayant été entreposés un certain temps, dont l'humidité soit inférieure à 20%.

Dans de nombreux pays sont par ailleurs classifiées les essences présentant une résistance naturelle à la destruction, comme par exemple le duramen du teck, du greenheart, de l'azobé, du chêne ou du robinier, ou, en Amérique, du robinier faux-acacia (black locust), du noyer noir (black walnut) ou du séquoia (redwood). > Chap. Croissance Ces bois peuvent être mis en œuvre, sans protection chimique, dans les parties de la construction les plus exposées à l'humidité. Une protection chimique s'avère toutefois indispensable en cas de contact avec le terrain naturel.

Protection constructive

Les mesures de protection de nature constructive sont principalement du ressort du concepteur. Le projet, et en particulier les détails, devraient être conçus de manière à éviter que les éléments en bois soient durablement imbibés. Le chapitre « Éléments de construction » reviendra de façon plus détaillée sur les mesures à prendre au niveau du soubassement, des fenêtres et des rives de toiture.

Protection chimique

On ne devrait recourir à une protection de nature chimique que si les autres mesures préventives se révèlent inapplicables ou insuffisantes.

Les moyens envisageables sont ici des produits d'imprégnation ou des enduits hydrosolubles, ou à base de solvants ou d'huile. Pour éviter les pollutions environnementales, le bois devrait être traité dans des installations hermétiquement fermées, par exemple en autoclave ou en cuve de trempage. On ne traitera sur le chantier que les surfaces de coupe et les trous de perçage.

Les moyens de protection chimiques à mettre en œuvre dépendront de la fonction statique de l'élément à traiter. À cet égard, on distingue entre :

— les éléments porteurs et raidisseurs
— les éléments non porteurs à faible stabilité dimensionnelle
— les éléments non porteurs à stabilité dimensionnelle élevée (portes, fenêtres).

Les <u>éléments porteurs</u> doivent faire l'objet de mesures de protection préventives. Que celles-ci doivent être ou non de nature chimique dépend entre autres, selon le droit national en vigueur, de la classe de risque à laquelle appartient l'élément concerné.

■ **Astuce:** Il convient à cet égard d'appliquer, non seulement dans la construction en bois, mais ici tout particulièrement, la triple règle suivante :

1. Tenir l'humidité à l'écart (avant-toits, retraits de façades, larmiers).

2. Assurer l'écoulement de l'eau (légère inclinaison des surfaces horizontales).

3. Ventiler les éléments exposés à l'humidité (lame d'air).

○ **Remarque:** Dans toute construction, on évitera que le bois touche le terrain naturel et soit de ce fait durablement imbibé, un tel contact entraînant en effet un risque d'attaque biologique maximal. Pour ce faire, les constructions en bois sont souvent séparées du terrain par un soubassement d'environ 30 cm de hauteur.

Lorsque le bois utilisé est résistant et que l'élément est peu exposé ○
aux attaques biologiques, il est possible de renoncer à une protection
chimique.

N'admettant, pour fonctionner correctement, que de faibles variations de dimensions, les fenêtres et les portes extérieures sont des éléments non porteurs, mais <u>à stabilité dimensionnelle élevée</u>, requérant
une protection accrue contre l'humidité. On pourra cependant renoncer
à une protection chimique en utilisant du bois de duramen appartenant
à une classe de durabilité suffisante.

Quant aux éléments non porteurs admettant des <u>variations dimen-
sionnelles</u> plus <u>importantes</u>, comme les bardages à recouvrement, les
clôtures ou les pergolas, ils peuvent être mis en œuvre sans protection
et sans peinture, pour autant que l'on s'accommode d'un grisaillement
du bois. En intérieur, aucun traitement chimique ne devrait jamais être
appliqué sur de grandes surfaces.

« Les bâtiments en bois doivent être construits, ceux en pierre peuvent être dessinés », écrit un jour l'architecte suisse Paul Artaria. Sans doute cette formule quelque peu provocatrice visait-elle moins à dénier à la construction en maçonnerie toute rationalité constructive qu'à mettre en lumière la spécificité de la construction en bois, la logique propre à l'assemblage de ses éléments linéaires et le caractère systématique de ses structures.

STABILITÉ

Pour répondre à l'exigence élémentaire de stabilité statique, la construction en bois offre plusieurs systèmes, possédant chacun son propre fonctionnement statique et ses propres modes d'assemblage au niveau des nœuds.

Avant de présenter, dans cette deuxième partie, les principaux de ces systèmes, il convient de passer brièvement en revue les différentes exigences auxquelles doit répondre toute structure porteuse.

Système porteur

La stabilité d'une construction dépend de divers facteurs. Il faut d'une part que la capacité porteuse des matériaux utilisés soit suffisante, et que les éléments soient dimensionnés de manière à pouvoir reprendre les <u>charges verticales</u> issues des murs, des planchers et de la toiture. Mais il faut aussi que le sol de fondation présente une texture qui lui permette de porter ces charges.

Hormis les charges verticales, un bâtiment est en outre soumis à diverses <u>forces horizontales</u>. Celles-ci sont principalement dues au vent, mais il peut aussi s'agir de chocs.

○

Contreventement

L'une des possibilités envisageables pour reprendre les charges horizontales est l'<u>encastrement</u>. > III. 10 Ici, les poteaux sont noyés dans les fondations, de manière à empêcher tout glissement latéral ou toute

○ **Remarque:** Ce thème est traité de façon approfondie in Alfred Meistermann, *Basics Systèmes porteurs*, Birkhäuser, Bâle 2007.

déformation. La forme d'encastrement la plus simple et la plus archaïque consiste à enfoncer des pieux dans le sol. Dans la construction en béton armé, l'encastrement des poteaux de béton dans des fondations en forme de carquois a fait ses preuves. Lorsque les poteaux sont en bois, par contre, ce type de fondation se révèle problématique du point de vue de la protection du matériau.

La manière adéquate de contreventer une construction en bois consiste à prévoir, dans les trois dimensions, des <u>parois</u> et des <u>planchers rigides</u>, assemblés en une structure stable. On peut se représenter la chose à travers l'exemple d'un simple carton, qu'il est assez facile de déformer en losange tant que le couvercle horizontal manque, mais qui devient un parallélépipède stable et rigide dès que celui-ci est posé. > III. 9

○
Contreventement
triangulé

L'élément de base d'une surface rigide est le triangle indéformable. Dans la construction en bois, il est relativement facile d'assembler des poutres pour former un tel triangle. On parle alors de contreventement triangulé, le bâti rectangulaire de la paroi constituant ainsi un voile indéformable. L'illustration 10 présente les diverses manières possibles de contreventer une paroi. L'une consiste à prévoir deux <u>écharpes</u> travaillant en compression, sollicitées en alternance, selon le sens dans lequel agissent les forces horizontales. Si l'on opte pour une <u>diagonale</u> unique, celle-ci sera sollicitée tantôt en compression, tantôt en traction. Quant aux <u>câbles de contreventement</u> en acier, ils ne peuvent travailler qu'en traction, le sens d'application des forces horizontales déterminant à nouveau lequel des deux sera mis à contribution.

Il est en outre possible de raidir une paroi au moyen d'un bardage à lames diagonales ou d'un <u>voile travaillant</u> composé de panneaux en dérivés du bois dotés d'une résistance adéquate.

D'un point de vue formel, ces différentes mesures ont profondément marqué la construction en bois, les systèmes présentés ci-après pouvant

○ **Remarque:** D'un point de vue statique, un élément bidimensionnel, paroi ou plancher, fonctionne comme un « voile » lorsqu'il reprend sans se déformer des forces agissant dans son propre plan. Si le même élément est sollicité par une force de même ampleur perpendiculairement à son plan, sa résistance sera sensiblement inférieure et il fléchira. On parlera alors de « dalle ». Qu'un élément fonctionne comme voile ou comme dalle dépendra du sens d'application des forces auxquelles il sera soumis (voir III. 9).

III.9 : Schéma dalle/voile

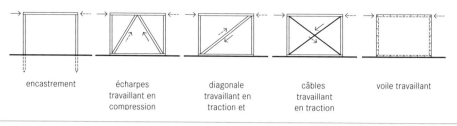

| encastrement | écharpes travaillant en compression | diagonale travaillant en traction et | câbles travaillant en traction | voile travaillant |

III.10 : Systèmes de contreventement des parois

du reste se distinguer les uns des autres d'après le mode de contreventement mis en œuvre. Si le contreventement triangulé est emblématique des anciennes constructions à colombage, les câbles en croix de saint André contreventant les constructions modernes à poteaux-poutres constituent, eux aussi, un détail caractéristique.

SYSTÈMES DE CONSTRUCTION EN BOIS

Les méthodes de construction se développent sous l'influence de différents facteurs : climat, contexte culturel, matériaux, outils et savoir-faire artisanal disponibles, etc. Alors que le sud de l'Europe, pauvre en bois, a vu se développer la construction en pierre, le nord, disposant de vastes forêts, a vu naître la construction en bois. Cette dernière a cependant elle-même pris des formes différentes selon les régions. Dans les régions alpines et de moyenne montagne, mais aussi en Europe du Nord, la profusion de résineux à tronc droit a conduit au développement de la construction en bois empilés, consistant à réaliser des parois de bois massives. En Europe centrale et orientale, en revanche, la prédominance des feuillus a donné naissance à la construction à pans de bois, dite aussi à colombages.

Au XIXe et plus encore au XXe siècle, des technologies et matériaux nouveaux ont profondément transformé la construction en bois européenne. La construction industrialisée a fait succéder aux techniques d'assemblage artisanales de très performants organes d'assemblage en acier exploitant mieux les sections de bois, principalement utilisés dans la construction à poteaux-poutres. En Amérique du Nord s'est par ailleurs établie la construction à ossature bois, dont les éléments sont assemblés par simple clouage.

Aujourd'hui, l'industrie du bois ne cesse de mettre sur le marché de nouveaux matériaux et produits, de nouveaux moyens de transport et des exigences accrues en matière d'isolation thermique entraînant, une fois encore, de profondes transformations dans le domaine.

Depuis la construction en bois empilés jusqu'aux structures à poteaux-poutres, en passant par la construction à pans et à ossature bois, l'histoire de la construction en bois était, jusqu'ici, celle de principes d'assemblage d'éléments linéaires. Aussi est-il indispensable de connaître et de comprendre ces différents systèmes, décrits ci-après, même si de nouvelles méthodes de construction, mettant principalement en œuvre des panneaux porteurs, élargiront à l'avenir l'éventail des possibilités.

Construction en bois empilés

Dans la construction en bois empilés, les pièces se croisent et s'emboîtent à leurs extrémités.

Ce mode de construction se caractérise par une forte consommation de matériau et l'important tassement des bois empilés. Les résineux à tronc droit ayant connu une croissance régulière sont ici les mieux adaptés. À l'origine, les parois se constituaient de rondins dont les surfaces de pose étaient légèrement aplanies. Les joints entre les troncs étaient calfeutrés avec de la mousse, du chanvre ou de la laine.

Au niveau des angles et des raccordements de parois perpendiculaires, les madriers sont entrecroisés et, en général, entaillés à quart de bois, de manièrc à créer un assemblage résistant à la traction. Du fait de cet entrecroisement, les deux parois, dont les bois sont décalés d'une demi-hauteur, forment une sorte d'appareil. > III. 11

À mesure que se perfectionnaient les outils, augmentait le niveau de façonnage artisanal. Les joints, désormais à rainure et languette, devinrent plus étanches. Le fait d'utiliser des bois équarris au lieu de rondins permit d'obtenir des sections de parois constantes. Aujourd'hui, les madriers sont dotés d'un profilage très élaboré. > III. 12

Assemblages   Les assemblages caractéristiques de la construction en bois empilés sont celui à rainure et languette entre madriers superposés, celui à quart de bois au niveau des angles du bâtiment, et celui en queue d'aronde, résistant à la traction, au niveau des raccordements entre
o   parois intérieures et extérieures. > III. 45, page 74

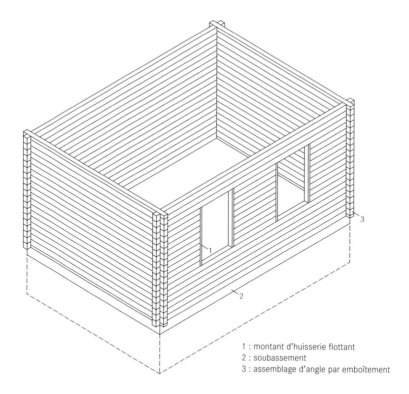

1 : montant d'huisserie flottant
2 : soubassement
3 : assemblage d'angle par emboîtement

III. 11 : Construction en bois empilés

La section d'une paroi composée de simples madriers ne permettant pas d'assurer le niveau de protection thermique aujourd'hui exigé, les constructions en bois empilés modernes sont dotées d'une isolation supplémentaire, qu'il convient de préférence, pour éviter toute condensation, de poser du côté extérieur. On ne retrouve dès lors plus l'aspect

○ **Remarque:** Dans un assemblage à mi-bois, les extrémités des pièces sont entaillées de moitié et assemblées à faces affleurantes. L'assemblage à quart de bois, obtenu en pratiquant une entaille sur les chants inférieur et supérieur de chaque pièce, est, lui, capable de reprendre des efforts de traction. C'est aussi le cas de l'assemblage en queue d'aronde, de forme conique.

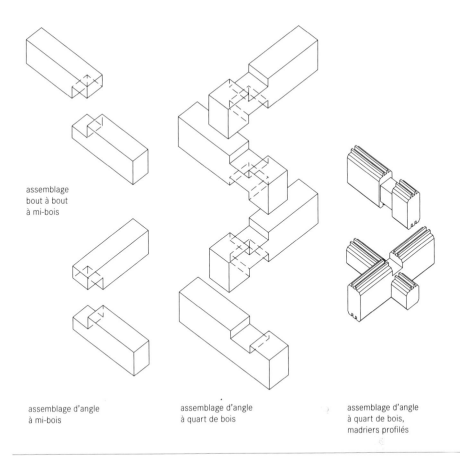

assemblage
bout à bout
à mi-bois

assemblage d'angle
à mi-bois

assemblage d'angle
à quart de bois

assemblage d'angle
à quart de bois,
madriers profilés

Ill. 12 : Assemblages par emboîtement

caractéristique des bois empilés que si l'on prévoit une seconde paroi de madriers, servant à protéger l'isolation thermique des intempéries. Aujourd'hui, l'industrie du bois offre des parois en bois empilés multi-couches, se présentant sous la forme d'éléments sandwich composés de madriers et de couches d'isolation.

Tassement   Le fait que les bois soient sollicités en compression transversale-ment aux fibres entraîne un <u>tassement</u> pouvant atteindre 2 à 4 cm par étage, qu'il s'agit de prendre en compte au niveau des portes et des fenêtres. Aussi les huisseries intégrées aux baies pour protéger les madriers doivent-elles présenter, à leur extrémité supérieure, assez de jeu pour pouvoir reprendre ce tassement sans contraintes. > Ill. 13 À cet effet, on ménagera aussi un joint couvert entre dormants de fenêtres et

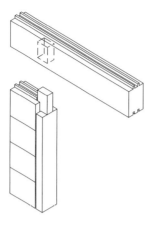

III. 13 : Fenêtre avec montant d'huisserie flottant et joint
de tassement

III. 14 : Construction en bois empilés – angle extérieur, raccordement d'une cloison
intérieure, fenêtre

linteaux, toutes les conduites ou cheminées traversant verticalement
l'édifice devant par ailleurs être raccordées à la construction de façon
non rigide. On voit donc que la construction en bois empilés, toute pri-
mitive qu'elle paraisse au premier abord, exige en réalité beaucoup de
savoir-faire et d'expérience.

En termes de projet, ce mode de construction requiert une organisation en plan orthogonale, simple et rigoureuse. Lors du dessin des
façades, on veillera à ce que la structure des parois ne soit pas trop per-
turbée en prévoyant des ouvertures aussi petites et peu nombreuses que
possible. Opter pour des façades percées de fenêtres semblables à celles

qui caractérisent l'architecture en maçonnerie traditionnelle est a priori le plus adéquat, la construction en bois empilés étant en effet, par nature, un mode de construction massif. > III. 14

Construction à pans de bois

Dans la construction à pans de bois, dite aussi à colombages, il est possible de « lire » distinctement le chemin suivi par les forces, raison pour laquelle on en parle parfois, dans la littérature, comme d'un « style ». La distinction claire entre éléments porteurs et non porteurs, entre bois de structure et matériaux de remplissage, fait tout le charme de ce mode de construction.

Remplissage Historiquement, les vides entre les éléments porteurs d'un pan de bois étaient remplis de maçonnerie (hourdis) ou de glaise appliquée sur un entrelacs d'osier (torchis). Aujourd'hui, les exigences en matière de protection thermique nécessitent de remplir les pans de bois d'isolation, laquelle requiert un bardage extérieur la protégeant des intempéries, mais aussi un revêtement intérieur.

Le remplissage n'assumant aucune fonction statique, il est aussi possible de traiter les vides des pans de bois comme des baies. Pour autant

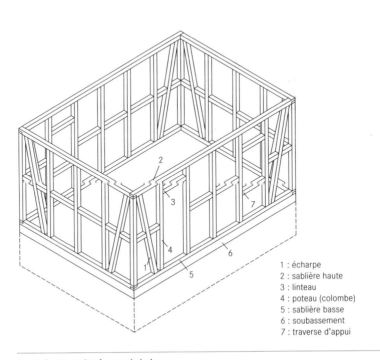

1 : écharpe
2 : sablière haute
3 : linteau
4 : poteau (colombe)
5 : sablière basse
6 : soubassement
7 : traverse d'appui

III. 15 : Construction à pans de bois

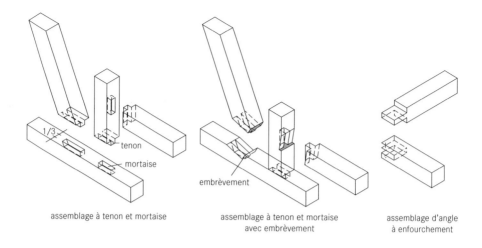

assemblage à tenon et mortaise

assemblage à tenon et mortaise
avec embrèvement

assemblage d'angle
à enfourchement

Ill. 16 : Assemblages à tenon et mortaise, embrèvement, enfourchement

qu'elles respectent la trame de construction choisie, les fenêtres peuvent être prévues en grand nombre, les locaux des bâtiments en pans de bois bénéficiant de ce fait d'un meilleur éclairage naturel que ceux des constructions en bois empilés.

L'assemblage typique de la construction à pans de bois est l'assemblage à <u>tenon</u> et <u>mortaise</u>, où les faces latérales des bois sont affleurantes. Pour assurer une meilleure transmission des efforts, il arrive souvent que l'on pratique aussi un embrèvement. Les sablières hautes et basses, elles, sont assemblées soit à tenon et mortaise, soit à mi-bois.

Assemblages

> Ill. 16 et Chap. Construction en bois empilés

Les pans de bois, édifiés étage par étage, se composent de poteaux verticaux (colombes), de traverses horizontales et d'écharpes obliques, maintenus ensemble par une sablière basse et une sablière haute. Les bols étant surtout sollicités en compression, on recourt d'ordinaire à des

○ Sections

○ **Remarque:** Les tenons et les mortaises sont découpés au deuxième tiers de l'épaisseur des pièces à emboîter. Pour ne pas trop affaiblir les sections correspondantes, la profondeur des mortaises ne devrait pas dépasser 4 cm.

sections carrées de 10/10, 12/12 ou 14/14 cm, les sablières présentant aussi souvent une section rectangulaire, posée à plat.

Il existe aussi des pans de bois s'étendant sur deux ou plusieurs étages, auquel cas le tassement – de toute façon bien moins important que dans la construction en bois empilés, les seuls bois horizontaux étant ici les sablières – se trouve encore considérablement réduit.

Planchers Les solives du plancher reposant sur la sablière haute, on en voit la tête à l'extérieur tant que la construction n'est pas habillée. Elles supportent à leur tour les pans de bois de l'étage suivant, commençant à nouveau par une sablière basse. Lorsque les pans s'étendent sur deux ou plusieurs étages, les planchers sont suspendus entre les parois.

> III. 50, page 79

Les colombages d'antan étaient en bois dur, de préférence en chêne. Les modes de construction varient d'une région à l'autre. En Allemagne, par exemple, on distingue entre les colombages franconien, alémanique et saxon, la dénomination des différents éléments de construction variant souvent, elle aussi, d'une région à l'autre.

Trame L'entraxe entre poteaux se monte en général à 100–120 cm. Il existe cependant des exemples où les colombes sont moins espacées, ou au contraire bien davantage. Malgré les contraintes constructives qui lui sont inhérentes, le pan de bois offre de multiples possibilités, qui ont été exploitées non seulement sur le plan technique, mais aussi sur celui de l'expression architecturale. La protection du patrimoine s'efforce de préserver dans les villes anciennes la richesse formelle des constructions à pans de bois traditionnelles, si bien qu'il est indispensable pour les architectes intervenant dans des sites historiques d'en connaître les principes.

Dans la construction à pans de bois moderne, les nombreux poteaux, écharpes et traverses nécessaires multiplient les joints et rendent de ce fait des plus laborieuse la pose de l'isolation dans les vides de la charpente. Cet inconvénient est toutefois compensé par le fraisage à commande numérique des pièces de bois, permettant de faire l'économie de l'important travail autrefois requis par les assemblages artisanaux.

Construction à ossature bois

La construction à ossature bois est originaire d'Amérique du Nord. L'urbanisation fulgurante du pays le long des nouvelles voies ferrées appelait une méthode de construction simple, économique et rapide. Avec le bois, on disposait d'un matériau adapté à toutes les zones climatiques du continent.

Dès la première moitié du XIXe siècle, les techniques industrielles se mirent à influer sur la construction en bois. Les scieries à vapeur et la fabrication industrielle des clous modifièrent les modes de construction, restés jusqu'alors très proches du pan de bois européen.

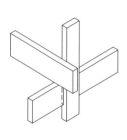 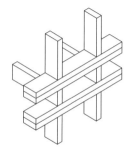

noeud d'assemblage,
ossature continue
(« balloon-frame »)

noeud d'assemblage,
ossature à plate-forme
(« platform-frame »)

III. 17 : Nœuds d'assemblage, ossature continue / ossature à plate-forme

Des bois de section uniforme, semblables à des madriers, supplantèrent les sections très hétérogènes qui prévalaient auparavant. Aux assemblages artisanaux requérant un travail considérable, succédèrent des assemblages cloués, qu'il était possible d'exécuter sans outils spéciaux, selon une technique relevant quasiment du « do it yourself ». Les minces sections de bois étaient ici clouées latéralement pour former une ossature à la trame plus serrée qu'un pan de bois, et s'étendant sur toute la hauteur du bâtiment. À l'origine, le terme de « balloon-frame » raillait la légèreté inusitée de telles constructions.

En Europe, ce mode de construction se fit connaître sous le nom d'ossature continue.

Les inconvénients de cette technique, à savoir le fait qu'il était devenu plus difficile de se procurer du bois et de monter des éléments aussi hauts, ainsi que les problèmes de transmission phonique dus aux montants continus, favorisèrent le développement d'un mode de construction étage par étage, qui se répandit en Amérique sous le nom de « platform-framing ». Ici, en effet, dalle de fondation et planchers intermédiaires servent de plate-forme pour le montage des ossatures suivantes.

Dans la construction à ossature bois, développée à partir du « balloon-frame », des montants de section mince et très rapprochés sont assemblés, au sol, en ossatures qui, si elles ont en général la hauteur d'un étage, peuvent aussi s'étendre sur deux niveaux.

Construction
à ossature bois

Au début du XXe siècle, l'architecture moderne européenne était principalement focalisée sur le béton. Aussi fallut-il attendre, pour voir s'imposer la construction à ossature bois, les années 1980, où l'on cherchait des méthodes de construction plus économiques, et où l'on se souvint de la construction en bois américaine. La section standard « two by four »

Sections

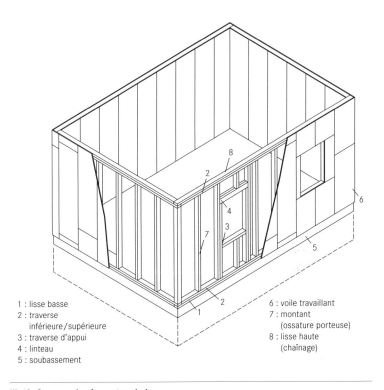

1 : lisse basse
2 : traverse
inférieure/supérieure
3 : traverse d'appui
4 : linteau
5 : soubassement

6 : voile travaillant
7 : montant
(ossature porteuse)
8 : lisse haute
(chaînage)

III. 18 : Construction à ossature bois

inches, correspondant à peu près à du 5 × 10 cm, inspira en Europe le
6 × 12 cm, une section un peu plus robuste que l'américaine.

Assemblages

L'assemblage caractéristique de la construction à ossature bois est
l'assemblage à joint vif, la liaison entre les pièces étant réalisée par
clouage. Les pièces perpendiculaires sont clouées obliquement, de

> ○ **Remarque:** Le « two by four » (inches) est une section
> éprouvée, qu'il est possible de mettre en œuvre et de
> combiner de multiples façons. Il arrive que l'expression
> « two by four » désigne la construction à ossature bois
> elle-même. Du fait des exigences accrues qu'impose
> le climat d'Europe centrale en matière d'isolation
> thermique, les sections s'y rapprochent aujourd'hui
> davantage d'un rapport de « two by six ».

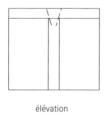

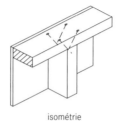

élévation   isométrie

III. 19 : Assemblage à joint vif et par clouage

manière à ce que la liaison se fasse le plus possible transversalement aux fibres. L'ossature n'atteint toutefois sa rigidité qu'une fois contreventée par des panneaux en dérivés du bois (voile travaillant), des mesures particulières devant ici être prises pour empêcher l'arrachement des clous. > III. 19

La trame serrée de la construction à ossature bois est, la plupart du temps, définie en fonction de la largeur des panneaux de contreventement, un entraxe de 62,5 cm étant courant. > Chap. Matériaux dérivés du bois La trame peut cependant aussi être déterminée par la largeur des isolants disponibles.   Trame

Ce qui caractérise toutefois la construction à ossature bois, c'est que la longueur totale d'un bâtiment ne doit pas forcément correspondre à un multiple exact de l'entraxe choisi. Il arrive souvent que le rythme de la trame soit rompu à l'extrémité des parois, au profit d'un entraxe qui en déroge. > III. 20 Tout aussi libre est l'agencement des fenêtres et des parois intérieures, dont la position n'est pas déterminée par la trame, comme c'est par exemple le cas dans la construction à pans de bois, mais par les seuls impératifs du projet. Dans la construction à ossature bois, la trame sert moins à garantir un ordre constructif et esthétique qu'à assurer une mise en œuvre économique des matériaux, très peu de restrictions étant ici imposées, par rapport à d'autres systèmes constructifs, à la conception des plans et des volumes.

Lors du montage, les bois de construction ne sont plus assemblés debout, comme dans la construction à pans de bois, mais cloués, à plat, en ossatures qui sont ensuite dressées, sans engin de levage particulier, sur la lisse basse ancrée à la dalle de fondation, puis fixées par clouage. Le doublement des bois horizontaux (traverses et lisses) est une caractéristique typique de la construction à ossature bois, qui préfère aux assemblages compliqués la simple juxtaposition ou superposition de pièces dont les sections sont ainsi doublées, voire triplées. > III. 21   Montage

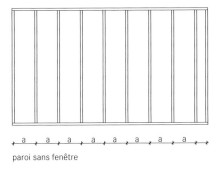

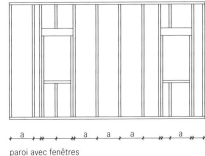

paroi sans fenêtre   paroi avec fenêtres

III. 20 : Élévation d'une ossature bois sans / avec fenêtres

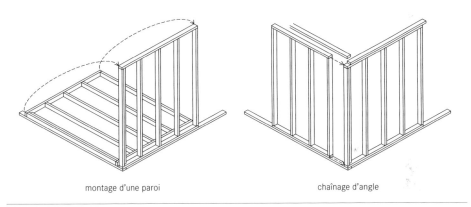

montage d'une paroi   chaînage d'angle

III. 21 : Montage et chaînage des ossatures bois

La solidarisation des parois ainsi montées obéit au même principe : sur les traverses supérieures des ossatures sont clouées des lisses supplémentaires, appelées <u>lisses hautes</u>, qui viennent ceinturer les parois et assurer un chaînage résistant à la traction.

Planchers   Le solivage que l'on pose ensuite sur les parois se compose lui aussi de sections minces, dont la hauteur dépend de la portée du plancher. Une poutre de rive de même hauteur, clouée aux solives, empêche celles-ci de basculer, mais le plancher n'est tout à fait stabilisé qu'une fois contreventé par des panneaux. Le solivage forme alors un voile rigide pouvant immédiatement servir de plate-forme de montage pour l'étage

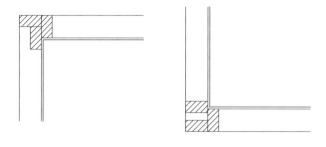

III. 22 : Solutions d'angle

III. 23 : Paroi à ossature bois, vue intérieure et extérieure

suivant, dont les parois sont dressées selon le même procédé. > III. 21 En Amérique, on construit selon le système du « platform-framing » des bâtiments pouvant compter jusqu'à six étages.   O

> O **Remarque:** Lors de l'assemblage des parois, il s'agit de placer les montants d'angle de manière à ménager pour le revêtement intérieur une surface de fixation d'une demi-largeur de section, soit de 3 cm, dans les deux directions. L'illustration 22 présente deux solutions envisageables.

Construction poteaux-poutres

Le système poteaux-poutres s'est développé à partir de la construction à pans de bois, dans le but de pouvoir organiser l'espace plus librement et ménager de plus grandes surfaces vitrées.

Le système consiste en une <u>structure primaire</u> composée de poteaux et de poutres, sur laquelle repose la structure secondaire des solives et des chevrons. Les parois délimitant les différents espaces sont placées indépendamment de la structure porteuse, ce qui permet une plus grande flexibilité dans l'agencement des plans et des façades. Ce mode de construction met en pratique l'idée de « <u>peau</u> » et de « <u>squelette</u> » prônée au XXe siècle par le Mouvement moderne.

Trame   Les poteaux porteurs sont ici sensiblement plus espacés que dans la construction à pans et à ossature bois. La structure porteuse reste la plupart du temps visible à l'extérieur ou à l'intérieur. Le bois lamellé-collé > Chap. Produits de construction en bois joue ici un rôle déterminant, lui seul permettant en effet de franchir les portées impliquées par les grandes distances entre poteaux.

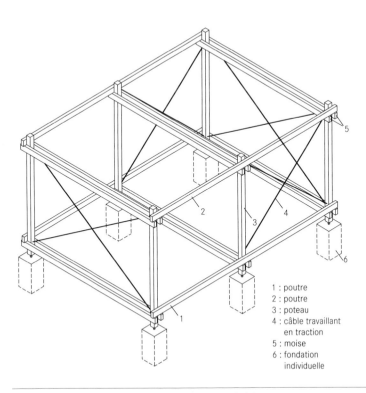

1 : poutre
2 : poutre
3 : poteau
4 : câble travaillant
    en traction
5 : moise
6 : fondation
    individuelle

Ill. 24 : Construction poteaux-poutres (assemblages moisés)

44

Les charges dues au vent sont en général reprises par des câbles ou des barres rondes en acier qui, ne pouvant travailler qu'en traction, sont disposés en croix. > Chap. Contreventement

Du fait de l'important espacement des poteaux, des fondations ponctuelles sont en général les plus appropriées. Les poteaux étant la plupart du temps détachés des parois, les pieds en acier zingué qui les fixent aux fondations constituent un détail caractéristique de la construction à poteaux-poutres.

Dans les bâtiments à plusieurs niveaux, le montage ne se fait pas étage par étage, mais au moyen de poteaux continus, auxquels les poutres horizontales sont raccordées soit sous forme de moises, > III. 24 et 25 soit à joint vif. > III. 26 et 27

Dans la construction à poteaux-poutres, les assemblages sont réalisés au moyen d'organes métalliques ne provoquant aucun affaiblissement notoire des sections de bois. À la différence des assemblages artisanaux caractérisant la construction en bois empilés et à pans de bois, les <u>assemblages industriels</u> faisant intervenir des connecteurs métalliques sont dimensionnés, d'après des tables, par l'ingénieur structure.

Assemblages

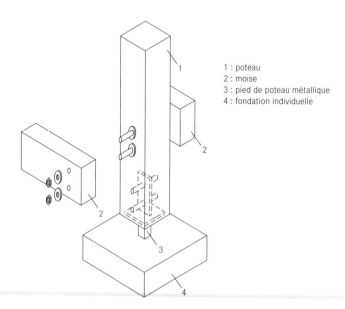

1 : poteau
2 : moise
3 : pied de poteau métallique
4 : fondation individuelle

III. 25 : Pied de poteau avec chevilles d'assemblage

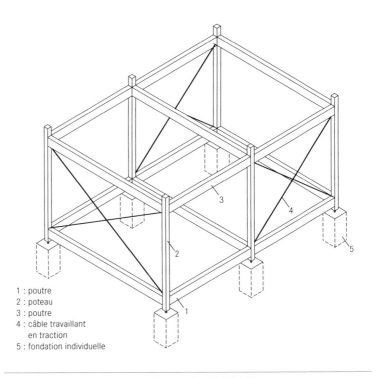

1 : poutre
2 : poteau
3 : poutre
4 : câble travaillant
    en traction
5 : fondation individuelle

III. 26 : Construction poteaux-poutres (assemblages à joint vif)

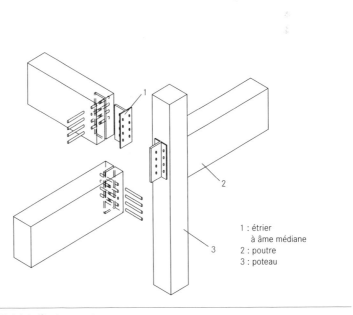

1 : étrier
    à âme médiane
2 : poutre
3 : poteau

III. 27 : Joint vif poteau-poutre

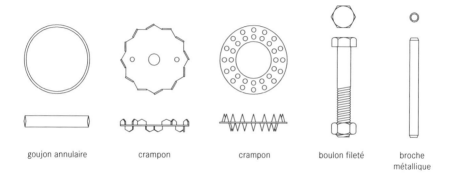

| goujon annulaire | crampon | crampon | boulon fileté | broche métallique |

III. 28 : Organes d'assemblage

Pour assurer une meilleure transmission des efforts entre pièces assemblées latéralement, > III. 25 on enfonce au niveau des surfaces de contact, soit dans un logement prévu à cet effet, soit à l'aide d'une presse, des anneaux ou des crampons > III. 28 permettant de répartir les charges sur un maximum de fibres, les liaisons étant ensuite assurées au moyen de boulons filetés.

Organes d'assemblage

Représentent un autre type d'organes d'assemblage les broches en acier rond, qui, enfoncées dans des trous prépercés, assurent la transmission des charges en association avec des étriers à âme noyée dans le bois. Cette solution permet de raccorder poteaux et poutres à joint vif, sans que les organes d'assemblage soient visibles de l'extérieur. > III. 27, 50 et Chap. Planchers

Construction en panneaux porteurs

Les avantages spécifiques de la construction en bois résident dans un montage rapide et « à sec », permettant de mettre en service les constructions dès leur achèvement. Or, la durée du chantier est encore réduite lorsque les différents éléments de parois, voire des modules entiers, sont préfabriqués en usine.

Si la construction à ossature bois se prête particulièrement bien à une préfabrication en atelier, les avantages de cette dernière, consistant à réduire au minimum les opérations à effectuer sur le chantier et à affranchir ainsi le processus de réalisation des conditions météorologiques, sont maximisés par la construction en panneaux porteurs.

Préfabrication

Ici, en effet, les éléments préfabriqués, allant en général du sol au plafond, sont déjà isolés et dotés de toutes les couches de construction nécessaires, y compris les revêtements extérieur et intérieur. Il ne s'agit donc plus, sur le chantier, que de les mettre en place et de les assembler, les joints entre éléments devant cependant faire l'objet d'un soin

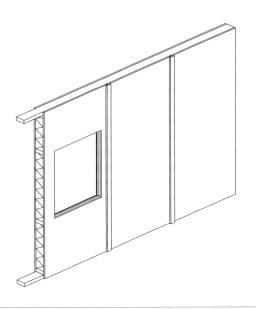

III. 29 : Panneaux porteurs préfabriqués

particulier. Les planchers intermédiaires, eux aussi préfabriqués, sont soit posés sur les éléments de parois, soit suspendus entre ceux-ci.

Tant que la construction en panneaux porteurs se base sur la construction à ossature bois, elle reste une technique relativement artisanale. On observe toutefois, depuis quelques années, une tendance à une industrialisation toujours plus poussée. Sont ainsi produits pour la construction en panneaux porteurs des éléments de parois massifs en bois contrecollé ou lamellé, assimilables à des panneaux en dérivés du bois de grand format.

De fait, alors que l'exigence d'utiliser la matière première de la façon la plus économique possible avait conduit à rationaliser les techniques basées sur l'assemblage d'éléments linéaires, des critères similaires de production industrielle et d'exploitation maximale du matériau > Chap. Matériaux dérivés du bois induisent aujourd'hui une réorientation de la construction en bois, amenée à se rapprocher de plus en plus de la construction massive.

Construction en panneaux
La construction en panneaux de béton, particulièrement répandue dans les pays d'Europe de l'Est et de Scandinavie, est bien connue. Du fait de leur poids élevé, les éléments préfabriqués se limitaient ici à une hauteur d'étage. Or le bois, beaucoup plus léger, permet de réaliser des éléments pouvant atteindre quatre étages de hauteur. Quant au danger d'une

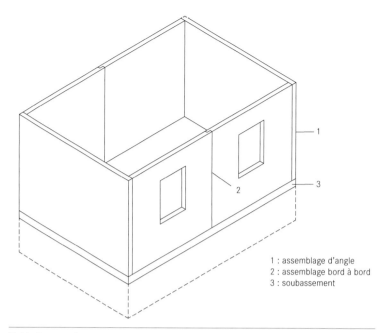

1 : assemblage d'angle
2 : assemblage bord à bord
3 : soubassement

III. 30 : Construction en panneaux massifs

architecture par trop stéréotypée – un problème récurrent lorsque l'on entend préfabriquer et normaliser les éléments de façade –, il peut être évité par une production individualisée, facilitée par la conception assistée par ordinateur et les nouvelles machines à commande numérique.

Construction en panneaux massifs

Les panneaux en bois massifs se composent de planches ou de madriers assemblés par collage, soit à fil parallèle, sous forme de bois lamellé-collé, soit à fil croisé, sous forme de bois contrecollé. Une autre possibilité consiste à clouer ensemble, face contre face, des planches disposées sur chant, pour obtenir des éléments en lamellé-cloué.

Ont par ailleurs été développées d'autres solutions encore, comme les parois composées de madriers verticaux assemblés en plusieurs couches sans colle ni organes métalliques, mais à l'aide de simples liteaux dotés d'un profil de type queue-d'aronde. Les fraiseuses à commande numérique garantissent ici la précision nécessaire. Aucune de ces constructions n'est sujette aux tassements.

Seront ici présentées plus en détail les constructions en panneaux contrecollés, aujourd'hui assez répandues. À la différence de la construction à pans de bois, à ossature bois et à poteaux-poutres, la construction en panneaux massifs ne requiert plus aucune trame. En termes de

III. 31 : Construction en panneaux massifs

conception, cela offre en principe une liberté accrue, car les dimensions des différents panneaux peuvent être adaptées au plan du bâtiment projeté. Sont en revanche déterminantes les contraintes statiques en matière de stabilité, de portées, de longueurs de flambage et de contre-ventement.

La hauteur des parois en panneaux contrecollés correspond au minimum à celle d'un niveau, mais souvent à celle de deux niveaux ou plus. La structure du bâtiment se compose ainsi d'éléments de paroi et de plafond massifs dont les dimensions maximales sont déterminées par les contraintes de transport et les capacités de production et de stockage de l'usine.

Le degré de préfabrication des éléments peut varier. L'option mini-male consiste à livrer sur le chantier des panneaux non isolés, où sont déjà percées les baies des façades. Il est cependant possible aussi de mettre en œuvre des éléments de paroi finis, déjà dotés de leur isolation, de leur bardage et de leurs menuiseries extérieures (portes et fenêtres). La préfabrication peut même aller jusqu'à la réalisation de locaux entiers en usine (« cellules » préfabriquées). Toutes ces options permettent de réduire la durée des travaux sur le chantier.

Les panneaux porteurs contrecollés utilisés dans le bâtiment sont similaires aux panneaux contreplaqués employés dans la construction de meubles. Mais alors que les seconds se composent d'un nombre impair de plis collés à fil croisé dont l'épaisseur est de l'ordre du milli-mètre > Chap. Matériaux dérivés du bois, les premiers se composent de couches dont l'épaisseur est celle d'une planche, et qui forment ensemble des éléments de paroi très résistants et rigides de 5 à 30 cm d'épaisseur.

Assemblages   Au niveau des angles et des raccords entre parois intérieures et extérieures, les différents éléments de paroi sont assemblés par vissage, à des intervalles en hauteur réguliers pouvant aller jusqu'à 30 cm. Comme

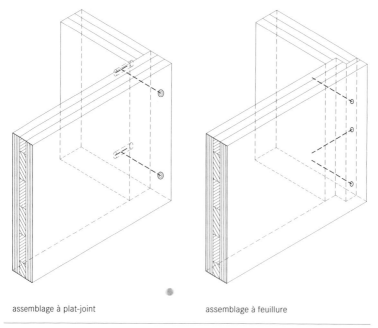

assemblage à plat-joint   assemblage à feuillure

III. 32 : Assemblages d'angle

l'orientation des planches varie d'une couche à l'autre, le vissage doit obéir aux mêmes conditions que celles qui s'appliquent au bois de bout. Cela signifie que, pour garantir une résistance suffisante à l'arrachement, les vis devront être <u>posées en biais</u>, tantôt vers le haut, tantôt vers le bas. Selon l'épaisseur des panneaux, leur inclinaison par rapport à l'horizontale pourra aller jusqu'à 45° au maximum. > III. 32

    Pour réaliser des assemblages en bout, un autre moyen consiste à recourir à des boulons à écrou transversal, semblables à ceux utilisés dans la construction de meubles.

Boulons à écrou transversal

    Composé d'un cylindre ou d'un demi-cylindre en acier percé transversalement et doté d'une rainure à l'une de ses extrémités, l'écrou est introduit dans un trou ajusté puis tourné, à l'aide d'un tournevis, de sorte que la tige filetée du boulon puisse être vissée dans le trou taraudé de l'écrou. Les efforts de traction sont ici transmis aux fibres du bois de manière uniforme sur toute la longueur du cylindre. > III. 34

    Les assemblages d'angle peuvent être exécutés à plat-joint ou à feuillure. Les raccords entre parois intérieures et extérieures sont en général réalisés à plat-joint. > III. 33 Quant à l'assemblage des panneaux juxtaposés bord à bord, il s'exécute en général à feuillure à mi-bois. > Chap. Construction en bois empilés Le vissage s'effectue ici à l'horizontale, c'est-à-dire

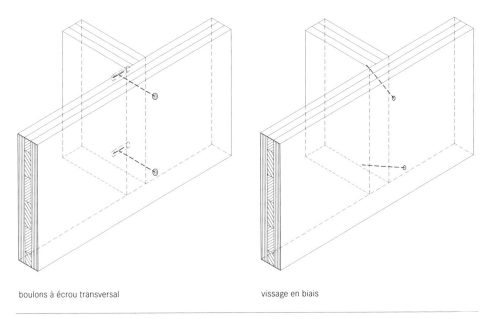

boulons à écrou transversal   vissage en biais

III. 33 : **Raccord entre parois intérieure et extérieure**

perpendiculairement aux fibres, ce qui garantit une liaison par friction suffisamment résistante.

Appuis de plancher L'exécution des appuis de plancher dépend de la hauteur des éléments de paroi. Si ces derniers vont de sol à plafond, les éléments de plancher massifs peuvent être directement posés et vissés sur ceux-ci, en en recouvrant toute l'épaisseur. Les parois de l'étage supérieur seront ensuite posées sur le plancher – comme dans la construction à ossature bois – et fixées à l'aide d'équerres métalliques.

Si la hauteur des éléments de paroi correspond en revanche à celle de deux ou plusieurs niveaux, les appuis de plancher ne pourront être réalisés qu'au moyen de lambourdes ou de profilés métalliques continus en équerre ou en U.

Au niveau des <u>toitures</u>, les appuis des éléments de toiture plate seront exécutés de manière similaire à ceux des planchers intermédiaires. Dans le cas des toitures inclinées, on pourra soit ériger sur le dernier plancher d'étage une charpente traditionnelle, soit opter pour la solution plus cohérente consistant à réaliser aussi les différents pans de toiture en panneaux de bois massifs.

Composition Si certains systèmes de construction bois mettent en œuvre des
des parois éléments en bois massif dans une épaisseur suffisante pour pouvoir se passer d'isolation thermique au niveau des parois extérieures, les

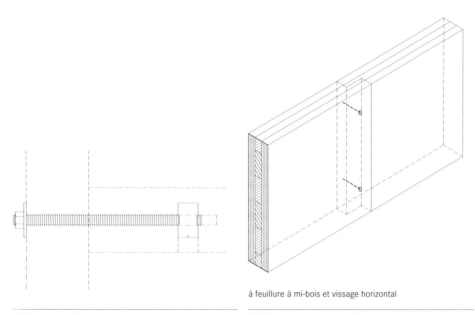

à feuillure à mi-bois et vissage horizontal

III. 34 : Boulon à écrou transversal vu en plan   III. 35 : Assemblage bord à bord

panneaux de bois massifs ne forment en général que le gros œuvre du bâtiment, qu'il convient dès lors de doter d'une isolation thermique rapportée et d'un bardage. De fait, la composition des parois se révèle, sur le principe, similaire à celle qui prévaut dans la construction en madriers empilés moderne. L'isolation, que des raisons de physique de la construction imposent de placer du côté extérieur, pourra par exemple être revêtue d'un bardage en panneaux dérivés du bois ou en liteaux ajourés. Les bardages à claire-voie nécessitent de poser, devant l'isolation, une barrière anti-humidité. > Chap. Parois extérieures Le lattage porteur pourra être directement fixé sur les panneaux contrecollés à l'aide de vis de longueur adaptée. Rien n'empêche par ailleurs d'opter pour un système d'isolation thermique extérieure crépie, d'autant que, dans le cas du bois contrecollé, les déformations dues au retrait et au gonflement sont négligeables. De manière générale, il est possible de renoncer à un pare-vapeur du côté intérieur des panneaux, de sorte que la question d'un éventuel revêtement intérieur dépendra en fin de compte de critères esthético-architecturaux. Il arrive toutefois souvent que soit ménagé, du côté intérieur, un vide destiné à accueillir des installations techniques et à être rempli d'une isolation thermique supplémentaire. Dans un tel cas, il sera nécessaire de prévoir un revêtement intérieur en plaques de plâtre cartonné ou en panneaux dérivés du bois.

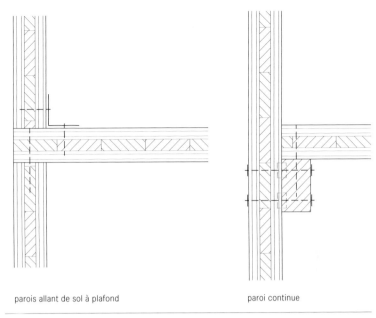

parois allant de sol à plafond   paroi continue

III. 36 : Appuis de plancher

Fondations   Dans le cas de la construction en panneaux massifs, l'exécution des fondations et du soubassement obéit, pour l'essentiel, aux mêmes principes que dans les autres systèmes de construction bois. Les éléments de paroi seront soit posés sur un radier en béton armé, soit fondés sur des semelles filantes sur lesquelles auront au préalable été posés, en guise de radier, des éléments en bois massifs. Les règles en matière de protection constructive du bois s'appliquent bien sûr aussi à la construction en panneaux massifs, le plus judicieux étant dès lors de prévoir, pour assurer la transition entre construction bois et terrain, un soubassement en béton.

Éventail des   La construction bois offre un éventail de possibilités assez étendu.
possibilités   Le choix d'un système dépendra de différents facteurs. Outre la décision fondamentale d'opter pour un système ouvert ou fermé – c'est-à-dire pour une construction à ossature ou pour une construction massive –, les contraintes techniques en matière de structure, de fabrication, de transport et de mise en œuvre sur le chantier revêtiront, elles aussi, une importance déterminante.

bardage en panneaux
lattage et ventilation
barrière anti-humidité
isolation thermique
panneaux contrecollés

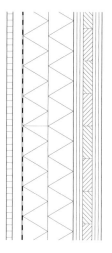

bardage en liteaux
lattage et ventilation
barrière anti-humidité
isolation thermique
panneaux contrecollés
isolation intérieure/
installations techniques
revêtement intérieur

III. 37 : Parois de composition différente

La construction bois n'a du reste pas fini de se développer. Aujourd'hui, le bois est aussi utilisé en combinaison avec d'autres matériaux – notamment le béton armé –, sous forme de constructions mixtes visant à exploiter au maximum les possibilités spécifiques offertes par chacun des matériaux mis en œuvre.

Éléments de construction

Dans cette troisième partie, nous examinerons plus en détail la construction, relativement complexe, des différents éléments que sont le soubassement, les parois, les planchers et la toiture, ainsi que leur rac-
○ cordement aux éléments contigus.

Les exigences et problèmes posés par chaque élément seront illustrés, à titre d'exemple, par des détails types de la construction à pans ou à ossature bois, représentés à l'échelle 1 : 10, sans qu'il soit nullement question de couvrir, tant s'en faut, le large éventail des solutions envisageables.

FONDATIONS

Pour assurer la <u>préservation du matériau</u>, la construction en bois proprement dite, reposant sur la dalle du sous-sol ou, en l'absence de cave, sur des fondations en béton ou en maçonnerie, devrait être surélevée d'environ 30 cm par rapport au terrain. Pour autant que la texture du sol ne requière pas de fondations spéciales, on pourra en principe recourir aux trois types de fondations suivants : > III. 38

— Fondations par dalle	=	fondations surfaciques
— Fondations filantes	=	fondations linéaires
— Fondations individuelles	=	fondations ponctuelles

Fondations par dalle

Sur une dalle de fondation (aussi appelée radier) peuvent être érigées des constructions exécutées selon n'importe lequel des systèmes présentés plus haut. Les fondations par dalle sont particulièrement appropriées aux constructions à ossature bois, où chaque «plate-forme» est utilisée pour le montage des parois. La dalle de béton pourra soit reposer de façon flottante sur un lit de gravier antigel compacté (gravier

○ **Remarque:** En ce qui concerne les toitures et les superstructures, nous n'aborderons ici que les problèmes de raccords avec les parois extérieures, le thème de la toiture étant en effet traité de façon approfondie in Tanja Brotrück, *Basics Construction de toitures*, Birkhäuser, Bâle 2007.

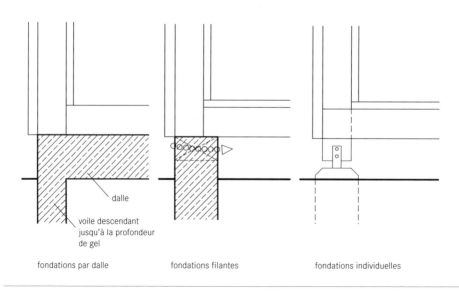

dalle

voile descendant
jusqu'à la profondeur
de gel

fondations par dalle   fondations filantes   fondations individuelles

III. 38 : Schéma des différents types de fondations

grossier), soit s'appuyer, sur tout son pourtour, sur des voiles de béton descendant jusqu'à la profondeur de gel.

Lorsque le bâtiment est excavé, la dalle du sous-sol, la plupart du temps construite en béton armé, remplace le radier.

Fondations filantes

Dans le cas de fondations filantes, le premier plancher devra être construit en bois. La protection constructive du bois, ici encore déterminante, nécessite de ménager sous le plancher un vide sanitaire. Celui-ci devra être inaccessible aux rongeurs, tout en laissant passer suffisamment d'air pour que le solivage soit constamment ventilé.

Un autre aspect important est la pose de l'isolation thermique. En effet, une fois les solives posées sur les fondations filantes, l'isolation ne peut plus être insérée que depuis le dessus, ce qui nécessite la pose préalable d'un lambrissage porté par des lattes fixées latéralement aux solives. > III. 41 Une autre solution consiste à mettre en œuvre des éléments de plancher préfabriqués, déjà isolés.

Dans les deux cas, les solives sont dimensionnées, comme celles des planchers intermédiaires, en fonction de leur portée. > Chap. Toiture

Fondations individuelles

Les fondations individuelles, permettant de réduire à un minimum la quantité de matériau à excaver, sont particulièrement adaptées à la construction à poteaux-poutres, où les charges sont transmises au sol de fondation de façon ponctuelle et concentrée.

Le premier plancher se construit selon le même principe que les planchers intermédiaires, soit, dans le cas d'une structure à poteaux-poutres, au moyen de poutres primaires et secondaires.

Pour assurer la transition entre poteaux et fondations, on trouve dans le commerce différents supports en acier zingué, garantissant la protection constructive du bois. Ce point de la construction étant cependant des plus sensible, on veillera à ce que le pied des poteaux reste en permanence aéré, et puisse s'égoutter librement. > III. 39 et Chap. Préservation du bois

Soubassement

Quel que soit le système constructif choisi, le soubassement d'un bâtiment est particulièrement sollicité, tant par les remontées d'humidité que par le rejaillissement de l'eau de pluie ou la neige en hiver. Aussi les parois extérieures en bois devraient-elles respecter, pour des raisons de protection constructive, une distance de 30 cm par rapport au terrain, la liaison avec les fondations devant être assurée par des matériaux résistants à l'humidité. > Chap. Préservation du bois

Le soubassement, souvent réalisé en béton apparent, a pour double fonction de marquer la limite extérieure du bâtiment et de protéger celui-ci contre l'humidité. Pour ce faire, la dalle de fondation se prolonge jusqu'au niveau de la façade. Grâce au matériau coulé qu'est le béton, le soubassement peut être conçu de telle manière que l'air puisse pénétrer sans obstacle dans le vide de ventilation de la façade. Pour éviter les

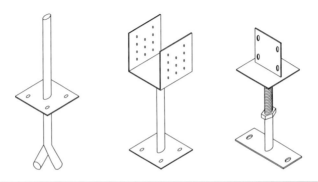

III. 39 : Pieds de poteaux en acier

construction de la paroi extérieure:

clins à recouvrement
lattage
voile travaillant/pare-vent
isolation thermique/
structure porteuse
pare-vapeur/pare-air
revêtement intérieur

construction du plancher:

revêtement de sol
chape sèche
isolation thermique
isolation contre les
bruits d'impact
barrière anti-humidité
dalle de fondation
lit de gravier

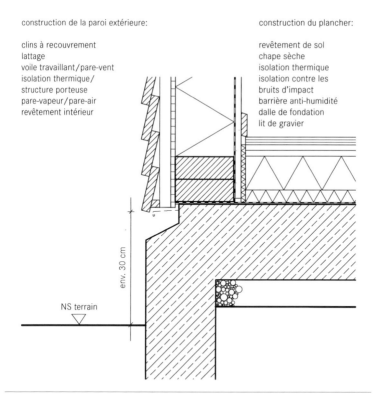

env. 30 cm

NS terrain

III. 40 : Soubassement d'une construction à ossature bois sur dalle de fondation

traînées de saleté, le soubassement ne devrait pas arriver tout à fait au nu du bardage, mais observer un léger retrait, de la profondeur d'un larmier. On fermera le vide de ventilation de la façade par une grille anti-insectes. > III. 40

Étant particulièrement exposées aux remontées d'humidité et aux rejaillissements, les lisses et traverses basses doivent se composer d'un bois dur, très résistant. On vérifiera dans les dispositions réglementaires du pays concerné s'il est possible, comme en Allemagne, de renoncer à une protection chimique du bois. Dans tous les cas, bois et béton devront être séparés par une barrière anti-humidité. C'est aussi à cet endroit que sont raccordés l'étanchéité du radier et le pare-vapeur de la paroi extérieure.

Préservation
du bois

○

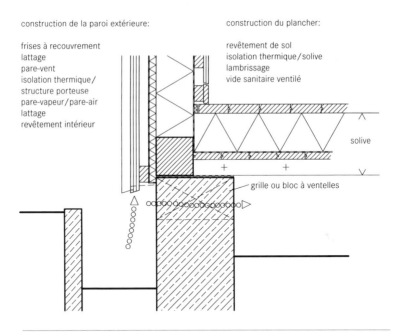

construction de la paroi extérieure:

frises à recouvrement
lattage
pare-vent
isolation thermique/
structure porteuse
pare-vapeur/pare-air
lattage
revêtement intérieur

construction du plancher:

revêtement de sol
isolation thermique/solive
lambrissage
vide sanitaire ventilé

solive

grille ou bloc à ventelles

III. 41 : Soubassement d'une construction à pans de bois sur fondations filantes

Dans la solution présentée à l'illustration 41, le soubassement est constitué de fondations filantes suffisamment larges pour que la sablière basse de la paroi extérieure et les solives du plancher puissent y prendre appui. Il est ici possible de renoncer à une barrière anti-humidité, pour autant que le vide ménagé entre terrain et plancher soit ventilé en permanence. À cet effet, on intègre dans les fondations des grilles ou des blocs avec ventelles.

○ **Remarque:** Les bâtiments en bois doivent être ancrés à leurs fondations. Pour ce faire, tant les lisses ou sablières basses que les montants sont fixés à intervalles réguliers sur le radier ou les fondations filantes, au moyen de goujons collés ou de chevilles pour charges lourdes.

Le soubassement apparent des bâtiments en bois en conditionne dans une large mesure l'aspect. Si l'on souhaite toutefois, comme dans l'exemple en question, faciliter l'accès au bâtiment et rendre le soubassement invisible en élévation, on pourra creuser en contiguïté immédiate du bâtiment une rigole périphérique, de manière à pouvoir abaisser le socle tout en assurant la protection constructive du bois. Pour des raisons de sécurité, on couvrira de telles tranchées par un caillebotis.

PAROIS EXTÉRIEURES

Les parois extérieures, constitutives de l'enveloppe du bâtiment, sont soumises à de multiples sollicitations. Elles doivent en effet protéger des influences extérieures que sont le vent, la pluie, les variations de température, le bruit et les rayonnements, tout en faisant face aux phénomènes de différences de température, de convection d'air, de transmission phonique et de diffusion de vapeur d'eau qui se produisent de l'intérieur vers l'extérieur.

Couches de construction

Dans la construction traditionnelle en bois empilés, reprise des charges, isolation, étanchéité et protection sont assurées, comme dans la maçonnerie, par un seul et unique matériau. Dans les constructions légères à ossature, en revanche, ces différentes fonctions sont attribuées à différentes couches et matériaux, qu'il s'agit, pour éviter les désordres et les points faibles, de placer dans le bon ordre et d'harmoniser les uns avec les autres. Chargé de déterminer la succession et l'épaisseur des couches et d'en étudier les raccords, l'architecte devra commencer par choisir entre une construction ventilée ou non. > III. 42

Dans une construction non ventilée, peau extérieure et ossature porteuse forment une paroi unique, tandis que, dans une construction ventilée, elles sont séparées par une lame d'air, chacun des deux complexes ainsi obtenus assumant des fonctions spécifiques :

Complexe extérieur	protection contre les intempéries, ventilation
Complexe intérieur	étanchéité au vent, isolation thermique / structure porteuse, barrière-vapeur / étanchéité à l'air, revêtement intérieur

Physique de la construction

L'exécution la plus sûre et, de ce fait, la plus fréquente, est la construction ventilée. La lame d'air a pour effet d'abaisser la tension superficielle et d'équilibrer la pression d'air, ce qui permet d'éviter les infiltrations d'eau de pluie. On devra cependant veiller à ce que celle-ci puisse s'écouler librement le long du bardage, la lame d'air ventilée assurant pour sa part l'évacuation de la vapeur d'eau provenant de

Vide de ventilation

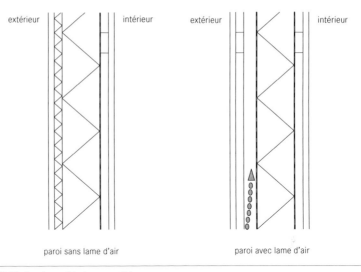

extérieur   intérieur   extérieur   intérieur

paroi sans lame d'air   paroi avec lame d'air

III. 42 : Paroi ventilée / non ventilée

l'intérieur du bâtiment ou de l'humidité provenant de l'isolation thermique. Le vide de ventilation offre en outre l'avantage d'évacuer de la façade, en été, une grande partie de l'air surchauffé.

La lame d'air doit présenter une épaisseur d'au moins 20 mm, aucun autre élément (fenêtre, soubassement, etc.) ne devant en interrompre ou en réduire la section. L'air doit pouvoir entrer au niveau du soubassement et ressortir au sommet de la paroi, en rive de toiture. On munira les orifices de ventilation d'une grille anti-insectes.

Étanchéité
au vent

L'écran pare-vent, appliqué sur la face extérieure de l'isolation thermique, protège celle-ci de trop forts refroidissements et empêche l'air extérieur de pénétrer, à travers les joints, entre isolation et construction.

En présence d'un bardage à claire-voie, > Chap. Bardage extérieur le pare-vent doit aussi protéger l'isolation des infiltrations d'humidité. Les couches de construction devant cependant présenter une perméabilité croissante à la vapeur d'eau de l'intérieur vers l'extérieur, le pare-vent doit être le plus ouvert possible à la diffusion de vapeur. Lorsque la structure porteuse est extérieurement revêtue d'un voile travaillant, cette fonction peut être assumée par les panneaux de contreventement, à condition que leurs joints verticaux soient dotés de feuillures. Dans le cas contraire, on posera des films ou des membranes pare-vent.

Si le bois rencontre aujourd'hui un grand succès auprès des maîtres d'ouvrage et des architectes, c'est, entre autres, parce qu'il répond bien mieux aux exigences croissantes en matière d'isolation thermique et d'économies d'énergie que d'autres matériaux comme, par exemple, la maçonnerie. Bien que des ossatures d'une épaisseur de 12 à 16 cm remplies d'isolant offrent déjà une isolation assez satisfaisante, on y ajoute la plupart du temps des couches d'isolation supplémentaires, soit à l'extérieur, soit à l'intérieur.

Isolation thermique/ structure porteuse

Peuvent être ici utilisés quasiment tous les isolants disponibles dans le commerce. Le polystyrène expansé (EPS) et extrudé (XPS) et tous les panneaux en mousse rigide présentent toutefois l'inconvénient de ne pas pouvoir s'adapter au retrait du bois. De ce point de vue, les produits les plus adéquats sont les isolants fibreux en plaques, dont la compressibilité permet de mieux compenser les mouvements du bois.

Une autre possibilité, souvent appliquée, consiste à isoler les parois avec des flocons de cellulose produits à partir de vieux papier. Mise en œuvre par soufflage ou insufflation, une telle isolation est tout à fait adaptée aux constructions à ossature bois, dont les montants et les voiles travaillants forment des compartiments fermés.

On veillera ici à protéger l'isolation de l'humidité, pour éviter que le gonflement du bois ne provoque des déformations de parois considérables et des dommages irrémédiables. Pour empêcher l'isolation de pourrir et la rendre moins facilement inflammable, on y ajoutera des sels de bore.

Dans le chapitre consacré à la protection du bois, nous avons montré que le bois devait être protégé de l'humidité. Cela ne vaut cependant pas seulement pour l'humidité provenant de l'extérieur, mais aussi pour la vapeur d'eau provenant de l'intérieur du bâtiment, susceptible de se déposer dans la construction sous forme d'eau de condensation.

Étanchéité à la vapeur d'eau et à l'air

■ **Astuce:** Une couche d'isolation supplémentaire, appliquée du côté intérieur ou extérieur, permet de couvrir les joints entre l'ossature porteuse et l'isolation dont elle est remplie. On utilise souvent ici, en raison de leur assez bonne stabilité propre, des panneaux de fibres tendres (voir Chap. Matériaux dérivés du bois) servant aussi, lorsqu'ils sont appliqués à l'extérieur, de pare-vent et, s'ils sont bituminés, de protection contre l'humidité.

De l'humidité peut pénétrer dans la construction soit par diffusion (vapeur d'eau), soit par convection (air ambiant), l'étanchéité à la vapeur d'eau et à l'air revêtant de ce fait, dans la construction en bois, une importance primordiale. Il s'agit d'empêcher, grâce à une couche pare-vapeur et pare-air, que l'effet isolant du mur soit réduit à néant par des phénomènes de condensation et de courants d'air.

Cela vaut tant pour les parois ventilées que pour les non ventilées, une enveloppe étanche à l'air, comportant le moins d'éléments traversants et de raccords possible, étant dans tous les cas requise. En général, les fonctions pare-vapeur et pare-air sont assumées par une seule et même couche, appliquée sur la face intérieure de l'isolation.

Résistance à la diffusion de vapeur d'eau

Les parois extérieures doivent être construites de manière à empêcher la diffusion de vapeur d'eau, et à évacuer l'humidité s'étant déjà infiltrée dans la construction. Aussi devra-t-on veiller à ce que la résistance des différents matériaux à la diffusion de vapeur d'eau (valeur sd) diminue de l'intérieur vers l'extérieur.

On établit à cet égard la distinction suivante :

Élément ouvert à la diffusion de vapeur d'eau	sd < 2 m
Frein-vapeur	sd 2–1500 m
Pare-vapeur	sd ≥ 1500 m

Dans les constructions ventilées, un frein-vapeur suffit. Composé de papiers spéciaux ou de films, celui-ci permet à la vapeur d'eau produite dans les locaux de diffuser à travers l'isolation thermique de façon dosée et contrôlée, pour être ensuite évacuée via la lame d'air.

Dans les constructions non ventilées, il est nécessaire de prévoir, à l'intérieur, un pare-vapeur constitué de membranes plastique ou de feuilles de métal étanches à la vapeur d'eau, empêchant cette dernière de diffuser vers l'extérieur.

Bardage extérieur

Dans la construction en bois, la protection contre les intempéries est en général assurée par une peau extérieure en bois ou en panneaux en dérivés du bois. Dans certains pays, comme en Amérique, il n'est cependant pas rare de trouver des revêtements composés d'autres matériaux, par exemple du métal ou du crépi. D'un point de vue constructif, il est toutefois plus judicieux de combiner des matériaux dotés de propriétés similaires. C'est particulièrement vrai pour un matériau vivant comme le bois, qui gonfle et se rétracte. À ces arguments s'en ajoutent par ailleurs d'autres, de nature esthétique, tout le charme de la construction en bois résidant en effet dans la force expressive, la chaleur et la texture propres à ce matériau.

Le bardage extérieur offre de nombreuses possibilités de mise en forme. Ainsi pourra-t-on choisir non seulement le type de bardage à mettre en œuvre, mais aussi l'essence et la qualité du bois, la largeur et l'orientation des lames ou des panneaux, ainsi que leurs finitions et patinage.

Bien qu'invisibles, les lattes portant les lames ou les panneaux constituent un élément essentiel du bardage. L'exécution de la sous-construction, fixée à la structure porteuse, dépendra de la présence ou non d'une lame d'air, et de l'orientation, horizontale ou verticale, du bardage. Quant à l'écartement des lattes, il sera déterminé par l'épaisseur des lames, et vice versa. > Tab. 8

○ Sous-construction

Lames et lattes devant être systématiquement croisées, un bardage vertical nécessitera un lattage porteur horizontal. Dans le cas d'une construction ventilée, il s'agira, pour garantir un flux d'air ininterrompu de bas en haut, de prévoir un contre-lattage ou lattage de ventilation supplémentaire. Dans le cas d'un bardage horizontal, cette fonction sera assumée par le lattage porteur vertical.

Les lames peuvent être fixées au moyen de vis, de clous ou de clameaux. Un clouage comportant toutefois le risque d'endommager tant la surface du bardage que la sous-construction, une fixation par vissage est plus sûre et plus facile à contrôler.

Fixation

Il n'est pas toujours nécessaire d'utiliser des matériaux résistants à la corrosion. Pour éviter cependant les coulures de rouille, on utilise

Tab. 8: Écartement des lattes porteuses

Épaisseur des lames [mm]	Écartement des lattes [mm]
18,0	400–550
22,0	550–800
24,0	600–900
28,0	800–1050

○ **Remarque:** La valeur sd d'une couche de construction correspond à l'épaisseur d'une couche d'air immobile présentant la même résistance à la diffusion de vapeur d'eau. Exprimée en mètres, elle correspond au produit de l'épaisseur du matériau (s) et de son coefficient de résistance à la diffusion μ : sd = $\mu \times$ s [m]. Plus grande est la valeur sd, plus la couche en question est étanche à la vapeur d'eau.

○ **Remarque:** Les propriétés et les effets esthétiques des revêtements en bois sont approfondis in Manfred Hegger, Hans Drexler, Martin Zeumer, *Basics Matérialité,* Birkhäuser, Bâle 2007.

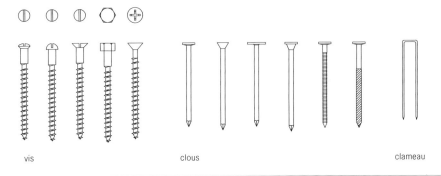

vis   clous   clameau

III. 43 : Organes de fixation

d'ordinaire des clous ou des vis en acier inoxydable ou en métal zingué. La fixation des lames ne devant pas empêcher le bois de gonfler ou de se rétracter, les pointes ne devraient, dans le cas d'un bardage à recouvrement, traverser qu'une seule lame. Quant aux couvre-joints, ils ne doivent être fixés qu'à une seule lame, ou alors dans les joints. Aucune pointe ne devrait jamais être enfoncée dans du bois de bout, même pour les éléments d'importance secondaire.

Parmi les bardages verticaux, on distingue entre : > III. 45

— les bardages en frises à recouvrement
— les bardages à couvre-joints
— les bardages en frises posées sur lattes
— les bardages en frises profilées.

■   Dans un bardage en frises à recouvrement, les lames de dessus re-

Bardage en frises à recouvrement couvrent les lames de dessous d'environ 20 mm. Lorsque toutes les lames sont de même largeur, il en résulte, en élévation, une alternance

> ■ **Astuce:** Dans le cas de frises à recouvrement, on peut renoncer à un lattage de ventilation, la section ininterrompue du vide compris entre lame de dessus et lame de dessous assurant une ventilation suffisante (voir III. 45).

> ■ **Astuce:** Dans un bardage en frises à recouvrement, la face des lames orientée vers le duramen devrait être tournée vers l'extérieur, de manière que les joints entre lames de dessus et de dessous restent fermés lorsque les frises se déforment en séchant (tuilage) (voir Chap. Humidité du bois).

III. 44 : Bardages verticaux : frises posées sur lattes, frises à couvre-joints, frises à claire-voie, frises profilées

de frises larges et plus étroites. À l'instar du bardage à couvre-joints, les frises à recouvrement produisent une surface assez fortement profilée.

Dans le bardage à couvre-joints, le joint d'environ 10 mm séparant les frises est couvert par une latte empêchant l'eau de pluie d'y pénétrer. > III. 44 et 45

Bardage à couvre-joints

Dans un bardage en frises posées sur lattes, les lattes fermant les joints sont posées du côté intérieur, ce qui produit, comme dans le cas d'un bardage en frises profilées, une peau extérieure sans ressauts, relativement lisse.

Bardage en frises posées sur lattes

Dans un bardage en frises profilées, les lames sont assemblées par feuillure ou bouvetage (rainure et languette), ce qui permet de rendre les fixations invisibles, soit en posant les clous dans les rainures, soit en utilisant des clameaux. Pour permettre aux lames de travailler, leur assemblage devra présenter un certain jeu. Alors que dans les autres types de bardages verticaux, les angles sont fermés par recouvrement des deux couches de lames et de lattes, le bardage en frises profilées nécessite la pose de lames ou lattes cornières supplémentaires. > III. 45

Bardage en frises profilées

○ **Remarque:** On fait la distinction entre bardages à joints fermés et bardages à joints ouverts ou à claire-voie. Dans ce dernier cas, l'écran pare-vent doit aussi faire office de barrière anti-humidité, pour empêcher l'eau de pluie de pénétrer dans le plan de l'isolation thermique.

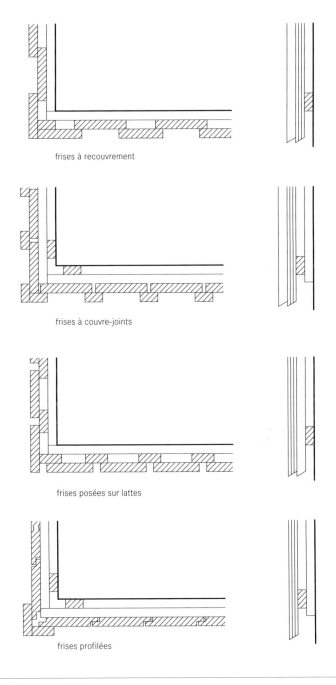

frises à recouvrement

frises à couvre-joints

frises posées sur lattes

frises profilées

III. 45 : Bardages verticaux

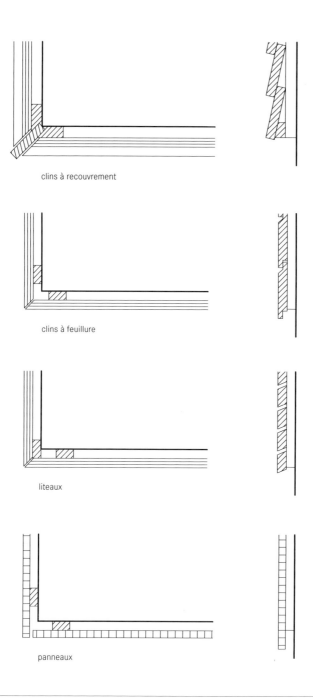

clins à recouvrement

clins à feuillure

liteaux

panneaux

III. 46 : Bardages horizontaux

III. 47 : Bardages horizontaux : clins à recouvrement, clins à feuillure, bardeaux, clins à claire-voie

Parmi les bardages horizontaux, on distingue entre : > III. 46

— les bardages en clins à recouvrement
— les bardages en clins à feuillure.

On trouve par ailleurs aussi :

— les vêtures en bardeaux
— les bardages en liteaux
— les bardages en panneaux.

Bardage en clins à recouvrement

Dans un bardage en clins à recouvrement, le chevauchement devra se monter à 12 % de la largeur des lames, mais à 10 mm au minimum. Les clins sont en général dépourvus de feuillures, mais il arrive qu'ils en présentent au niveau du chevauchement.

Qu'il s'agisse de frises ou de clins, le principe du recouvrement offre un certain jeu, qui facilite tant la répartition régulière des lames sur la paroi que les raccords au niveau des portes et des fenêtres.

> ■ **Astuce:** Du point de vue de la protection du bois, les bardages horizontaux ont l'avantage, par rapport aux bardages verticaux, de permettre un remplacement aisé des clins endommagés au niveau du soubassement, ce qui est d'autant plus utile que le socle du bâtiment est bas ou exposé.

Dans un bardage à recouvrement, une disposition oblique des lames requiert, au niveau des angles, des coupes en onglet géométriquement compliquées. Pour contourner cette difficulté, on fait souvent buter les lames du bardage contre une planche verticale placée en diagonale. > III. 46

Dans un bardage en clins à feuillure, en revanche, il est tout aussi facile de réaliser des assemblages d'angle en onglet que de dissimuler les fixations. Cela se fait, comme dans les bardages en frises profilées, soit au moyen de clameaux spéciaux, soit en posant les clous ou les vis dans les rainures. > III. 46 et 47

Les vêtures en bardeaux se composent d'écailles de bois clouées ou vissées à joints décalés sur un lattage. > III. 47, au milieu à droite Du fait de leur petit format (largeurs de 50 à 350 mm et longueurs de 120 à 800 mm), les bardeaux permettent de couvrir plus facilement des surfaces incurvées et de réaliser des transitions douces. On trouve dans le commerce des bardeaux <u>sciés</u> ou <u>refendus</u>. Les bardeaux refendus, dont la structure cellulaire n'est pas altérée lors de la taille, sont plus durables. Le mélèze est une essence appropriée à la fabrication de bardeaux. Pour permettre au bois de gonfler, on prévoira entre les bardeaux des joints de 1 à 5 mm, la pose pouvant se faire en deux ou trois couches. Les bardeaux peuvent aussi servir de matériau de couverture, pour autant que la toiture soit suffisamment inclinée (30 à 40°).

Les bardages en liteaux horizontaux ou verticaux sont des bardages à <u>claire-voie</u>, dont les joints ne sont pas couverts. > III. 46 et 47 Il est donc impératif de prévoir ici une lame d'air permettant d'évacuer l'eau de pluie s'étant infiltrée derrière les liteaux, le pare-vent devant quant à lui servir aussi de pare-pluie pour protéger l'isolation thermique. Il est judicieux, pour protéger le bois, de couper les liteaux horizontaux en biseau, une telle mesure n'étant en revanche pas nécessaire dans le cas d'un bardage vertical.

Dans le cas des bardages en panneaux, on veillera à ce que la classe de collage des panneaux choisis corresponde à une mise en œuvre exposée aux intempéries. > Chap. Matériaux dérivés du bois Se prêtent à un tel emploi les panneaux en dérivés du bois suivants :

— Panneaux contreplaqués de construction (BFU)
— Panneaux à trois plis en bois résineux (FSH)
— Panneaux de particules liés au ciment (ZSP)

Les <u>tranches</u> des panneaux de bardage, très sensibles, posent un problème particulier. Une solution sûre consiste à les protéger par des <u>couvre-joints</u>, dont il est possible d'accentuer le rythme en leur donnant, comme le font certains architectes, une couleur différente de celle des panneaux.

Bardage en clins à feuillure

■

Vêtures en bardeaux

Bardage en liteaux

Bardage en panneaux

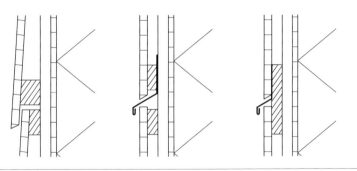

III. 48 : Joints horizontaux

Si l'on souhaite en revanche souligner l'aspect lisse et plat d'un bardage en panneaux, le plus efficace est de ménager entre ceux-ci des joints en creux d'au moins 10 mm, les tranches des panneaux devant alors être protégées de l'humidité par un enduit hydrofuge.

Au niveau des joints horizontaux, on biseautera le bord inférieur des panneaux selon un angle de 15°, de manière à former un larmier. On empêchera en outre l'eau de stagner sur le bord supérieur des panneaux en posant entre ceux-ci une bavette métallique inclinée de 15° vers l'extérieur. > III. 48

Les panneaux sont la plupart du temps fixés au moyen de vis apparentes en acier inoxydable. Pour rendre les fixations invisibles, on devra accrocher les panneaux à une sous-construction spécialement conçue, différents systèmes étant disponibles dans le commerce.

Lorsque les panneaux formant angle se rencontrent à joint vif, comme dans l'illustration 46, on veillera à ce que la tranche nue ne donne pas du côté le plus exposé aux intempéries.

○ **Remarque:** Les bardages en panneaux étant très sensibles, il est conseillé, pour réduire l'impact des intempéries, de prendre des mesures préventives de protection constructive, pouvant consister à orienter le bâtiment de façon judicieuse, à prévoir de grands avant-toits et/ou à réaliser des dalles de balcons continues sur tout le pourtour du bâtiment.

Finitions

En tant qu'éléments non porteurs ne devant répondre à aucune exigence particulière en matière de stabilité dimensionnelle, les bardages ne requièrent aucune protection chimique. > Chap. Préservation du bois

Il s'agit toutefois de prendre des mesures de protection physique, destinées à empêcher une absorption d'eau de pluie excessive et une altération superficielle du bois par le rayonnement UV. L'application d'une lasure pigmentée ou d'un enduit couvrant empêchera le bois de devenir gris avec le temps.

Grisaillement

Le grisaillement ne faisant cependant que modifier la couleur du bois, sans l'endommager, maints architectes s'en servent comme d'un véritable moyen esthétique. Ainsi les façades du Sea Ranch des architectes Moore, Lyndon, Turnbull & Whitaker, construit sur la côte Ouest des États-Unis > III. p. 73, ont-elles par exemple pris au fil des décennies, sous l'influence des rayons UV et des embruns, une patine gris argenté, grâce à laquelle les bâtiments paraissent aujourd'hui faire corps avec la nature. Lors de la conception, on tiendra compte du fait que d'éventuels retraits ou saillies en façade peuvent conduire, du fait des différences d'exposition qui en résultent, à des différences de coloration indésirables.

Peintures/ lasures

D'autre part, les enduits colorés peuvent constituer, eux aussi, un précieux moyen de composition, comme en témoignent les bâtiments en bois scandinaves peints dans des couleurs vives.

On pourra ici recourir tant à des lasures pigmentées qu'à des enduits couvrants. Les systèmes d'enduit se composent en général d'une couche de base, d'une couche intermédiaire et d'une couche de finition, la compatibilité des produits employés revêtant bien sûr une importance déterminante.

Revêtement intérieur et installations techniques

Le revêtement intérieur des parois pourra consister en lames de lambrissage ou en panneaux en dérivés du bois, par exemple en contreplaqué. Un revêtement composé d'une ou deux couches de placoplâtre,

■ **Astuce:** Les lames de bardage devraient toujours être peintes avant le montage, pour éviter que les parties non enduites n'apparaissent suite au retrait du bois. Pour prévenir le tuilage des lames (voir Chap. Types de débits), celles-ci devraient être au moins enduites des deux côtés d'une couche de base.

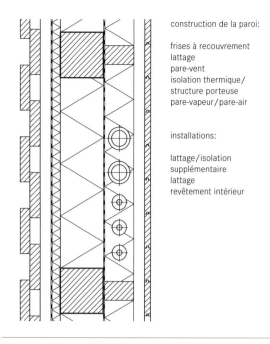

construction de la paroi:

frises à recouvrement
lattage
pare-vent
isolation thermique/
structure porteuse
pare-vapeur/pare-air

installations:

lattage/isolation
supplémentaire
lattage
revêtement intérieur

III. 49 : Couche destinée aux installations (plan)

aussi appelé <u>crépi sec</u>, permettra pour sa part d'améliorer, grâce à sa masse volumique relativement élevée, l'isolation phonique de la paroi extérieure.

Si le revêtement intérieur peut s'appliquer à même l'ossature porteuse, il est préférable de le fixer à un lattage, une telle sous-construction facilitant en effet une pose d'aplomb, tout en permettant une ventilation du revêtement.

L'intégration des installations techniques dans les parois extérieures constitue, dans la construction en bois, un problème récurrent. Pour éviter qu'elles ne traversent l'enveloppe du bâtiment, étanche à la vapeur et à l'air, les installations sanitaires, électriques et de chauffage devraient en principe être intégrées dans les parois intérieures. Comme il est cependant rarement possible de ne pas faire passer de conduites dans les parois extérieures, on leur ménage la plupart du temps, en augmentant la largeur des lattes à 4 ou 6 cm, une couche située avant le pare-vapeur, dont on pourra en même temps se servir comme couche d'isolation thermique supplémentaire. Dans les salles de bains et autres salles d'eau, on logera les installations dans des parois et des gaines leur étant spécialement destinées. > III. 49

Installations techniques

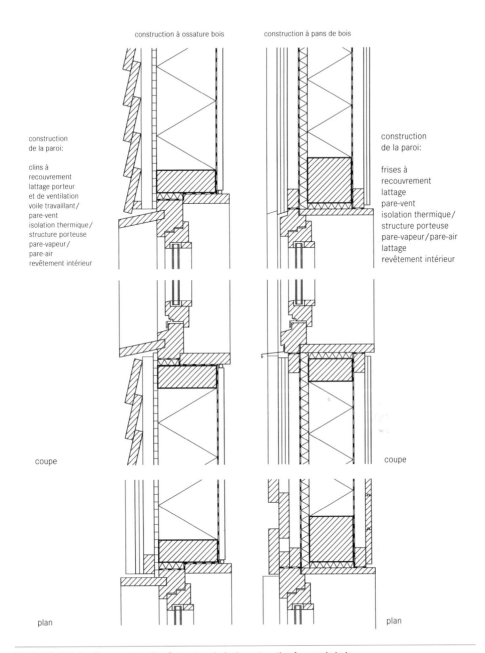

construction à ossature bois

construction à pans de bois

construction
de la paroi:

clins à
recouvrement
lattage porteur
et de ventilation
voile travaillant/
pare-vent
isolation thermique/
structure porteuse
pare-vapeur/
pare-air
revêtement intérieur

construction
de la paroi:

frises à
recouvrement
lattage
pare-vent
isolation thermique/
structure porteuse
pare-vapeur/pare-air
lattage
revêtement intérieur

coupe

coupe

plan

plan

III. 50 : Détail de fenêtre, construction à ossature bois / construction à pans de bois

76

Baies

Pour ne pas affaiblir la protection physique offerte par l'enveloppe du bâtiment, il s'agit de raccorder avec le plus grand soin aux baies (portes, fenêtres) toutes les couches dont se composent les parois extérieures (pare-vent, isolation thermique, pare-vapeur et pare-air), les transitions entre bardage et fenêtres méritant par ailleurs une attention particulière d'un point de vue esthétique.

Dans le détail de l'illustration 50, à gauche, le bardage en clins, assez fortement profilé, vient buter contre un cadre solidement fixé, sur les quatre côtés, au dormant de la fenêtre. Au niveau du linteau et de l'appui, les planches de ce cadre sont inclinées vers le bas, pour permettre l'écoulement et l'égouttement de l'eau de pluie.

Pour que la ventilation du bardage soit aussi assurée au niveau des raccords avec les fenêtres, on veillera à ce que l'air puisse s'échapper au niveau des appuis et entrer au niveau des linteaux. On protégera en outre le vide de ventilation par une grille anti-insectes. Ventilation

À l'intérieur, les joints entre dormant et structure porteuse sont couverts, comme à l'extérieur, par un cadre fermé.

À l'instar du pare-vent extérieur, le pare-vapeur doit être raccordé de façon étanche au dormant, le joint entre dormant et structure porteuse devant, quant à lui, être rempli d'isolation thermique. Pare-vapeur

Dans le cas d'une construction à pans de bois avec frises à recouvrement, > Ill. 50 à droite on pourra renoncer à un encadrement extérieur en plaçant la fenêtre dans le plan du bardage, le joint vertical entre fenêtre et bardage étant alors couvert par la lame de dessus correspondante.

La membrane pare-vent est raccordée de façon étanche au dormant au moyen d'une latte. Au niveau du linteau, on devra pratiquer dans le dormant une feuillure oblique, destinée à recevoir le bardage vertical. Pare-vent

À l'intérieur, la profonde embrasure sera délimitée par un cadre solidement fixé au dormant, auquel le pare-vapeur et le revêtement intérieur seront raccordés de façon étanche. Quant à la fenêtre elle-même, elle sera fixée à la structure porteuse au moyen de cornières en acier zingué.

PAROIS INTÉRIEURES
Couches de construction

Il convient d'établir une distinction fondamentale entre parois intérieures porteuses et non porteuses. Parois porteuses/
non porteuses

Les parois intérieures porteuses reprennent non seulement leur poids propre, mais aussi les charges issues des planchers et de la toiture. Sont aussi considérées comme porteuses les parois raidisseuses. Entièrement intégrées à la structure porteuse du bâtiment, ces parois doivent fonctionner comme des voiles rigides, en vue de quoi on les dotera soit de panneaux raidisseurs, soit d'écharpes. > Chap. Système porteur,

Contreventement Les cloisons non porteuses, elles, ont avant tout une fonction de séparation spatiale.

En général, les parois intérieures sont construites selon la même trame et le même système que les parois extérieures. Les montants porteurs, allant de plancher à plafond, sont reliés par des lisses basses et hautes. Sur les lisses hautes des parois porteuses reposent les solives du plancher suivant. L'espace compris entre les solives doit être fermé de la même manière que les parois intérieures.

Les parois intérieures ont pour principales fonctions physiques d'assurer la protection phonique et anti-incendie. Aucune protection thermique n'étant requise entre des locaux chauffés, l'épaisseur des parois intérieures ne se déterminera pas en fonction de l'isolation.

Protection phonique L'indice d'affaiblissement acoustique d'une paroi étant principalement déterminé par le poids surfacique de la construction, il augmentera avec l'épaisseur des panneaux de revêtement choisis (panneaux de placoplâtre ou de particules, par exemple), dont la masse volumique devrait être la plus élevée possible. Contribue pour beaucoup à l'isolation phonique l'amortissement acoustique obtenu en remplissant de fibres minérales ou de coco les interstices de l'ossature. Il suffit de remplir la paroi jusqu'à la moitié ou aux deux tiers de son épaisseur, l'espace restant pouvant accueillir diverses conduites techniques. On laisse la paroi ouverte d'un côté jusqu'à ce que toutes les installations soient posées, d'éventuels flocons de cellulose ne pouvant être insufflés qu'une fois les compartiments fermés. En cas d'exigences accrues en matière d'isolation phonique, on prévoira une construction à double paroi, dont l'une sera fixée de façon souple, afin d'empêcher la transmission des bruits solidiens d'un côté à l'autre de la cloison.

Raccordements

Les raccordements entre parois intérieures et extérieures devront faire l'objet d'une attention particulière. Il s'agira non seulement d'assurer entre elles une liaison solidaire, mais aussi de veiller à laisser, au niveau des angles rentrants, une surface de fixation suffisante pour le revêtement intérieur.

○ Remarque: Dans les pièces humides, on utilisera pour les parois soit des panneaux en dérivés du bois à collage spécial, soit des panneaux de placoplâtre imprégnés. Les panneaux de fibroplâtre, eux, pourront être mis en œuvre sans traitement particulier. Si les montants de la structure sont espacés de plus de 42 cm, on prévoira comme support de carrelage deux couches de panneaux de placoplâtre.

Dans la construction à ossature bois, les parois intérieures sont la plupart du temps raccordées indépendamment de la trame de construction, leur position n'étant déterminée que par des critères fonctionnels d'organisation spatiale. Pour ce faire, on ajoute dans la paroi extérieure deux montants supplémentaires, permettant d'assurer à la fois une liaison solidaire entre parois et la possibilité de fixer le revêtement intérieur.

> III. 22, page 43, et III. 51

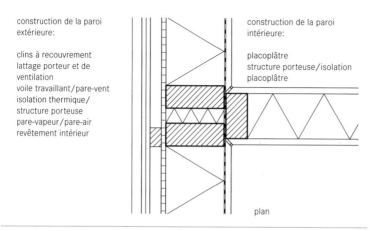

construction de la paroi extérieure:

clins à recouvrement
lattage porteur et de ventilation
voile travaillant/pare-vent
isolation thermique/
structure porteuse
pare-vapeur/pare-air
revêtement intérieur

construction de la paroi intérieure:

placoplâtre
structure porteuse/isolation
placoplâtre

plan

III. 51 : Raccordement d'une paroi intérieure, construction à ossature bois

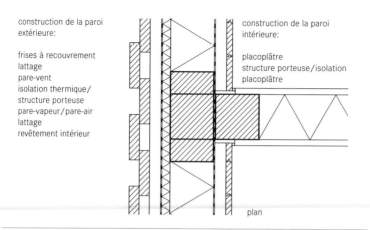

construction de la paroi extérieure:

frises à recouvrement
lattage
pare-vent
isolation thermique/
structure porteuse
pare-vapeur/pare-air
lattage
revêtement intérieur

construction de la paroi intérieure:

placoplâtre
structure porteuse/isolation
placoplâtre

plan

III. 52 : Raccordement d'une paroi intérieure, construction à pans de bois

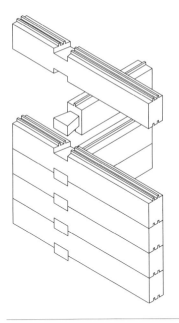

III. 53 : Raccordement d'une paroi intérieure,
construction en bois empilés

Dans la <u>construction à pans de bois</u>, la position des parois intérieures se conforme à la <u>trame</u> des poteaux porteurs, les raccordements se faisant dans l'axe de ces derniers. Les poteaux d'ossature concernés sont flanqués de deux <u>montants de renforcement</u>, auxquels est fixé le revêtement intérieur. > III. 52

Dans la construction en <u>bois empilés</u>, parois intérieures et extérieures sont, comme dans les angles sortants, entaillées <u>à quart de bois</u>. Pour garantir un raccord résistant à la traction, on exécute des assemblages à tenon et mortaise ou en <u>queue d'aronde</u>. > Chap. Construction en bois empilés Dans ce dernier cas, la position des parois intérieures est révélée, à l'extérieur, par le bout apparent de leurs éléments. > III. 53

PLANCHERS

Les planchers en bois peuvent être construits tant sous forme de solivages que de planchers massifs. Dans la construction traditionnelle en éléments linéaires, visant à limiter la consommation de matériau, les solivages dominent. Pour des raisons similaires à celles qui sous-tendent la construction en panneaux porteurs, en particulier pour permettre un montage plus rapide, on assiste cependant à la mise en œuvre toujours plus fréquente de systèmes de planchers en éléments massifs préfabriqués.

 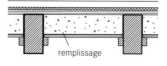 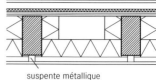

remplissage

suspente métallique

construction à une couche	construction à deux couches	construction à trois couches
revêtement de sol/ couche d'usure lambrissage solivage	revêtement de sol/couche d'usure chape isolation contre les bruits d'impact lambrissage remplissage (matériau en vrac) couche anti-écoulement solivage revêtement intérieur sur lattage	revêtement de sol/couche d'usure chape isolation contre les bruits d'impact lambrissage isolation solivage lattage (avec effet amortissant) revêtement intérieur

III. 54 : Constructions de planchers à une, deux et trois couches

Planchers à solivage

La protection phonique joue un rôle important dans la construction des planchers en bois. On fait à cet égard la distinction entre <u>bruits solidiens</u> et <u>bruits aériens</u>. On a par exemple affaire à la propagation de bruits solidiens lorsque le plancher vibre sous les impacts dus aux pas.

Quant aux bruits aériens, ils peuvent par exemple avoir pour source les voix humaines ou les sons émis dans une pièce par une radio, un téléviseur ou autre.

○ **Remarque:** Lorsque le revêtement de sol est totalement séparé du plancher et des parois latérales, on parle de construction flottante. On veillera ici à ce que les bruits ne puissent pas non plus se propager au niveau des bords, par les parois. Pour ce faire, on posera, outre une couche d'isolation horizontale contre les bruits d'impact, des bandes d'isolation verticales séparant la chape des parois (voir III. 57, page 85).

Couches de construction

Selon les propriétés requises en matière de protection phonique, les planchers seront exécutés en une, deux ou trois couches.

Bruits solidiens Dans une <u>construction à une couche</u>, le revêtement de sol est en contact direct avec la structure porteuse, les bruits solidiens se propageant donc sans obstacle lorsque l'on marche sur le plancher.

Dans une <u>construction à deux couches</u>, revêtement de sol et structure porteuse sont séparés par une isolation contre les bruits d'impact. Le revêtement doit donc être posé sur une couche porteuse spécifique, qu'il est logique d'exécuter, dans la construction en bois, sous la forme d'une chape sèche, pouvant par exemple se composer de deux couches de panneaux de fibroplâtre ou de panneaux de particules. > III. 54, III. 56 et

○ Chap. Matériaux dérivés du bois

Bruits aériens Pour répondre à des exigences accrues en matière de protection contre les bruits aériens, par exemple pour isoler des chambres à coucher de locaux particulièrement bruyants, on exécutera une <u>construction à trois couches</u>. Ici, la transmission directe des ondes sonores à travers le plancher entré en vibration sera interrompue par un plafond suspendu, fixé en sous-face de solivage au moyen de suspentes métalliques avec effet amortissant.

Le principal moyen de prévenir la propagation des bruits aériens consiste à augmenter le poids surfacique de la construction. Pour ce faire, on pose sur ou entre les solives des matériaux dotés d'une masse volumique relativement élevée.

Isolant de remplissage On pourra par exemple déverser dans les compartiments formés par les solives et le lambrissage inférieur un sable spécialement séché, > III. 54 ce qui réduira considérablement la hauteur apparente des solives. Pour éviter que le sable ne s'écoule entre les joints sous l'effet des vibrations, on posera sur le lambrissage un film de séparation.

Pour augmenter encore le poids du plancher, on pourra par exemple poser et coller sur le lambrissage des dalles de trottoir en béton, servant elles-mêmes de support à l'isolation contre les bruits d'impact, à la chape et au revêtement de sol.

Solivage

Portée Lors de la conception du projet, on fera en sorte que les solives aient la plus petite portée possible. La portée maximale des solives en bois massif est d'environ 5 m, les solives filant sur deux ou plusieurs travées étant plus économiques que les solives à deux appuis.

Dimensionnement La capacité porteuse des solives dépendant moins de leur largeur que de leur hauteur, on les pose sur chant, de manière à exploiter les sections au maximum. Un rapport largeur/hauteur de 1 : 2 ou plus est cou-

○ rant. La hauteur maximale des bois équarris se monte à 240–280 mm.

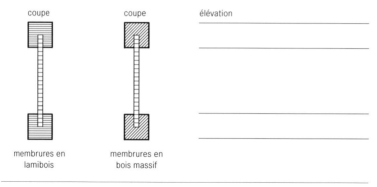

coupe	coupe	élévation

membrures en lamibois   membrures en bois massif

III. 55 : Poutres TJI

Les poutres TJI, du nom du fabricant <u>Trus Joist MacMillan Idaho</u>, Poutres TJI constituent un système des plus performant mais néanmoins bon marché, surtout utilisé dans la construction en bois américaine. Leur section en I se compose de membrures en bois massif ou en lamibois dans lesquelles est insérée et collée une âme en panneaux OSB, > Chap. Matériaux dérivés du bois conférant aux poutres, malgré leur faible poids propre, une capacité porteuse très élevée. En outre, la hauteur des âmes permet de faire passer assez facilement des conduites techniques transversalement au solivage ou à la poutraison, des réservations étant, à cet effet, prépercées en usine. Les planchers en poutres TJI sont, d'ordinaire, revêtus en sous-face. > III. 55

L'écartement des solives se monte en général à 60–70 cm. Il est Écartement des solives cependant judicieux de faire correspondre cet écartement avec la <u>trame</u> des parois, de manière que les charges du plancher soient transmises directement aux montants ou poteaux de l'ossature.

Dans la plupart des systèmes de construction en bois, les solives reposent sur les parois, la profondeur d'appui requise pouvant être déterminée en multipliant par 0,7 la hauteur des solives.

> ○ **Remarque:** Pour prédimensionner le solivage, on pourra se baser sur la règle empirique suivante :
>
> Hauteur h = portée/20
>
> Les solives d'une hauteur supérieure à celles que permet le bois massif devront être réalisées en lamellé-collé ou en dérivés du bois.

III. 56 : Systèmes de planchers : plancher à solivage, structure poteaux-poutres, poutre TJI

Trémies

Là où des gaines techniques, des cheminées ou des escaliers traversent les planchers, on ménage des trémies en interrompant les solives et en les reprenant par des chevêtres, comme cela se fait dans le
chevronnage des charpentes. > Basics Construction de toitures Intégrés dans le
plan du solivage, les <u>chevêtres</u> sont raccordés aux solives par des assemblages à tenon et mortaise, en général assurés contre le déboîtement par
des <u>clameaux</u>. Pour des raisons de sécurité incendie, on placera les
solives à au moins 5 cm des conduits de cheminées.

Appuis

Dans le détail typique de la construction à ossature bois, > III. 57 une
poutre de rive longeant le pourtour du bâtiment forme une sorte de cadre
empêchant les solives de basculer, tout en faisant office de <u>chaînage</u>
résistant à la traction et à la compression. Pour fonctionner comme un
<u>voile</u> au sens statique du terme, le solivage devra être raidi par des pan-
neaux agréés comme voile travaillant, par exemple en contreplaqué. On
veillera à poser ceux-ci à joints décalés, à la manière d'un appareil de
maçonnerie.

Pare-vapeur

Pour que les pare-vapeur des parois extérieures ne soient pas inter-
rompus au niveau des appuis de solives, ils devront contourner les rives
des planchers et être raccordés d'un étage à l'autre. Pour exclure la
condensation non seulement dans les parois, mais aussi au niveau des
appuis de planchers, on veillera en outre à ce que l'isolation thermique
ne soit pas interrompue ou affaiblie à cet endroit. > Chap. Physique de la
construction

Sabots/étriers

Dans le détail de l'illustration 58, le solivage de la construction à
pans de bois est suspendu entre les parois. Les assemblages à joint vif

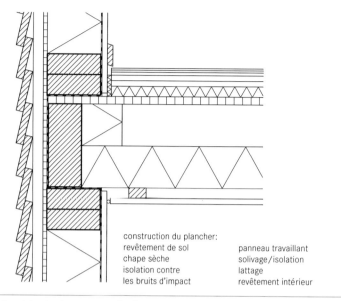

construction du plancher:
revêtement de sol
chape sèche
isolation contre
les bruits d'impact

panneau travaillant
solivage/isolation
lattage
revêtement intérieur

III. 57 : Appui de plancher, construction à ossature bois

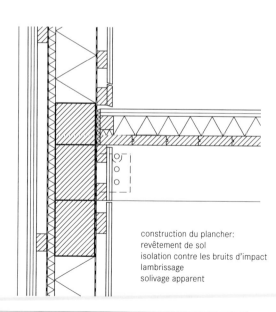

construction du plancher:
revêtement de sol
isolation contre les bruits d'impact
lambrissage
solivage apparent

III. 58 : Appui de plancher, construction à pans de bois

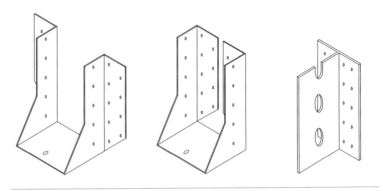

III. 59 : Sabots et étrier

sont, dans ce cas, assurés par des <u>sabots</u> ou des <u>étriers</u> en acier, disponibles dans le commerce en différentes dimensions.

Les assemblages à joint vif sont rendus possibles par une poutre
de rive posée à la hauteur du solivage. Le pare-vapeur, s'étendant ici
verticalement et sans interruption, devra être raccordé aux sabots ou
étriers de façon étanche à la vapeur d'eau. Dans le détail présenté, où le
solivage est apparent, on a opté pour des étriers à âme noyée.

Appuis
intérieurs
Lorsque le plancher n'est pas suspendu entre les parois, mais
repose sur ces dernières, il est possible de créer un appui intérieur en
rapportant contre la construction de la paroi extérieure une seconde
couche porteuse, pouvant par ailleurs servir de couche d'isolation supplémentaire, de logement pour les installations techniques et de sous-
construction pour le revêtement intérieur. > III. 49, page 75

○ **Remarque:** Les sabots étant visibles, on y recourra
en général dans le cas de solivages revêtus en sous-
face. Lorsque les solives sont destinées à rester
apparentes, on utilise de préférence des étriers dont
l'âme, insérée dans une fente pratiquée en tête de
solive, est maintenue en place par des chevilles trans-
versales (voir III. 27 et 56 au milieu).

Planchers massifs

Au cours de l'évolution ayant mené de la construction en bois empilés aux structures à poteaux-poutres, la quantité de bois mis en œuvre n'a cessé de diminuer. Or, comme nous l'avons vu, > Chap. Construction en panneaux porteurs la tendance s'est aujourd'hui inversée. C'est particulièrement vrai pour les planchers, où toute une série de nouveaux systèmes permettent de faire bénéficier la construction en bois des <u>avantages</u> de la construction massive, à savoir :

— Montage accéléré
— Fabrication simple, la plupart du temps industrialisée
— Hauteur de construction réduite grâce à la diminution de la section des planchers
— Isolation thermique et phonique accrue entre les étages

En outre, la sous-face lisse et continue des planchers massifs facilite leur raccordement aux parois.

La composition des planchers massifs ne diffère pas fondamentalement de celle des planchers à solivage, si ce n'est par le fait que des mesures d'amélioration de l'isolation thermique et phonique, comme la pose de matériaux destinés à augmenter le poids surfacique du plancher, sont ici superflues.

Comptent parmi les constructions massives les <u>poutres-caissons</u>, préfabriquées industriellement à partir de planches. Tout à fait appropriés au franchissement de grandes portées, ces éléments sont dotés de doubles rainures et languettes et assemblés en planchers sur le chantier.

Poutres-caissons

Le fait qu'ils soient produits en série garantit une qualité constante et une grande précision d'ajustement. Les poutres-caissons ont une largeur standard de 195 mm et sont disponibles dans des longueurs allant jusqu'à 12 m. Les hauteurs vont de 120 à 280 mm, par augmentations graduelles de 20 mm.

Tab. 9: Valeurs de prédimensionnement des poutres-caissons

Portée	Hauteur des éléments
3,8 m	120 mm
4,5 m	140 mm
5,2 m	200 mm

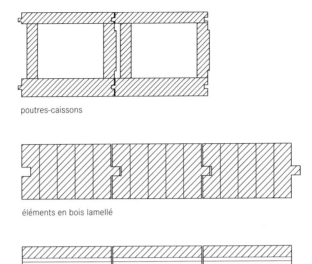

poutres-caissons

éléments en bois lamellé

éléments en bois contrecollé

III. 60 : Éléments de planchers massifs

Le tableau 9 donne les valeurs de prédimensionnement applicables pour une charge de 3 kN/m².

Éléments en bois lamellé   La construction en <u>bois lamellé</u> permet de tirer parti des planches débitées sur dosse et du bois d'éclaircie inapte à servir de poutre ou de bois équarri. Posées en long et sur chant, les planches sont clouées latéralement sans collage, selon un schéma de clouage bien précis. Les joints entre planches aboutées doivent être décalés. Les éléments ainsi obtenus, dotés de feuillures sur leurs longs côtés, sont assemblés sur le chantier en parois ou en planchers. > III. 60

Durant le chantier, il est indispensable de protéger les éléments de l'humidité, car le <u>gonflement</u> que provoquerait la pénétration d'eau dans les planches compromettrait toute possibilité de mise en œuvre.

La plupart des fabricants produisent des éléments de dimensions standard, dont l'épaisseur va de 100 à 220 mm, la largeur jusqu'à 2500 mm et la longueur jusqu'à 17 m.

Le tableau 10 donne les valeurs de prédimensionnement applicables pour une charge de 3 kN/m².

Éléments en bois contrecollé   Le <u>bois contrecollé</u> se compose de planches de résineux superposées d'une épaisseur de 17 ou 27 mm, assemblées à entures multiples

Tab. 10: Valeurs de prédimensionnement des éléments en bois lamellé

Portée	Hauteur des éléments
3,6 m	100 mm
4,3 m	120 mm
5,0 m	140 mm

Tab. 11: Valeurs de prédimensionnement des éléments en bois contrecollé

Portée	Hauteur des éléments
3,8 m	115 mm
4,6 m	142 mm
6,4 m	189 mm

et collées à fil croisé. Les éléments ainsi obtenus ont une forme très stable, et se prêtent de ce fait aussi très bien à la construction de parois. Pour améliorer la surface des éléments, on pourra réaliser les couches de parement dans un autre matériau que les couches intérieures.

Selon la nature de leurs parements et le nombre de leurs couches, les panneaux présentent une épaisseur variant entre 51 et 297 mm, leur largeur maximale se montant à 4,8 m. Les éléments sont fabriqués, en fonction des applications, dans des longueurs allant jusqu'à 20 m, ce qui permet par exemple de réaliser des parois d'une hauteur de quatre étages.

Le tableau 11 donne les valeurs de prédimensionnement applicables pour une charge de 3 kN/m^2.

Les trois systèmes de plafonds massifs décrits ci-dessus sont souvent utilisés aussi, suivant les mêmes principes, dans la construction de parois en panneaux porteurs massifs, un domaine dans lequel le nombre de nouveaux produits mis sur le marché ne cesse d'augmenter. Le principe de construction des parois est, ici, similaire à celui de la construction en bois empilés moderne, les parois porteuses massives étant, dans les deux cas, recouvertes d'une isolation thermique et d'un revêtement protégeant contre les intempéries.

TOITURE

Le domaine d'application de la construction en bois s'étend même aux bâtiments en maçonnerie, les toitures inclinées se présentant souvent, surtout dans la construction de maisons individuelles, sous forme

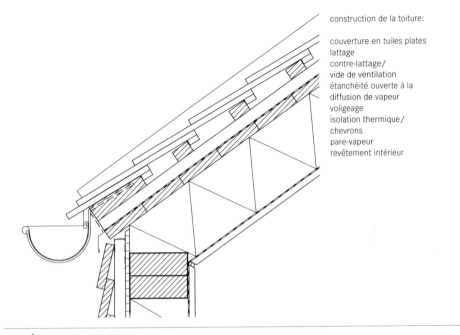

construction de la toiture:

couverture en tuiles plates
lattage
contre-lattage/
vide de ventilation
étanchéité ouverte à la
diffusion de vapeur
voligeage
isolation thermique/
chevrons
pare-vapeur
revêtement intérieur

III. 61 : Égout sans avant-toit

de charpentes en bois. Poser une charpente en bois sur un bâtiment en maçonnerie représente cependant une technique mixte, combinant ○ construction légère et massive, sèche et humide.

Toitures inclinées

Dans la construction en bois, toiture inclinée et parois extérieures sont conçues selon le même principe.

Couches de construction

Les fonctions et l'ordre des différentes couches sont en effet identiques dans les deux cas, à savoir, depuis l'extérieur : <u>protection contre les intempéries</u>, <u>étanchéité</u> à l'eau et au vent, <u>isolation</u>, <u>pare-vapeur</u> et <u>revêtement intérieur</u>. Il s'agit dès lors de raccorder ces couches de

> ○ **Remarque:** Les termes techniques employés ci-après
> sont expliqués dans le volume déjà cité de Tanja
> Brotrück, *Basics Construction de toitures*.

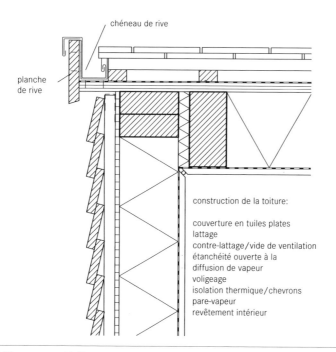

chéneau de rive

planche
de rive

construction de la toiture:

couverture en tuiles plates
lattage
contre-lattage/vide de ventilation
étanchéité ouverte à la
diffusion de vapeur
voligeage
isolation thermique/chevrons
pare-vapeur
revêtement intérieur

III. 62 : Rive sans avant-toit

manière à obtenir une enveloppe continue, remplissant toutes les fonctions physiques requises sans interruptions ni points faibles.

C'est par ailleurs au point de jonction entre toiture et parois que les charges issues de la première, composées du poids propre de la construction et, en hiver, des charges dues à la neige, doivent être transmises aux secondes. Il s'agit par ailleurs d'ancrer la toiture dans les parois, de manière à ce qu'elle puisse résister à la succion due au vent, à laquelle elle est particulièrement exposée. Ancrage

On n'oubliera du reste pas, outre ces nombreuses exigences techniques, l'enjeu esthétique que représente le raccord entre toiture et parois. La manière dont sont conçus l'égout et les rives de la toiture marque en effet fortement l'architecture d'un bâtiment, la présence ou l'absence d'avant-toits étant à cet égard déterminante.

Les coupes de détail des illustrations 61 et 62 présentent une manière assez simple de raccorder les différentes couches de construction de la toiture et des parois. Les revêtements en placoplâtre des deux éléments sont certes séparés par un joint, mais la masse à élasticité durable qui l'obture est à peine visible si on lui donne la même couleur qu'aux parois. Physique de la construction

La continuité de l'enveloppe pare-vapeur et pare-air des combles aménagés est assurée par collage des films au niveau des angles intérieurs entre égout et rives.

Les couches d'isolation comprises entre les montants des parois et les chevrons de la toiture se trouvent dans le prolongement direct les unes des autres, la limite supérieure des parois étant marquée par les lisses hautes de l'ossature.

Appuis

À la différence de la construction en maçonnerie, il n'est pas nécessaire de prévoir une panne sablière au niveau de l'égout, les chevrons pouvant reposer à même l'ossature de la paroi. Au niveau des rives, on veillera, pour éviter un grave pont thermique, à bourrer d'isolation le joint entre paroi pignon et chevron de rive.

○

Peau extérieure

L'isolation entre chevrons est couverte par un voligeage et une étanchéité ouverte à la diffusion de vapeur (sd < 2 m), celle des parois étant protégée par un voile travaillant en contreplaqué. La peau extérieure de la toiture et des parois est ventilée. Chaque lame d'air constitue un dispositif de ventilation indépendant, doté de ses propres ouvertures d'amenée et d'évacuation d'air.

Rives du toit

L'absence d'avant-toit souligne le volume et la corporéité du bâtiment, toiture et parois contribuant dans une mesure à peu près égale à l'effet plastique de celui-ci. Cet effet pourra être renforcé par la mise en œuvre d'un bardage à clins et d'une couverture en tuiles plates, tous deux basés sur le principe du recouvrement.

Les rives des façades pignon, particulièrement exposées à l'action du vent, seront protégées par une planche de rive. Celle-ci ne pouvant être vissée dans le bois de bout des voliges, elle sera fixée sur le voligeage au moyen d'une cornière en acier zingué.

Entre la couverture et la planche de rive, l'eau de pluie sera collectée et envoyée dans la gouttière de l'égout par un chéneau de rive en tôle.

○ **Remarque:** À la différence des parois longitudinales du bâtiment, les parois pignon ne sont pas délimitées par une lisse haute horizontale, mais par une lisse oblique, suivant l'inclinaison de la toiture. Les représentations en coupe des rives se feront selon un plan perpendiculaire à celui du versant, de manière à ce que les sections ne soient pas déformées (voir III. 62).

construction de la toiture:

couverture en tuiles à emboîtement
lattage
contre-lattage
étanchéité ouverte à la diffusion de vapeur
voligeage
isolation thermique / chevrons
pare-vapeur / pare-air
lattage
revêtement intérieur

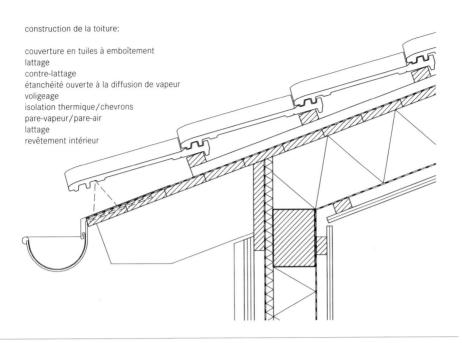

III. 63 : Égout avec avant-toit

Avant-toits — Un bâtiment doté d'avant-toits produit un effet tout différent. Un toit en saillie aura en effet tendance à se détacher du reste du volume, l'autonomie de la toiture et des parois pouvant être encore renforcée par la mise en œuvre de matériaux différents pour la couverture et les bardages.

Un débord de toiture continu sur tout le pourtour du bâtiment contribue de façon déterminante à la préservation du bois, en protégeant efficacement des précipitations le bardage des parois. Cette solution comporte toutefois un inconvénient : les chevrons traversent dans ce cas l'enveloppe extérieure du bâtiment. En coupant en biseau la tête des chevrons, on parviendra à en soustraire le bois de bout, particulièrement sensible, à l'influence directe des intempéries.

Raccordement toiture / parois — Pour éviter de devoir adapter les frises à recouvrement au chevronnage, on arrêtera le bardage sous les chevrons, et on insérera entre ceux-ci un madrier pouvant en même temps servir à fixer la partie supérieure du bardage. > III. 63 et 64 L'air assurant la ventilation du bardage pourra ici s'échapper par les vides entre lames de dessus et madriers.

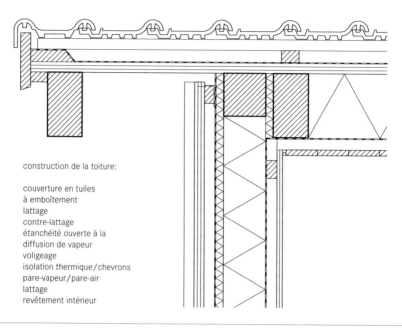

construction de la toiture:

couverture en tuiles
à emboîtement
lattage
contre-lattage
étanchéité ouverte à la
diffusion de vapeur
voligeage
isolation thermique / chevrons
pare-vapeur / pare-air
lattage
revêtement intérieur

III. 64 : Rive avec avant-toit

Rives

Au niveau des rives, en revanche, le bardage s'arrêtera juste sous le voligeage, par rapport auquel il devra cependant observer une distance de 2 à 3 cm, permettant à l'air de s'échapper du vide de ventilation vertical.

Au niveau des pignons, l'avant-toit ne peut être réalisé qu'au moyen de pannes en porte-à-faux, servant d'appui aux <u>chevrons volants</u> qui, cette fois, ne peuvent reposer à l'intérieur du bâtiment. Cette fonction sera assumée par les sablières hautes des parois longitudinales, que l'on prolongera, à cet effet, au-delà de la façade pignon. On dimensionnera ces pièces en fonction de l'ampleur du porte-à-faux, les sections carrées habituelles étant, dans ce cas, avantageusement remplacées par des sections rectangulaires posées sur chant.

À la différence de l'exemple précédent, où la couverture se composait de tuiles plates, le détail de l'illustration 64 ne requiert pas de <u>chéneau de rive</u>, l'évacuation des eaux pluviales étant ici assurée par des <u>tuiles de rive</u> de forme spéciale, fermant avec la planche de rive l'extrémité de la construction. La planche de rive est vissée à des lattes posées sur et sous le voligeage, dont les bords se trouvent ainsi renforcés.

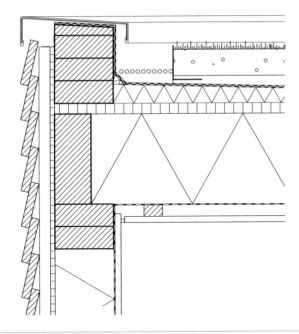

construction de la toiture:
végétalisation/couche filtrante/
couche drainante/protection
anti-racines
étanchéité
isolation à pente intégrée
panneau travaillant
isolation thermique/solivage
pare-vapeur
lattage
revêtement intérieur

III. 65 : Acrotère, plancher à solivage – construction à ossature bois

Toitures plates

Si les toitures plates, éléments caractéristiques de l'architecture moderne, ont la plupart du temps été réalisées en béton, elles font aujourd'hui partie intégrante du répertoire formel de l'architecture en bois contemporaine.

Acrotère   Dans le détail de l'illustration 65, le bardage à clins monte jusqu'à l'acrotère. Une planche de rive est ici superflue, la protection nécessaire étant assurée par l'acrotère, dès lors qu'il forme par rapport à la couverture un rebord d'au moins 10 cm de haut. L'acrotère et le revêtement de façade sont protégés par une couvertine inclinée vers l'intérieur, devant permettre à l'air ventilant le bardage de s'échapper vers le haut.

Appuis   La construction et les appuis du plancher de toiture sont exécutés comme ceux d'un plancher intermédiaire, > III. 57 même les lisses superposées qui constituent l'acrotère rappelant celles des ossatures reposant sur les planchers d'étages.

L'isolation est posée entre les solives du plancher de toiture, comme elle l'est entre les montants d'ossature. Le reste de la construction étant

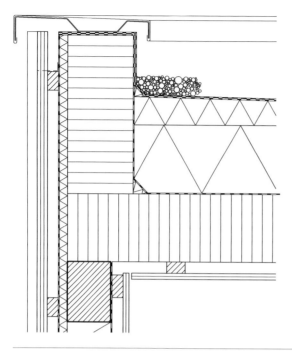

construction de
la toiture:

gravier
étanchéité
isolation à pente
intégrée
isolation thermique
pare-vapeur
éléments en bois
lamellé
lattage
revêtement intérieur

III. 66 : Acrotère, plancher en bois lamellé – construction à pans de bois

cependant conçu selon le principe de la <u>toiture chaude,</u> c'est-à-dire sans
ventilation, le pare-vapeur posé en sous-face d'isolation revêt une importance déterminante. Pour que l'eau parvenue jusqu'à l'étanchéité
résistante à la pénétration des racines soit systématiquement évacuée
vers les écoulements, on ajoute sur le lambrissage de la toiture une
couche d'isolation à pente intégrée, pouvant par ailleurs couvrir d'éventuels points faibles de l'isolation thermique sous-jacente. Des granulats
déversés en vrac sont ici on ne peut plus appropriés.

    L'assez faible capacité d'accumulation thermique des planchers de
toiture en construction légère pourra, dans une certaine mesure, se compenser par une <u>couche de protection végétalisée.</u> Pour des raisons de
protection anti-incendie, celle-ci devra être séparée des rives du toit et
des autres éléments en bois par des bandes de gravier d'au moins 50 cm
de largeur.

    Les détails d'acrotères présentés aux illustrations 65 et 66 ne consti-
tuent que deux solutions parmi d'autres, tant en ce qui concerne l'aspect
extérieur des rives que la composition du plancher de la toiture.

On notera en outre que, si les toitures plates sont souvent exécutées selon le principe de la toiture chaude, elles peuvent aussi l'être, à l'instar des toitures inclinées, selon celui de la toiture froide.

L'exécution d'un plancher de toiture en <u>bois lamellé</u> > Chap. Planchers se rapproche beaucoup, tant du point de vue de la composition que des détails, de celle d'une construction en béton armé. > III. 66 Une exécution en bois massif permet d'améliorer à la fois l'isolation et la capacité d'accumulation thermique de la toiture. Les éléments en bois lamellé reposent sur la sablière haute des pans de bois, le rebord de l'acrotère étant lui aussi réalisé en bois lamellé.

Couches de construction

Dans l'exemple présenté, les couches de construction sont posées sur le plancher en bois massif selon le principe de la toiture chaude, comme s'il s'agissait d'une dalle en béton armé. Dans ce cas de figure, le pare-vapeur se situe sous l'isolation thermique, séparée de celle des parois par les éléments massifs. Il est possible d'éviter les ponts thermiques en rapportant une couche d'isolation supplémentaire à l'extérieur de la structure porteuse.

Conclusion

En conclusion de ce volume, il convient de souligner une nouvelle fois la spécificité du bois, que Gottfried Semper qualifiait, dans le chapitre consacré à la tectonique de son ouvrage *Le Style*, de « matériau originel des constructions en éléments linéaires ».

Construire en bois, c'est en effet assembler des éléments selon une logique et des principes constructifs clairs. À la différence des ouvrages massifs, les ossatures des constructions en bois permettent une lecture et une étude immédiates du flux des forces. Aussi une bonne compréhension de la construction en bois livre-t-elle la clé de nombreux autres systèmes constructifs utilisés en architecture. La parenté avec la construction en acier, qui consiste elle aussi à assembler barres et plaques, est évidente. Il en va de même des façades en verre-métal, qui ne représentent qu'une transposition des constructions à montants et traverses en bois. Même le matériau coulé qu'est le béton s'inspire des principes tectoniques de la construction en bois, dont il reprend les structures à poteaux-poutres. Et l'on comprendra mieux le fonctionnement statique d'une dalle de béton armé en se représentant les fers d'armature comme autant de solives.

Si de nombreuses écoles d'architecture ont placé la construction en bois au début de leur cursus, c'est précisément parce qu'elle permet mieux qu'aucune autre de comprendre les principes fondamentaux de la construction, tout en offrant un champ d'activité varié et fascinant.

Annexes

NORMES

Construction en bois en général

NF EN 338	Bois de structure – Classes de résistance
NF EN 384	Bois de structure – Détermination des valeurs caractéristiques, des propriétés mécaniques et de la masse volumique
NF EN 1995-1-1	Eurocode 5 : Conception et calcul des structures en bois – Partie 1-1 : Règles communes et règles pour les bâtiments
SIA 118/265	Conditions générales relatives à la construction en bois (2018)
SIA 265	Construction en bois (2012)
SIA 265/1	Construction en bois – Spécifications complémentaires (2018)

Préservation du bois

NF EN 335	Durabilité du bois et des matériaux dérivés du bois – Définition des classes de risque d'attaque biologique
NF EN 350	Durabilité du bois et des matériaux dérivés du bois – Durabilité naturelle du bois massif
NF EN 351	Durabilité du bois et des matériaux dérivés du bois – Bois massif traité avec produit de préservation
SIA 257	Peinture, teintage du bois, revêtements muraux (2005)

Protection contre le feu

Documentation SIA 84	Protection incendie dans la construction en bois (1998)

Protection thermique

SN EN ISO 10211	Ponts thermiques dans les bâtiments

Protection phonique

SN EN 12354	Acoustique du bâtiment

RÉFÉRENCES BIBLIOGRAPHIQUES

Werner Blaser, *Holz-Haus. Maisons de bois. Wood houses,* Wepf, Bâle, 1980

Andrea Deplazes (dir.), *Construire l'architecture,* 2e édition augmentée, Birkhäuser, Bâle, 2013

Dominique Gauzin-Müller, *Construire avec le bois,* Le Moniteur, Paris, 1999 (réimpression 2005)

Thomas Herzog, Julius Natterer, Roland Schweitzer, Michael Volz, Wolfgang Winter, *Construire en bois,* 3e édition entièrement revue, Presses polytechniques et universitaires romandes, Lausanne, 2005

Ernst Neufert, *Les Éléments des projets de construction,* 10e édition française revue et augmentée, Dunod, Paris, 2010

René Vittone, *Bâtir,* 2e édition entièrement revue et augmentée, Presses polytechniques et universitaires romandes, Lausanne, 2010

CRÉDITS ICONOGRAPHIQUES

Illustration page 12 : Johann Weber
Illustration page 28 : Ludwig Steiger
Illustration 14 : Ludwig Steiger
Illustration 23 : Jörg Weber
Illustrations : 30–37 : Jörg Rehm
Illustration page 55 : Ludwig Steiger
Illustration 44 : Anja Riedl
Illustration 47 : Anja Riedl / Jörg Rehm
Illustration 56 : Ludwig Steiger / Jörg Weber
Illustration page 73 : Ludwig Steiger
Illustration page 93 : Architekturbüro Fischer + Steiger
Dessins : Florian Müller / Jörg Rehm

L'AUTEUR

Ludwig Steiger, dipl. ing. Univ., architecte, chargé d'enseignement en construction et aménagement intérieur à l'Université technique de Munich, associé du bureau d'architecture Fischer + Steiger à Munich

Jörg Rehm, Dr. Ing., UT Munich, participation au chap. *Construction en panneaux massifs*

Directeur de collection : Bert Bielefeld
Conception éditoriale : Bert Bielefeld,
Annette Gref
Traduction de l'allemand : Léo Biétry
Maquette et conception graphique de la
couverture : Andreas Hidber
Mise en page et production : Amelie Solbrig
Coordination éditoriale : Annette Gref

Papier : Magno Natural, 120 g/m²
Imprimerie : Beltz Grafische Betriebe GmbH

Library of Congress Control Number:
2020938924

Information bibliographique de la Deutsche
Nationalbibliothek
La Deutsche Nationalbibliothek a répertorié
cette publication dans la Deutsche National-
bibliografie ; les données bibliographiques
détaillées peuvent être consultées sur Internet
a l'adresse suivante : http://dnb.d-nb.de.

ISBN 978-3-0356-2125-9
e-ISBN (PDF) 978-3-0356-2129-7
e-ISBN (EPUB) 978-3-0356-2132-7
ISBN édition imprimée allemande
978-3-0356-2124-2
ISBN édition imprimée anglaise
978-3-0356-2126-6

© 2020 Birkhauser Verlag GmbH, Bâle
Case postale 44, CH-4009 Bâle, Suisse
Membre de De Gruyter GmbH, Berlin / Boston

9 8 7 6 5 4 3 2 1

www.birkhauser.com